Thief!

Thief!

The Gutsy, True Story
of an Ex-Con Artist

WILLIAM "SLICK" HANNER
and CHERIE ROHN

To Margery
Have a Good read.
Wm Slick Hanner

BARRICADE
BOOKS

Published by Barricade Books Inc.
185 Bridge Plaza North
Suite 308-A
Fort Lee, NJ 07024

www.barricadebooks.com

Library of Congress Cataloging-in-Publication Data
A copy of this title's Library of Congress Cataloging-in-Publication
Data is available on request from the Library of Congress.

ISBN 1-56980-317-x

First Printing

Designed by India Amos, Neuwirth & Associates, Inc.
Manufactured in the United States of America

I dedicate this book to my family, the loved ones
I ignored during the early years of my life.
—WILLIAM "SLICK" HANNER

CONTENTS

Part Three: Las Vegas 1970–1993

INTRODUCTION

HAVING RECENTLY WRITTEN a book called *Superthief,* I was intrigued when I heard there was a book called *Thief!* coming out. When Cherie Rohn (co-author with William "Slick" Hanner) told me the story also had a Mafia/Las Vegas backdrop, I was anxious to get my hands on a draft.

As the drummer for Sammy Davis Jr. in the early 1980s, I spent much of my time playing in Vegas. That was before I became a police officer and began writing about the Mafia. Like most people, I have a natural curiosity about the extremes of life—from the cesspit of the human population that serial killers and child molesters inhabit, to the high-society venues of the rich, famous, and powerful. Perhaps because it embodies elements from both of these extremes, such as violence, disdain for the law, and a tendency toward an ostentatious lifestyle, the Mafia is an ongoing object of fascination for a large percentage of readers, television watchers, and moviegoers.

My interest in the Mafia was more personal than most. I first learned about the origins of this ruthless, far-flung and deeply-rooted organization during research into the murder of my grandfather, Raymond Porrello, and three of his brothers, Prohibition-era mob leaders. That research would snowball into my first title, *The Rise and Fall of the Cleveland Mafia*, which would be put out by Barricade Books, publisher of the book you are reading.

In the course of my research, I was astounded to learn what had been going on behind the Las Vegas gaming and entertainment scenes that I'd never given a second thought to while drumming for Sammy—casino profit skimming, cheating, government corruption, murder and the involvement of mob figures like Tony Spilotro and Frank "Lefty" Rosenthal. In reading *Thief!* I have revisited this darkly fascinating piece of American history—all from the perspective of Slick Hanner, wise-cracking and ambitious, colorful and skilled, good-humored and nervy con-artist and cheat.

Most often the inside stories of the Mafia come from the perspective of informants, cooperating witnesses or law enforcement officials. But in *Thief!* we meet neither a lawman nor a turncoat in the shape of our protagonist. Slick was a thrill-seeking, seat-of-your-pants, adrenalin junkie who entertained mobsters with his "I don't give a shit" sense of humor. They trusted him like an insider because he kept his mouth shut. But that was then, when telling tales could get you killed. Now Slick Hanner guides us (with the superb collaboration of Rohn) through his story as he crisscrosses the country during a most fascinating era. *Thief!* takes us from the headquarters of the Chicago "Outfit" to the plush and not-so-plush gaming rooms of Las Vegas, from his boat *Knot Guilty* to the Windy City's seedy strip joints, from Mafia hit men, casino managers and prostitutes, to fat-wallet suckers, comedians and even Jerry Lewis. Add inside knowledge about the murders of Marilyn Monroe, Bugsy Siegel, and JFK, and Hanner's roller-coaster life reveals more than the superficial antics of some happy-go-lucky con artist.

When it comes to crime, murder is the ultimate transgression, but theft is the most common. Burglary, fraud, cheats, scams, shoplifting—Slick Hanner has done them all. But while he also lives for fast, easy and big money, his disdain for murder distinguishes him from the New York and Chicago wiseguys with whom he associates. He knows his place in this treacherous underworld in which even perceived slights are often resolved with two bullets to the brain. Hanner treads lightly with these characters.

No doubt Slick Hanner is ambitious. He accepts almost every opportunity to make a score. One exception is noteworthy: He turns his back on a substantial sum and faces contempt from his cohorts, all because the victim reminds Slick of his mother. Such is the personality of this thief with his refreshing capacity to love and be loved.

But ultimately it's the love of money and excitement that defines Slick Hanner's life. And in that life he has the ability to laugh off his constant screw-ups, pick himself up, and set off on his next adventure and score. With resilience like that, it's no wonder Slick Hanner has the drive to go to work and teach current Las Vegas poker dealers how to spot the thief.

—Rick Porrello
Police Lieutenant, Jazz Drummer and Author of
Superthief: A Master Burglar, the Mafia and the Biggest Bank Heist in U.S. History

PROLOGUE

THE CHINESE HAVE a saying that goes something like this: *May you live in exciting times.*

Well, that fits me like a glove.

The Chicago I grew up in was tough, but I wouldn't trade it for any place in the world. Life was one thrill after another for a nervy guy with street smarts and a yen for excitement. First, there were the noisy streetcars I used to sneak aboard as a kid. When I was older, joy rides in stolen black sedans were my thing. I was so busy getting in trouble, I hardly noticed World War II come and go.

Later, I hung around with Mafia figures all over the country. Every night some sucker on the make went broke in the mob-owned strip joints where I tended bar. Miami was still a tropical paradise when I lived there—loaded with tan gangsters puffing Cuban cigars.

I was part of Las Vegas when it was nothing but a two-bit town that grew into the glitziest mob hangout the world's seen. Then I watched it all change as organized crime was wiped out by the authorities.

All that's gone now. But when I put on the old music and close my eyes, it's like it happened yesterday.

PART ONE

Chicago
1932–1961

"The toughest neighborhood in the world."
That was Wilson and Broadway, just two blocks
from the Green Mill Bar where Joe E. Lewis
was appearing when he got his throat cut.

IN THE MIDDLE of a fitful sleep, I grew conscious of Lucio shaking me. "Come on," he said. "We have business."

"What time is it?" I asked, trying to focus.

"About 2:00 a.m.," Lucio answered. "We got a job to do for Dominick. He wants to take your boat."

I didn't like the sound of this. It might be a setup. I eased my .25-calibre Beretta into my pants pocket when Lucio wasn't looking. My mind was made up. If this was it, I was gonna take Lucio along with me and any of the Lucchese thugs that stood in my way.

"I'm low on gas," I lied, trying to sound matter-of-fact. "Why don't we take your car?" I figured if Lucio drove, he'd be the easier target.

"Okay," he said. "By the way, does your boat have a full tank?"

"Yeah, it's full," I said, aware this was gonna be more than a short pleasure cruise.

We arrived at Haulover, south of Miami Beach, around 3:00 a.m. It was so quiet I could hear my watch ticking. The longer we waited, the more I sweated in the muggy night air. Finally, the infamous Mauro Brothers appeared out of the blue fumes from the idling motors. They wrestled a heavy, black canvas bag aboard the *Knot Guilty*.

"What's in the bag?" The words spilled out of my mouth before I could check myself.

"You don't want to know," one of the goons grunted. "Just think of it as garbage."

I was thankful for the moonless night because the sweat was pouring down me like Niagara Falls. My hand automatically closed around the Beretta in my pocket. I was so jumpy, the snap of a twig was all I needed to shoot all three of them. If they were going to do what I figured, they couldn't leave any witnesses, especially an outsider like me.

We had entered international waters, just beyond the 12-mile limit, when I heard the order I'd been dreading. "Okay, you can stop." My grip tightened on the semi-automatic still in my pocket. I held my breath and waited. There was shuffling followed by a giant splash, then silence. I was gonna be fish food in about two seconds . . .

Yeah, it's like you always hear people say. When a guy's about to die, his whole life flashes before him. How did I get into this stupid mess with these Lucchese killers anyway? Just when everything seemed to be going good for a change, trouble hit like a punch in the solar plexus. In fact, my earliest memories are always of me in some kind of trouble. . . .

It all started when my parents, Charlie and Mary, migrated from the South in the early thirties. They set out for California, went broke in Chicago, and that's where they settled, on the North Side. I arrived without fanfare on May 5, 1932, in Cook County Hospital. It's where all the poor people go who can't afford to pay. They baptized me William Ronald Hanner, but everyone called me Billy. By that time my sister, Louise, was eighteen and my brother, Tom, sixteen. I guess I was kind of a surprise.

My folks were part of the melting pot of nationalities that migrated to the area looking for work. I'm Irish and Scottish.

Our neighbors were Jewish, Italian, Polish, Indian, Asian, and everything else. In fact, most were rednecks who didn't know what the hell they were.

When I was a kid, my neighborhood still had some class. The Aragon Ballroom on Lawrence and Winthrop was so popular, folks lined the sidewalk for an hour on a busy Saturday night. The inside looked like the courtyard of a Spanish castle. Puffy clouds filled the dark blue "sky" that flickered with a handful of tiny stars, like they'd just come out for the evening. Sparks of light shooting off the stars made everyone look glamorous.

The Uptown Theater on Lawrence and Broadway showed all the latest movies, but the big screen wasn't the only attraction. Us kids competed to see who could make out in every one of the Uptown's dark balconies without getting caught. I knew all the good hiding places—away from the prying flashlights of the horny, pimple-faced ushers.

The Great Depression hit our country and left almost everyone out of work. By the early 1930s the neighborhood started attracting undesirables for two main reasons: Cheap, furnished apartments were as common as houseflies, and there were plenty of ways to hit on people to get money. Growing up was thrilling and dangerous in what *Esquire* magazine called "the toughest neighborhood in the world." That was Wilson and Broadway, just two blocks from the Green Mill Bar where Joe E. Lewis was appearing when he got his throat cut.

I remember one time in particular when I was six or seven years old. Me and the other kids from my neighborhood were playing kick-the-can in an alley off Kenmore and Leland Avenue in broad daylight.

"Quit hogging it, Jimmy."

"Hey! Get your fat elbow out of my ribs, you moron."

We were minding our own business while three adult males dragged some old, boozed-up guy into an alley. They beat and kicked the hell out of him, only 10 feet from our game, after they relieved him of his few dollars. We hardly glanced over 'cause it was nothing to see a guy roughed up. Years later I saw a TV news program about kids in Vietnam playing around dead soldiers. As I watched, I got a flashback of the one-sided fight in that alley. I knew exactly how those Vietnam kids felt—that's just the way it is.

Me and my family lived at 1139 Leland Avenue, one block north of Wilson Avenue near Lake Michigan. Our simple three-bedroom walk-up occupied the entire third floor of a large, brown brick building. It was a carbon copy of every building in the neighborhood—peeling wallpaper inside, dingy brown brick outside. Many times a family would run a business on the first floor and live above their store, or rent out the upper floors to poor working families like ours.

You reached our front door by climbing the skinny stairs past our noisy neighbors, Mr. and Mrs. Del Campo, who rented the second floor. It wasn't really the Del Campos who were noisy. The problem was the wrestlers who clomped through the Del Campos's apartment like a herd of angry buffalo.

It all started when Sam Del Campo, a featherweight, happy-go-lucky version of Poncho Villa, was dying to shoot the breeze with the Mexican wrestlers he met down the street at the Rainbow Arena. Sam lured the big guys to his home with his homemade chilies rellenos. Sure enough, the wrestlers took the bait. Now Sam had 250 pounds of flesh hitting the mat, better known as Sam's threadbare living room carpet, at one in the morning. This did nothing to cement relations with my father.

My dad would lose it. He'd thump on the floor shouting at the top of his lungs, "Them fuckin' Mexicans!"

Sam called off the late night visits which saved him from a fate worse than a piñata—not my father, but the brutal tongue-lashings of Mrs. Del Campo. Now when Sam felt like bullshitting, he retreated to the tough-talking, "men only" atmosphere of the Rainbow Arena.

Two meaty giants, Cyclone Anaya and the Great Montezuma, hung out at the Del Campos's before Sam chickened out. I swear, together these guys must have weighed over 500 pounds. The whole building shimmied when they practiced their body slams in the Del Campos's living room. Every time I was in a hurry to get down our narrow steps, I'd run into the wrestlers on their way up. "Coming through," I'd warn. The Great Montezuma would pluck me one-handed from the stairs, like I was no more than a piece of carpet lint, and set me on the step below.

"Eat your spinach, baby boy. Maybe you'll grow up to be a wrestler."

It was bad enough calling me baby boy, but their bouts of uncontrolled laughter made me want to kill them. My fists flew like a windmill whiffing air, a miniature human fan held captive by Montezuma's gorilla-sized mitts. If my friends had seen me, I was dead meat. Cyclone and Montezuma were okay, though. Sometimes they even gave me free tickets to a match.

Our apartment was nothing special. In fact, I didn't spend much time there—too many drunken relatives hanging around. The neat thing was that our back porch had outside stairs going down to a square yard enclosed entirely by buildings—my playground. All the stores had back doors leading to the trash-littered yard. One door went into the Greek restaurant, one into Lee's Lounge, another led into the butcher shop, and so on. Sharp aromas drifting from the open doorways mingled to form a sort of backyard stew. The pungent scent hung heavy in the air. Nothing can describe that complicated, indefinable smell that made me feel so good.

As I got older, me and my friends climbed the nearby roofs. We took turns leaping across unknown territory. I pretended I was Spiderman from my favorite comic book, complete with scarlet cape snapping sharply behind me. My spider powers pulverized the mad scientist so I could rescue the pretty girl. So what if we actually jumped across the tops of three-story buildings that were five feet apart, and my cape was really the red sweater my mom gave me last Christmas tied around my neck. A hero is still a hero.

Our neighborhood hummed with activity. It's where everyone shopped. In fact, the whole world traded at Goldblatts Department Store across from our apartment. The place had so much stuff that if Goldblatts didn't have it, you didn't want it. No working class neighborhood would be complete without a bar on every corner. I guess that meant we had a regular working class neighborhood. Aside from the ghostly groans that rattled through our decaying building, all night long the El, an elevated train, roared on platforms above Wilson Avenue. Streetcars screeched to a halt up and down Broadway, a block away. Then there were the wrestlers raising the dead with their body slams. None of this fazed me. I could sleep if a bomb went off under my bed.

In 1938 I started Catholic school at St. Thomas of Canterbury. My parents were so busy working to pay the rent and feed us kids, they didn't have time to see that I made it to first grade, four blocks away. By the end of my first year, I was a real delinquent. I flunked and had to repeat first grade because I cut school maybe three times a week. If that wasn't bad enough, I took other kids milk money. Our family couldn't afford the two cents a bottle for milk. I got disciplined a lot.

One Polish sister really cared about me though. Her name was Sister Mary Stanislaus, but I called her Sister "Santa Claus." As far as looks go, if Santa was a female, he'd be Sister Mary's twin. Every time I looked at that plump face it reminded me of my mom's geraniums in the kitchen window. Even if it was raining, those pink flowers made it seem like the sun was shining full blast.

When I got in trouble (at least once a day), the nuns and priests performed their religious duty and beat the hell out of me. But if Sister Santa Claus caught me playing a trick, on some sissy for instance, it was another story. She looked me steadily in the eye, not one hint of anger wrinkling that calm, gentle face. "William, if you just try to be good, God will help you and so will I." There was no doubt in my mind. She really believed that stuff.

I remember when I was in second grade and it was a week before Christmas. My father bought us a tree but there was no money for ornaments. That puny tree was the sorriest thing I ever saw, but an idea hit me. A beautiful manger, with statues of the wise men and animals and everything, decorated a table in front of our classroom. If my family had that manger, our tree wouldn't look so naked. So I sneaked back into the classroom after school, snatched the manger and stuff and beat it.

On the way home this fat-ass kid, Casper, spotted me carrying the manger. He just watched me. I knew his squinty little horn-rimmed eyes followed my every move on account of the sweat that was breaking out all over my body.

The next day in school twenty-five outraged little voices cried, "What happened to the manger?"

Right about now a smug looking Casper whispered in sister's ear. That was it. He was ratting me off. Boy, would I fix him! After school I wasn't one bit surprised when Sister Santa Claus said, "William, I want to talk to you."

It was hard to believe, but we just talked. She wasn't even mad at me. Instead, her motherly voice explaned, "I know you took the manger, William, but it isn't fair to the other children. You know, some aren't as lucky as you are to have a Christmas tree." I figured if she wasn't mad at me, how could I be angry at Casper for squealing?

The next day in school I sneaked a peek at Casper when he was looking the other way. Maybe Casper's eyes weren't quite as close together as I thought. I never heard another word about the manger.

Almost the exact moment I reached third grade, the authorities at St. Thomas had enough of me and threw me out. That forced my parents to enroll me in public school. By then I hated school.

What a waste of time. Instead of going to school, I hung out where three major streets intersected: Montrose, Broadway and Sheridan. Between the clanging streetcars on Broadway crossing the double-decker buses on Sheridan Road, plus all the regular car noise, a guy could go deaf. It was at this traffic-jammed crossroads I discovered the excitement I secretly craved.

Next to Chicago's largest bowling alley, the 26-lane Bowlium, stood Helsing's Restaurant and Vaudeville Lounge. The place attracted every breathing person within a half-mile. From white-collar types on their lunch hour to local housewives out to buy two pounds of hamburger then kill a little time, Helsing's drew them all. It was the neighborhood's unofficial meeting place. Me and my friends ignored the "no loitering" sign out front. The snazzy dressers in their uptown suits offered us hour after hour of free entertainment. Not everyone was light-hearted. Murmurs of "Germany" and "European crisis" sometimes rose above the hubbub.

The first thing that grabbed your attention in the Vaudeville was the gaudy, gold stage curtain. Too often, that's all that was worth watching. Bored patrons lounged at tables littered with stained glasses and chipped ashtrays overflowed with stale butts. Filtered through a perpetual blue haze, tired comics ground out their slapstick routines. Sometimes a customer would shout, "Go back to the Catskills, you jerk! You ain't even funny."

Once in a while, a performer turned out to be the genuine article. Us kids would crouch behind the red velvet drapes at the rear of the theater, eight wide eyes riveted on the sad figure center stage. I was too young to catch the full meaning, but the sight of some guy exposing his broken heart in front of all those people sent goose bumps up and down my arms.

"Ach, you kids get the hell out of here!" Rudy, the manager, descended on us. German-sausage legs propelled Rudy's Jello-like body unsteadily down the hall, a good ten feet behind us. His enormous patent leather shoes squeaked in time to the music.

Once inside the restaurant, our sides ached from laughter at how we ditched the enemy.

Everyone thought Helsing's was a coffee shop but I knew better. It was really a hotbed of neighborhood gossip. "Agnes! You don't mean to tell me Charlie's in bed with that one?" In less time than it took to gulp down a coffee and Danish, you knew who was cheating with who and how long they'd been doing it. That's how I got the first inkling my father was "up to no good."

On another corner, near the Arcadia Roller Rink, there was a drugstore that was so busy, customers spun through its revolving door like a merry-go-round gone haywire. That's where I met Jack Bailey, a kid my age. Jack's parents, both alcoholics, were as dirt poor as the rest of us. In fact, most of the guys I hung with came from broken homes where someone hit the booze heavy. They didn't realize it, but our parents—basically good people with shattered dreams—did us kids a real favor. They turned us into expert survivors.

Besides hanging around Helsing's, the fast-paced Wilson El Station attracted me like a magnet attracts metal filings. I'd scramble onto a roof that leads under the main platform where the passengers waited for the trains. If I was lucky, people would drop change that found its way through the wide cracks in the platform. Once in a while I got an unexpected treat just by looking up—sort of my own *Playboy* magazine.

On the spur of the moment, I jumped out on the tracks, avoiding the electric third rail. (I once saw an old guy roasted on that thing when he accidentally stepped on it.) I threw my skinny leg onto the train platform and hoisted myself up. A train screeched to a stop. Nobody was looking so I sneaked on board.

I soaked up every detail on the way to the South Side. Mostly there was mile after mile of smoke-stained apartments. The nickname "dirty shirt town" hit home. Wash never seemed clean on lines strung from back porches in need of more than a fresh coat of paint. Jagged, gaping windows exposed gray piles of who knows what heaped inside abandoned warehouses. The dingy mess left me feeling empty.

Then something hit my face. All at once the sun's warmth poured over me, a welcome relief from the gloom we left behind. Lake Michigan showed up like an old friend, a blue mirror dotted with toy boats. The sight made me restless. I longed to escape—to bust out of my same old neighborhood—see what this world had to offer a kid who's been nowhere.

Jolting brakes jarred me back to the South Side of Chicago. End of the line, time to get off. The largest building in the Universe loomed in front of me, only a block away. It was a swell place called the Rosenwald Museum of Science and Industry.

Once inside, I took a chance and stood in line with these silly school kids. The half-hour wait was more than worth it. A real Pennsylvania miner's car whisked us through an authentic coal mine. I couldn't wait to tell my new friend, Jack Bailey. The museum was loaded with all the latest technology. There was a brand new invention called television where real people talked to one another inside this little box. The recorded voice explained: "Television is going to change the entire world." but I didn't think it would catch on. What could possibly beat the big screen?

The very next day I brought Jack to my "secret place." Everything was perfect except for one minor setback. Jack was goofing around, slipped and fell off this ten-foot ledge that circled the outside of the museum, and broke his arm.

The following week we investigated Jack's favorite place, the Arcadia Roller Rink at 4444 Broadway. The rink offered skating every single night with matinees on the weekend. Jack, the best skater I'd ever seen, was so good the girls were all over him like bees around honey. I couldn't believe this guy. He glided up to a cute redhead whose bottom was about to make contact with the wooden floor. "Hi! Want some help?" Without waiting for an answer, Jack scooped up the surprised girl, swung her easily around with his good arm, and planted her neatly in a swarm of giggling girlfriends. To top it off, Jack was a dead ringer for the actor John Garfield. Some guys have all the luck.

When he wasn't sweeping girls off their feet at the Arcadia, the pair of us killed time at the drugstore down the block sitting at the newsstand for hours. We wolfed down the hot dogs we mooched from the little Greek guy who peddled them on the sidewalk. Our eyes undressed the girls who dared to wander into range. Zap! Another pair of gorgeous tits exposed with our x-ray vision. Every time we spotted a worthy target we chimed in, "Must be jelly 'cause jam don't shake like that."

I was horny ever since second grade when a fast little blonde with big blue eyes let me peek under her dress. The only thing she offered after that was the cold shoulder, so I had to find other ways to satisfy my growing urges. "Eight-pagers," pornographic comics bootlegged in the high school print shop, helped ease the pain. I learned more about sex from my favorite cartoon characters than from real life. I guarantee it wasn't Popeye's bulging biceps that made Olive Oyle smile. Besides, the little pamphlets were ten times easier to lay our hands on than the prick-teasing neighborhood girls. It was all part of my education along with fighting and hanging out.

It was December 7, 1941. Above the din a paperboy croaked, "Read all about it. The Japs just bombed Pearl Harbor." I thought where the hell is Pearl Harbor?

IMET OTHER GUYS from the neighborhood with the same routine, skipping school and hanging out. There was Leroy Smolen, Sonny Clark, Bob Thor, Loreny Rodgers, Gilbert Chester, Buddy LaRue and Jack Kearns. We stuck together which meant if one guy got in a fight, we were all in the fight.

For transportation, all we had to do was grab the taillights or spare tire of a stopped car and jump on the bumper. We called it "skitching" a ride. It was important to jump on exactly when the car pulled away or the driver would notice the rear end of the car dipping from our weight. We raced to see who could make it to the Drake, a fancy hotel, and back before the other guys. Our starting point was the Outer Drive, a freeway that winds along the shore of Lake Michigan. Getting off was easy. We pounded on the fender, whump, whump, whump, like the car had a flat. When the driver stopped to investigate, we jumped off.

One time a guy yelled, "Hey, you crazy kids! Don't you know you can get yourselves killed?" What was he talking about? I was nine years old. I couldn't die.

The corner of Montrose and Broadway was our favorite meeting place. From there we skitched a ride and pulled the flat tire bit at Montrose Harbor, our destination. Running past this big park, we swung along the edge of a city golf course by the beach. In less than ten minutes we were swimming in Lake Michigan off these rocks. For hours we entertained ourselves diving for poor suckers' golf balls or other kinds of junk that littered the dark bottom. You wouldn't believe the things that wound up in that harbor.

Jack Bailey burst from the water sputtering, "There's a guy wrapped in chains down there!" Heart pounding, I frog-kicked my way along the bottom, searching for the grizzly body. Nothing. He was just putting us on. But my imagination was on a roll. Maybe one day I'd find a pair of cement booties attached to some guy who couldn't keep his mouth shut, like in the movies.

We raced one another across this long, deep channel that connects the lake to Montrose Harbor. The threat of being caught in the channel's treacherous current turned us into expert swimmers. Because it's so far north, the temperature in Lake Michigan hovers around sixty degrees even in summer. Sometimes I'd shiver, but not from the icy water. I can still see the two guys they once pulled from that murky water— blue faced and battered.

In the late afternoon a reddish summer sun blazed brightly then sank behind the familiar Chicago skyline. We swam out to an empty yacht and stretched our chilled bodies on the still warm deck. Long into the night we boasted about our adventures, each guy's story bigger than the last guy's. We exaggerated so much, I almost fell overboard from laughing so hard. Pretty soon, my head began to nod. I couldn't hold it up a second longer. My eyes slammed shut.

Another summer turn-on was the Wilshore, an open-air ballroom on Wilson and Claredon near the lake. Saturday evenings us guys strained to hear the hot, live music drifting over the wall from the musicians playing riffs on the other side.

"Hey, Leroy," one guy would say. "I dare you to climb on top."

"Whatsa matter, you chicken?" another guy piped in.

One by one we scaled the bricks. Perched on top of the wall, we had the perfect vantage point. We jabbed one another, mocking the dreamy-eyed couples swaying below. I didn't let on, but secretly I envied them. I imagined myself down there dancing with the best looking girl in the place. She laughed at my funny jokes while I pressed her close. It was just a daydream, but I knew one day it would come true.

Darker things happened around the Wilshore. On one of those sticky summer nights, the kind that made you feel jumpy for no reason, this guy and his girl were walking slowly by the ballroom. Jack Bailey let out a wolf whistle.

The guy spun around to face Bailey. "Get off the corner you punk."

"Who says?" I piped in, my smart-mouth always in gear. In a flash, the guy whipped out his police-issued Smith & Wesson and pointed it straight at me. No fooling. How was I supposed to know he was an off-duty cop? The sound of my feet hitting the pavement echoed down the street, this crazy cop in hot pursuit. As I turned west on Leland, a bullet grazed the heel of my right loafer. I made a dive under a parked car and held my breath. The trigger-happy cop rushed by. We named this nut-case "Jesse James." But there were dozens of cops with just as many short-circuited brain cells. Cops like that made us fearless and tougher than tungsten steel.

Speaking of tough, one of our gang was Jack Kearns whose world-famous father promoted and managed Jack Dempsey in bout after moneymaking bout during Dempsey's heyday. "Doc" Kearns also handled guys like Mickey Walker and Joey Maxim to round out a card that read like a *Who's Who* of boxing. It was a well-known fact that Kearns was the biggest fight promoter in the entire country. He was the kind of guy who made a million dollars, went broke, made another million, went broke, and so on. Someone said Doc was like one of those inflated shmoo dolls with a weighted base. It kept popping up no matter how hard you punched it.

Young Jack was a natural bullshitter just like his old man. When it came to fighting, Jack took a lot and gave a lot. He was as fearless as a male lion defending his harem.

One lucky Thursday—a day seared into my memory—Jack invited our gang over to Helsing's to meet his father. It was the first time I set eyes on a hundred dollar bill. Doc threw money around the table like he minted it in his basement. I got a knot in my stomach the size of a man's fist just eyeballing all that cash. If a working stiff took home a hundred bucks a month, I guarantee, he was President of the United States.

Not only did Doc treat us guys to lunch, he casually peeled off a ten spot for each of us—fifty bucks just like that. My hand shook as I reached for mine. That was more than my father made in a week. It was funny Doc Kearns was so free with his money because, rumor had it, he was in one of his broke spells. After that meeting, Jack never lost a fight.

I WAS JUST a nine-year-old squirt pacing my El platform waiting for a train. It was December 7, 1941. Above the din, a paperboy croaked, "Read all about it—the Japs just bombed Pearl Harbor." I thought where the hell is Pearl Harbor? The next day, huddled around the radio, me and my family listened to President Roosevelt declare war. I didn't understand what it all meant until, within a month, every male from eighteen to forty wore a uniform. With few exceptions, if a guy wasn't in uniform, he was either a 4F or FBI man.

My father at nearly 50 was too old for the draft. But the slim, sharp-looking Irishman, the "bantam rooster" as his cronies called him, not only threw a mean belt with his fists, he could belt down his whiskey with the best of them. My dad played around a lot so I didn't see him much. I knew he had other women because I overheard the grownups around the neighborhood click their tongues and whisper, "How can Charlie cheat on Mary, she's such a good woman?"

Sometimes when my dad stumbled in late—shirt torn and bloodied, a woman's scent hanging heavy on his clothes—I heard Mom cry and plead with him, "Charlie, ain't I good enough for you?" The silence hurt my ears. Of course my brother and sister knew what was going on, but what could they do? I tried not to think about it.

Once in a while I visited my dad at the Madison Avenue barbershop where he worked for as long as I can remember. I walked in just as Johnny, a loyal customer, sank into the barber chair. "Hey Charlie, give me the usual cut with a razor trim around the ears—not too short." Those were the exact same words the nearly bald Johnny had used for ten years.

"Okay, Johnny—just the way you like it," my dad said reassuringly as he snapped out a clean, white sheet. He took care to tie the ends around the old guy's neck the way a man knots a favorite necktie.

My father didn't encourage my visits. I guess he was afraid I'd walk in on him and one of his girlfriends, but I never did.

A terrible thing happened to our family when I was around 12. My father's coughing spells grew so bad, soon he was housebound with TB. The neighborhood gossips said maybe he got what he deserved for fooling around, but it meant something different to me. Now I had to have my hair cut by a stranger. Worse yet, I had to pay for it.

My dad never said much, which made it hard to get to know him. On one rare occasion I was sitting it out in the police station. My father came for me even though he was weak with TB. "If it wasn't for your poor mother, I'd leave you here." He shot me that look of his. I got the silent treatment all the way home on the streetcar. The next day my father forgot I was even alive. That was okay. At least he came down to the station to get me.

My mother's brother, Uncle Cameron, a brash, alcoholic cop from Louisville, Kentucky, informed my mother he was going to pay us a visit. My father had a different slant on the situation. "You mean we gotta put up with that loud-mouthed deadbeat? He sure knows how to sweet-talk your mother."

One night I was eating supper minding my own business. Out of the blue, Uncle Cameron knocked my hat off my head with a blind-sided swat that took me by surprise. "Don't you know you're not supposed to wear your hat inside?" he yelled.

My father rallied to my defense, barely able to stand. "Don't you raise your voice to my son," he rasped. "And if anybody's gonna hit him, it'll be me."

Sensing danger, my mother stepped between the two men. "What are you doing, Cameron?" My mother's steady gaze hit its mark. Uncle Cameron flinched like a wounded animal, ashamed he upset the one who raised him.

Uncle Cameron cut his vacation short. It was his last visit. When a subdued Uncle Cameron kissed my mother goodbye and finally closed the door, my father screwed up his face and mumbled something about stinking fish and guests, but I didn't catch the meaning. It was guys like Uncle Cameron, plus all my other alcohol-swilling relatives, who turned me off on drinking.

With my father too sick to work, my mother took his place as the main breadwinner for the family. She found a job in a defense plant, a former pencil factory, called Auto Point. It was converted into a war material factory. No matter what they actually did, women in defense plants were nicknamed "Rosie the Riveter." When she was white with fatigue after a long shift, I tried to cheer Mom with a "Hi, Rosie." She'd bounce right back with her sweet laugh.

Pretty soon, they drafted my brother. I stole a flag with a star in the middle of it, which meant someone in your family was serving in the armed forces. Our gang was very patriotic. We never broke a window with one of those flags pasted in it. There was a kid in our group, Tom Nakanasi, a Jap. He was just one of the guys. Next thing you know, they shipped him and his family to California. It was some camp for the American Japs. What a way to leave the neighborhood.

Us kids had no role models since most adult males served in the war. We lived for today. Nothing else mattered. The cops called us incorrigible, "incapable of being reformed." Without realizing it, a beast of defiance lurked inside each of us. Most of the time we kept our rage under wraps, but once authority entered the picture, the sleeping tiger awakened. "Back off!" it snarled. Then all hell broke loose. There was no stopping us. We became more daring with each new score and so strong that no lousy cop could break us.

Seeing that we were tough, we had to look the part. Our favorite "clothing store" was Maxwell Street, a Jewish neighborhood on the South Side. Block after block of outdoor tables spilled their contents onto the cracked sidewalk. Everything was wholesale but that didn't matter because we never paid for a thing. It was part of our code. One gang member distracted the owner while the others grabbed a bunch of clothes and ran.

The colored guys would flaunt their coolness in bright, pinstriped "zoot suits." We dug the look so much we tried a tamed-down version. That's how our gang wound up with outer-seam pants from Maxwell Street. We had the legs tapered to eight inches at the bottom, one inch wider than the colored guys wore theirs. It was outer-seam peg pants. Funny, they never sold outer-seam pants at Goldblatts or Sears. It must have been some kind of closeout the Jewish merchants latched onto. To the pegs we added a bright, three-button cardigan jacket with padded shoulders. We swung a gold chain attached to our belt, keys dangling from the end. Alligator shoes and a wide-brimmed fedora cocked over one eye completed the look.

Since there was no one around to keep me in line, I became an accomplished shoplifter. I stole from Goldblatts for years and never got caught. With the aid of traps—nothing more than big grocery bags tucked inside the front of our pants—stealing was as easy as skitching a ride. When the coast was clear, we pulled our pants out and stuffed merchandise down the front. Anything we couldn't use, we fenced.

The closest I ever came to messing up was the night I thought I was all alone in the store. I crouched inside the bottom of a display case till the place was dark and quiet. I sneaked out of my hiding place, grabbed a pillowcase and started to load up. All

of a sudden there was a shout, 'Hey, what are you doing there!"
It was a cleaning guy. I dropped the pillowcase and took off. I
navigated through the empty isles between waves of clothing
racks. A display window appeared ahead. Freedom. It took only
a few seconds to wield a mannequin battering ram through the
plate glass window.

The instant my feet touched the sidewalk, a police car made
a U-turn a few blocks down. Don't know if they spotted me
yet. I ran like hell, my heart doing a two-step on my rib cage.
By some miracle I made it to the hallway of my building a split
second before the cops turned the corner, siren screaming. They
flew by. I was safe.

Our gang beat restaurants, movies, everyone—with one exception. We had to pay to get in the Arcadia Roller Rink because the
manager, Eddie Anderson, knew us. Walkaround money came
easy. We jack-rolled people and pulled petty burglaries—anything to make a buck—then spent it before it could burn a hole
in our pockets.

School wasn't so good. They finally kicked me out of public
school and demoted me to Hogan Vocational School. It was
the last stop before reform school. At 10 years old I was already
branded a juvenile delinquent. Hogan was out on Montrose
Avenue a good 10 or 15 miles from my place. There were no school
buses, so you had to get there any way you could. I managed by
hanging onto the back of streetcars. If a guy got kicked out of
Hogan, he wound up in Parental School, a reform school where
the maximum stay was six weeks. After that, it was a much
longer stint at St. Charles Reform School. Lots of guys from
the Arcadia took that trail.

I started skipping from Hogan, so the school officials sent for
my mother. While I was in the sheet metal shop, one of the guys
in my class said he saw my mother heading for the principal's
office. As soon as I heard that, I took off out the window.

Later my mother confessed what happened. I couldn't look

her in the eye. "Son," she whispered, "Hogan wants to send you to Parental School. The principal gave me a big lecture."

I glanced sideways at Mom, startled to see the tears well up in her eyes. Then the tears were brimming over, landing in spatters all over the faded kitchen linoleum.

"I pleaded with the principal," she sobbed. "Please give my son another chance."

No one got to me like my mother. I tried to shrug it off, but we both knew it was no use. Maybe what I was doing was wrong, but I couldn't stop. Still, there were some things I could never do. A lot of guys I knew had no morals, no conscience. They worked their way up to the rank of hitmen—big-time gangsters. That wasn't my thing. It made me sick to see innocent people hurt. A guy like me who couldn't stomach killing would make a lousy gangster. But vicious guys didn't faze me. They knew I wasn't afraid of them. These animals that could do brutal acts—I could do worse to them—especially when I knew they'd kill my own mother just for the sport, as if they were taking potshots at a sitting duck in a penny arcade.

That was it. I quit Hogan. Nobody was going to send me to reform school. Once in a while the school authorities gave my family the third-degree regarding my whereabouts, but no one squealed.

Without school hanging over my head, life was one thrill after another—like the night me, Jack Kearns and Sonny Clark were walking along Sheridan Road. Jack nudged me. "Look, the keys are in that car." At ten years old, Jack's feet barely reached the pedals. But he knew how to drive, so Jack jumped behind the wheel. The cops nailed us in Evanston just north of Chicago. A scowling policeman poked his head in the window, giving us the once-over. "Whose car is this?" he asked.

Jack pointed at me, I pointed at Sonny and Sonny pointed at Jack, so the cop arrested all three of us. We sat it out in the Evanston Police Station lockup. That was the first night I spent in jail. It wouldn't be my last.

The next morning a paddy wagon hauled us down to the state attorney's office on Twenty-sixth and California. Jack's father arrived while we were in the auto theft department. You'd think God himself walked in the way everything changed for the better. We crammed our faces with so many cheeseburgers and milk shakes I thought I was going to throw up. Doc Kearns sprang us in record time. I doubt that God could have done any better. When my folks heard it was the famous Doc Kearns who came down to the station, they didn't believe it. "If you play your cards right, I'll introduce you," I said.

The older we got, the bolder we got. One day a bunch of us were hanging out at Wilson Avenue Beach. Bill Young, a professional thief, and Chester, a nice-natured nervy guy, pretended to leave. Instead, they strolled over to the hot dog stand, calmly put a knife to the attendant's throat and emptied the cash register. Bill and Chester made a run for it. The customers created such a ruckus they attracted the attention of the park district police who happened to be cruising by. The two were arrested a block away. It was straight down to JDH for them—Juvenile Detention Home on Ogden and Roosevelt.

A few weeks later, with only one guard on duty, Bill Young made a break for it. He found a cord that fit neatly around the guard's neck. When the guard blacked out, Bill and another guy from the neighborhood beat it. It was in all the newspapers: "Juveniles Escape from Detention Home!" Bill couldn't go home because he would have been arrested in no time. He had to find a place to stay till the heat was off. I knew just the spot.

Very late one night, me, Bill and Sonny dropped by a streetcar barn on the corner of Diversey and Clark where they kept the streetcars that weren't running. No watchman on duty—a good sign. The three of us hung out in a musty streetcar in this barn for maybe a week. Time dragged by so slowly we started to get on one another's nerves.

The following Sunday evening we were laying around listening to the rain beat a boring rhythm on the barn's tin roof. Sonny glanced up at the ceiling. "I'm not really sure, but maybe this is one notch better than watching the grass grow." Sonny started fiddling with the streetcar's controls absentmindedly. He discovered that if he turned a lever, the streetcar moved forward—he pulled it back, the streetcar stopped. Following his lead, I pulled a switch next to the tracks. Earlier I'd noticed that the switch turned the tracks toward Clark Street. I jumped aboard as the streetcar quickly gained speed.

Once we were on Clark Street Sonny gave it full throttle. What a thrill . . . until heavy traffic put an end to our little ride. We jumped off when some fool passenger tried to board the thing.

Now Bill was forced to stay with an uncle. Sure enough, the cops caught him and he wound up in St. Charles Reform School. After that, Bill did a lot of hard time in prison.

Due to the fact that nearly all adult males were in the war, I could get away with almost anything. It seems that people have a tendency to believe everyone acts and thinks the way they do, like my mother for instance. My mother never, and I mean *never*, told a lie. Naturally, she thought everyone was an angel like she was. In order to be a good liar, you had to practice lying a lot like I did. If you never told a lie, you were usually gullible. That was my mother—gullible. There was just one problem. It was almost impossible to give my mother anything because she always wanted to know where I got the money. So I invented "Reggie," some rich kid from the Gold Coast, a swanky neighborhood on Marine Drive. Well, Reggie would give me this or that and my mother would fall for it. At twelve years old I had more money than my entire family.

Sunday matinees were my mom's favorite entertainment, her only day off, so I said I'd take her to a movie. She smiled but wouldn't budge. "Why won't you go with me, Mom?"

"I made a promise to God," Mom answered smoothing her apron. "If God stopped Tommy's seizures, I solemnly swore I'd never go to a movie on Sunday again."

You see, my brother Tom was an epileptic, but he didn't have a single attack after Mom's promise. And, true to her word, my mother stopped going to Sunday matinees. That sort of thing didn't work for me since I was no angel. Later that same night I took in a movie at the Uptown with about eight of the guys. I didn't make any promise to God. Each guy told the window attendant the last guy had the tickets. When the last guy got to the window he said, "I don't know those guys."

It was 1945 and the war was winding down. Doc Kearns packed Jack off to St. Joseph's Military Academy west of Chicago so he'd stay out of trouble. Little did I know what wild adventures were in store for us when me and Jack met by accident many years later.

I didn't mind being down there too much because none of the girls had any underwear on.

IT WAS 1947 and I had a string of burglaries hanging over my head. With the war over, better technology meant they could keep track of guys like me. Younger authorities, now in the system, hounded my relatives trying to find me.

"Look Billy," my brother Tom said. "You have a bunch of warrants out for your arrest. Why don't you join the army?"

"But I'm only fourteen. They ain't gonna take me," I told him.

"Don't worry," he said. "I'll get you a phony birth certificate that'll make you seventeen and I'll sign as your legal guardian." Next thing you know, I was in the U.S. Army Air Corps.

By the time I got to basic training at Lackland Airbase in San Antonio, Texas, they had divided the Air Corps into two separate branches of the military. I was one of the first guys to be in the Air Force as it was now called. As an aviation engineer, my job was building parking lots. That was about as far from flying as you can get.

After basic, they transferred me to Albrook Field in the Panama Canal Zone. What a paradise, especially to a kid straight out of Chicago's concrete jungle. Technicolored tropical flowers and palm trees popped up everywhere, and the strange bird sounds reminded me of the Lincoln Park Zoo. You sure didn't see this stuff on the corner of Montrose and Broadway! It smelled a whole lot better, too.

On base we lived in a brick barracks. Imagine the local five-foot-tall San Blas Indians peeling our potatoes wearing little more than loin clothes? It looked like someone rounded up a bunch of midgets for a Hollywood movie. Seeing as how the kitchen was in the same building as our barracks, we didn't have far to go for food. Eating was my second favorite pastime. Behind the barracks an Olympic-sized swimming pool, complete with high dive, cooled our sweat-drenched bodies. But that wasn't the best part.

A one-hour bus ride from Panama City took you to a place called the Rio Abajo that hid a wonderful secret. Locals and outsiders alike craved its treasures: the world's two finest whorehouses. The brothels grew fat on a steady diet of sex-starved Americans swatting their way through the mosquito-infested interior. The men were all in search of just one thing—a piece of ass. As luck would have it, Rio Abajo was strictly off limits to military personnel. Right then I knew I had to find some excuse to get there.

I learned through the grapevine that if you joined special services, especially if you fought on the boxing team, you had many privileges including a class "A" pass with unlimited leave. That same day I rushed to sign up. The first chance I got, I sneaked off to Rio Abajo. It didn't bother me one bit that I'd probably get court-marshaled if I was caught. At 14 years old, my hormones called all the shots.

A dusty bus ride brought me to the first whorehouse, a vine-covered mansion called the Vive L'Amour. Inside its fortress-like walls classy whores in all shapes, colors and sizes strutted their stuff. Their bag of sexual tricks included French moves to please even the hard to please. Only problem was, variety didn't come cheap.

There was a local place further down the road called the Felix Bar. This bordello on stilts rose above the thick jungle like a tree house out of the mist. In the yard, chickens scratched out a meal under a crummy tin sign that read, "Lucky Strike es Primero." Six rickety stairs led to a thatch-roofed bar. Inside, a few Casablanca ceiling fans aimlessly stirred the muggy air. The small barroom, lit only by the faint light filtering through a few louvered shutters, could seat maybe twenty people. Six shabby but clean tables filled what space remained next to a tiny blue-tiled bar. The two customers, obviously locals, barely glanced over when I took a seat on one of the wooden bar stools. I guess they were used to seeing *gringos* from the airbase.

A slender, dark-haired girl washing glasses behind the bamboo bar winked and offered me some liquor, but I asked for a Coke. I was already reeling under the heady aroma of over-ripe flowers and the oppressive humidity. Loud Spanish music blaring from the jukebox in the corner started to make my head throb. From its bar stool perch next to me, an orange, yellow and green parrot squawked Spanish obscenities to anyone who cared to listen. I let out a laugh when it called me *cabron* and *pendejo*.

I don't know what made me sweat more, the sticky jungle air or the three females competing for my attention. Ranging from about 15 to 20 years old, the trio wore simple peasant dresses that accentuated their ripe, young bodies. Their dark hair and expressive eyes made my heart thump louder than a bongo drum. I was sure everyone in the joint could hear it. Maria, the one in the white gauzy dress, cast a lazy smile in my direction. Those liquid brown eyes seemed to bait me with their directness. The French girls over at the Vive L'Amour were really something, but a guy could get laid here for a lot less. That did it. One twist from Maria's shapely hips and my mind was made up. I decided to make the Felix Bar my regular hangout.

Before long the Spanish *putas* fell for me. I was only 14—just a kid with hormones in overdrive. My blue eyes and blond hair, plus my trim build, made me something of a novelty. The whores called me "pretty blue eyes" and fought over me. I didn't complain much.

Maria became so obsessed with me she stopped charging me for her services. She even tried to push money on me. Of course

I refused. I never could take money off a woman. I asked to see Maria one time and the girls said "which one?" There were no fewer than five Marias who worked at the Felix Bar, so my Maria made me call her *cara una.*

After we were lovers for a while, Maria hid me in her closet behind these bamboo blinds when she was with a customer. She got a thrill out of my watching her. The flickering candle on the table beside the bed exaggerated the shadows on the wall made by the rhythmic movements of Maria and her partner. The erotic images blocked out all distractions, even my fear of the scorpions I was dead certain lurked somewhere in the dampness behind me. The way Maria moaned and clenched her partner with those strong legs of hers, I suspected she was totally caught up in her work. But when I waved at her from behind the blinds, she wriggled her fingers at me like she was drying her nails. I snickered into my hand, afraid I'd give myself away. My thoughts wandered.

Maria taught me everything about sex—stuff the guys at home didn't know existed—like what really excites a woman. She showed me by using my hand on her body as if it were her own. I discovered all the places where women love to be touched. I also learned a lot about hookers. They have emotions like anyone else—love, hatred, fear, jealousy. They just happen to hook for a living. It's strictly business. For example, the girls often screwed their johns under a religious picture or a cross. To them having sex is like eating or sleeping, just a natural part of life.

The fevered pitch of animal sounds from Maria and her lover threatened to drown out the tinny radio playing Spanish music in the next room. Aroused, I closed my eyes. In my mind I became the object of Maria's passion. I opened my eyes to find myself gazing at a statue of the Virgin Mary in a wall niche not two feet from Maria's bed. I wondered what the Madonna with the blue veil could be thinking, the sad one who never blinked. The girl with the same name was doing things that would make any virgin blush. It excited me to watch her long, dark hair brush against the man's face and chest every time she moved up and down in her slow, even rhythm. I could swear Maria threw in a few sexy maneuvers just to make me jealous.

After the john had paid and left, I could hardly wait for Maria to repeat everything she did earlier, but this time with me. Was I imagining it or was she really as passionate about me as she seemed? Shit, who cared!

It wasn't all fun and games. One time me and this Puerto Rican boxer José were on our way to Rio Abajo. In Panama City we caught a mini-bus called a *chiva*. I was told *chiva* is the word for female pig, but I couldn't make the connection. The *chiva* was like a long station wagon decked out with colored lights, the sort you put on a Christmas tree. Loaded to the roof with squealing pigs, clucking chickens, screaming babies and wall-to-wall passengers, the stuffy bus made breathing hard for me. José squeezed me into a corner like a sausage in a casing. My dark-skinned friend blended in with the crowd but my blond hair, blue eyes and light skin were a dead giveaway if the military police stopped us. Secretly, I jammed my civilian hat down on my head as far as it would go.

We careened down the highway and I felt kind of woozy with all the commotion. Suddenly, bouncing lights appeared ahead of us. If it was the MPs, we were in big trouble. Our driver slowed down so we could make a quick exit. In a single calculated move, me and José rolled off the bus, scrambling for the welcome cover of the thick jungle. My heart pounded wildly as I lay on my belly holding my breath. We could make out the uniforms now. The driver and passenger were the dreaded Panamanian Police, worse than big trouble. They answered to no one.

The angry staccato of foreign words cut through the silence. I didn't need José to translate that these guys were going to kill us if we didn't haul our asses out immediately. We stayed put. The zing of bullets ricocheting off nearby trees quickly changed our minds. José shouted in Spanish. He said something like, "Don't shoot. We're coming out."

Grabbing me by the collar, he dragged my unwilling body with him. Cautiously, we made our way out of the tangle of vines, hands in the air. I expected we weren't gonna get too far. The whole time José bargained in Spanish seemed like a lifetime. I was as jumpy as a blind man in a snake pit.

José hissed, "Give me your money and wrist watch, quick!"

"Why?" I asked.

"Don't argue."

Before I could do anything stupid, José grabbed my stuff. Together with his, he shoved the whole lot at the police. The dark-skinned officers in their steel-gray uniforms eyed me with hatred during their rapid-fire exchange. Clearly, they were deciding our fate and the fact I was a *gringo* put us at a decided disadvantage. The Panamanians despised the *norte americanos* in the Panama Canal Zone, especially since we were screwing around with their women.

When at last the two shrugged and moved on, I gulped air like it was in short supply. Sweat soaked my once crisp shirt. I glanced at José, surprised a guy with such dark skin could turn so pasty white. "The bastards were dead set on shooting us," he volunteered, voice shaking. "I told them we weren't worth the effort. I've seen them kill American soldiers just for fun," José added with a grimace. A shiver ran through me even though it was ninety degrees in the shade.

Whenever women were around, trouble wasn't far off, so I was in trouble a lot. One time in the Felix Bar it was just me and three girls flirting around a table drinking Panamanian coffee. Heavy footsteps on the stairs startled us. This time it was the MPs. Before they crossed the threshold, I made a dive under the table. The girls hid me by dropping the large table cloth down to the floor on the side facing the door.

Pretty soon my eyes adjusted to the dim light. I didn't mind being down there too much because none of the girls had any underwear on. It was like sitting in the middle of a forest admiring all the different bushes and trees. What a sight! I explored a little, probing here and there. The girls squirmed but held their cool. Too bad the MPs couldn't stay a little longer.

I had to admit that boxing no longer motivated me. Besides, I'd been a screw-up all my life. Now I was dying to get out of special services. In the fights I did have, I was in the ring with guys ten years older than me who trained all the time. I was lucky they didn't kill me. My superiors finally threw me out of special services because I fought so lousy. They called me "a disgrace to the Air Force." My commanding officer "volunteered" me for my old job—building parking lots in the tropical heat. He said I deserved it. I couldn't argue on that score.

It was 1948 and the U.S. military just opened Las Vegas Air Force Base in Nevada. Later it was renamed Nellis Air Force Base after some big shot. They needed guys who could work in a lot of heat, so I was transferred to Las Vegas. No one heard of the place. One guy said, "I think they made a mistake. Las Vegas is in New Mexico." He was right. At that time Las Vegas, Nevada, was barely more than a man-made bump in the desert.

I nearly wet my pants when I stepped off the train in downtown Las Vegas, or Glitter Gulch, as it's known. From the station where the Union Plaza now stands, I surveyed the night scene down Fremont Street. Nothing I'd seen could compare to all the glitz. The glare, from what seemed like a million blinking light bulbs, temporarily blinded me. Out of the blur a giant sign shaped like a waving cowboy caught my attention. I spotted a military truck ready to take us to the base about 17 miles away. It might as well have been a laundry truck for all I cared. I had to go down that street. The "Howdy Pardner" from that sign was all the temptation I needed.

Dazed, I stumbled into the Golden Nugget only a few steps from the train station. My knees turned to jelly when I realized the entire floor was inlaid with silver dollars, the bar too. A jolt went through me like I'd stuck my finger in a 220-outlet. It wasn't just the sight of all that money. Dazzling lights, air thick with cigarette smoke, the clink, clink of slot machines—the atmosphere sent sparks of electricity shooting through my veins. Hell, I got a hard-on just watching.

Across the street in the Eldorado Club, the action made all the card games I'd ever seen pale by comparison. What could beat this? Deep in my gut I knew I'd found the place I'd been dreaming about, this shot of adrenaline, way out in the Nevada desert.

Four hours later my circuits were on overload. Mustering nerve, I called the base and told the guy on duty I was lost. When he finally stopped laughing, he told me they'd come pick me up. The MPs carted me back. They slapped me with a "104," which I think is one step below a court-marshal. My PFC stripe came off one more time. If Velcro had been around, it would have come in handy.

With each passing day my obsession to see Las Vegas grew like the giant knot in my stomach. Finally, my 30 days of hard labor were up. I was allowed to go into town like any other guy. My racing heart ran a red light at the thought of seeing all that action again.

To set the scene, travelers heading for L.A. from back East passed through town on Las Vegas Boulevard. It would become one of the most famous stretches of commercial real estate in the world, the Las Vegas Strip. As you drove in a southwesterly direction, the first casino you hit on Las Vegas Boulevard was the El Rancho Vegas, several miles out in the country. I caught sight of the El Rancho marquee as our brown military truck passed by. *"Frankie Laine Now Appearing."* I whistled for the driver to drop me off.

Once inside, I quickly spotted the singing sensation himself talking to some admiring fans. I heard Frankie was from Chicago, too. Armed with the confidence only youthful ignorance brings, I marched up to him, hand outstretched. "Hi, Frankie," I beamed. "My name's Bill Hanner and I'm from Chicago." He could have brushed me off. Instead, he treated me like I was really somebody. Maybe Frankie sensed that the skinny kid in the big uniform was just plain homesick.

"Hey, that's great, kid. What part of Chicago are you from?"

Frankie, with the turned-up brim and toothy smile, turned out to be even better than his songs. Sometimes I cruised around Las Vegas with Frankie and Carl Fisher, Frankie's long-time friend and piano player. One time Frankie invited me along when they entertained the kids at Las Vegas High School. If guys like Frankie Laine visited my school, maybe I wouldn't have quit. Now every time he spotted me at the El Rancho Frankie told his staff, "Give the kid anything he wants." I became kind of a celebrity on account of his generosity. I didn't let it go to my head, though. Everyone said Frankie was the greatest, from stagehands to big shots. Nasty rumors followed many Las Vegas headliners, but not Frankie Laine.

When I first laid eyes on Las Vegas, it was mostly a scattering of seedy "no-tell" motels and a handful of bustout joints. Only three casinos broke up the desert monotony along Las Vegas Boulevard: The El Rancho Vegas, the Last Frontier, and finally, Bugsy Siegel's showplace, the Flamingo. Bugsy made a big splash when he built the Flamingo in 1947, just one year before I got there. But his exit wasn't so great in June of that same year. I always thought it was a shame Bugsy couldn't hang around to see the Flamingo take off. Before Bugsy's blood had clotted, the mob's new team had taken over the Flamingo.

Years later Mafia insiders told me that Bugsy was murdered by mob hitmen Gussie Alex and Frank "Strongy" Ferraro in Beverly Hills. Frankie Carbo, the point man from New York, made the positive ID. For his trouble, the Outfit rewarded Gussie with the booming First Ward in downtown Chicago to support his loansharking, brothel, strip joint and bookmaking operations.

It was unheard of for a Greek to gain so much power within the organization, unless he performed an outstanding service.

On June 17, 1960, the El Rancho burned down, allegedly set by Marshall Caifano, Sam Giancana's henchman. The motive for the arson was hazy, but when the smoke finally cleared, one thing was certain—greed played a major role, just like Bugsy Siegel and his Flamingo. Most everyone knows that once greed gets in your blood, there's no stopping it. From the moment I learned the power of greed, I started to make a lot of money.

All of a sudden Moretti pulled out his gun to kill
Pomeroy. I could tell by the veins popping out all
over Moretti's face that he was going goofy.

IT WAS 1948 and I was a worldly guy of 17. With my discharge
papers in my hand after my 18 months were up, and about three
hundred dollars in mustering-out pay, I made a bee-line straight
back to Chicago. I moved in with my mom who still lived on the
third floor on Leland Avenue across from Goldblatts Department
Store. It was the same old place. Aside from the sad fact that my
father had died from TB, nothing much had changed.

When you turned the lights on in our place, you couldn't miss
the thousands of cockroaches knocking one another over to get
out of sight. Sometimes when I was fixing a sandwich, I caught a
roach move out of the corner of my eye. There went my appetite.
This wasn't my mother's fault. She was the cleanest person I ever
met. After she scrubbed our floors on her hands and knees every
day, she went to the factory to work her regular job. Roaches
were just part of living in a poor neighborhood.

Since my Irish/Scottish family liked to drink and fight, my
sister Louise made sure there was always a bottle of Old Fitzgerald on the table. I don't know exactly why I never drank, maybe
I'd seen too many drunken relatives, but Louise could hold her
own with the best. In fact, she could down a fifth and not even
show it. Louise married Lee Griffin who owned Lee's Lounge
around the corner. Not a bad match for a girl who liked to drink.
I guess that left the fighting part to me.

An important person entered the picture around this time. We met by chance at the Sheridan Rec Pool Hall across the street from my dad's barber shop in the Sheridan Plaza Hotel. If pool wasn't your thing, the place featured "short" cards like gin rummy, hearts and pinochle.

Bob Mauro, an accomplished card mechanic, made the pool hall his second home. Maybe a couple of years older than me—trim with dark hair and decent features—Bob had only one minor problem. Not that Bob was a slob, but once in a while he gave off a faint odor, like Friday night's fish on Saturday morning.

I didn't shoot pool too well, but cards came easy. Seeing my interest, Bob showed me how to manipulate the cards. Pretty soon I was dealing the second card off the deck, making it appear to be the first. Next, I mastered how to false cut a deck. Before I knew it, we were taking off live card games. Even though Bob was a loner, we got on great. I talked guys into playing, then Bob would step in with his amazing sleight-of-hand.

Imitating my favorite Bogart character after our first big score, I lisped, "Louie, I think this is the beginning of a beautiful friendship."

Bob scratched his head and said, "Who the hell is Louie?"

Pretty soon I was back in the old routine, hanging around the drug store then going out in teams of three or four. We'd burglarize a joint or pull a holdup, as the mood struck us. Then it was back to the Arcadia to divide up the loot, which meant we always had walk-around money. The cops called us "cowboys," a better-dressed version of the "Dead End Kids" we copied from all those movies. Our gang was a rough and tumble lot with our own fearless sense of loyalty.

That kind of loyalty nearly got me killed. Mike Moretti, a detective with the state attorney's office, was a real nut-case. His brother Sal, another screwball, worked for the city park police and moonlighted as Sam Giancana's chauffeur and bodyguard.

Anyway, Loreny Rodgers from our gang allegedly raped the Chicago crime commissioner's daughter, of all people. While out on bail Loreny contacted me and Bob Hopkins to be his witnesses. Bob was a guy we hung out with sometimes but he was too square to be in tight with our gang. Loreny cooked up a story that the girl was willing to gang bang a bunch of us guys in the park. Rape wasn't something I'd do, but we always stuck up for one another. I always felt sorry for that girl even though I never met her.

When Loreny's case came up, me and Bob Hopkins waited in court for our turn as witnesses. In marched Mike Moretti, his eyes shooting off sparks in all directions. Clearly he was itching for a fight. He reminded me of a hand grenade just waiting for someone to pull his pin. Out of the blue, Moretti arrested me and Bob on a trumped up charge. "Crimes against nature" he called it, better known as oral sex.

Moretti was shoving us toward the elevator when Loreny's attorney, Paul Pomeroy, stepped in. He grabbed Moretti by the lapels screaming, "You can't do that. These are witnesses for my client."

Moretti exploded. He threw all three of us in the waiting elevator. Now the court was on the third floor, the lockup was in the basement. On the way down, Moretti and Pomeroy got into a heated argument. All of a sudden Moretti pulled out his gun to kill Pomeroy. I could tell by the veins popping out all over Moretti's face that he was going goofy. I knew if Pomeroy went, I didn't stand a chance. Moretti sure as hell couldn't leave any witnesses. Here I was handcuffed to the useless Bob Hopkins who looked like he might faint any minute. If I was quick enough, I could stop Moretti from bringing his gun down to shoot.

Desperately, I pulled Bob's arm up with mine. I hit Moretti's hand. For a nerve-wracking second the gun see-sawed nearly out of Moretti's grasp, but he managed to regain control of it. Just then, the elevator door burst open. Police rushed at Moretti before he could fire. What a relief. I couldn't believe I was actually overjoyed to see the cops.

Me and Bob were locked in a holding cell till the police sorted things out. When Pomeroy told the judge what took place in the elevator, the judge had a fit. In a few hours we were out on signature bond, direct orders from the judge. We went on to testify for Loreny who beat the rap this time, and all charges against me and Bob were dropped. There were no thanks from Loreny. It was just something we did for one another.

Moretti's career ended with a bang. In a fit of anger, he pulled a gun and killed two innocent bystanders in a parking lot on Taylor Street. A third victim who was only wounded positively ID'd Moretti. At Moretti's trial, Paul Pomeroy had the satisfaction of describing Moretti's little temper tantrum in the elevator. This plus other damning testimony practically guaranteed Moretti would get the electric chair for murder. But thanks to his considerable juice with the Chicago Outfit, he squeezed out a better deal for himself—life in Stateville Prison. By an odd quirk of fate, Loreny and Moretti got acquainted in the joint years later while Loreny was serving ten years for armed robbery. Seems Loreny had a habit of cheating Moretti at cards and winning.

Brother Sal Moretti got nailed sometime later. His bloated body was found stuffed in the trunk of a car, shot four times in the head after he was tortured. Sal was murdered Mafia-style—"trunk music" the mob called it—after he screwed up on an assignment from Willie "Potatoes" Daddano, head of Giancana's burglars.

That's the way it was in Chicago—the Mafia guys in cahoots with the crazy Chicago cops. The line between the good guys and the bad guys fuzzed over due largely to the fact that the Outfit "owned" the Chicago aldermen who hired all the city workers including the police. It was no big secret that Chicago corruption started at the top and slithered all the way to the bottom.

On the South Side there was a colored cop named Sylvester Washington. He had the nickname "Two Gun Pete" on account of the two pistols he wore strapped to his waist. And on the North Side, there was this white cop Frank Pape whose trigger finger got a major workout. These two cops had a nasty habit. Shoot

first and ask questions later. Pape and Washington competed
to see who was the meanest and baddest. It was a real toss-up.
But they did what they wanted and nobody stopped them—just
like a couple of junkyard dogs. Later Pape headed security for
Arlington Race Track northwest of Chicago, a cushy job. It
just goes to show how far you can climb when you have juice in
high places.

With police officers like these on the force and mostly nuts,
us cowboys needed eyes in the back of our heads. Still, we woke
up every morning eager to have fun then share our stories with
one another . . . like the night we went out to pull a robbery.

We were cruising by this YMCA about 3:00 a.m. Me, Leroy
and Bob Thor decided to go inside and check it out. Except for
this elevator operator, an old guy sleeping on a couch, everything
looked deserted. Leroy and Thor entered the office while I kept
an eye on the old guy. We couldn't see one another.

After ten minutes Leroy called in a loud whisper, "There's a
safe in here. We're trying to get the night clerk to open it."

While I was guarding the operator, the elevator bell started to
ring, meaning somebody upstairs wanted to come down. Holding
a gun on the old guy I told him, "Stay right where you're at."

What sounded like sharp claps of thunder startled me. Huge,
ominous shadows appeared on the stairwell wall above our heads.
I relaxed a little when I realized it was just four or five guys in
white coats tromping down the stairway. They must have been
doctors or interns going to work. I had them face the wall with
their hands on their heads while the old guy frisked them. I
ordered him to give me the money he collected.

Meanwhile, the elevator bell kept ringing. Then four or five
more guys came down the stairs. Once again I covered them
and made the old guy empty their pockets and hand over the
dough. I spun around to see three more guys coming down. I
was getting nervous. I yelled at Thor to get out here. Him and
Leroy were still trying to open the safe.

Wouldn't you know? Here came five more guys down the

stairs. It was a fucking army. If they decided to attack, I didn't stand a chance. Besides, the gun I had was really a prop. I knew I couldn't shoot anybody. I stood there like an idiot until Leroy and Thor finally showed up.

Thor calmly surveyed the scene. "What are you guys having out here, a convention?"

In the car going home, the guys admitted they couldn't get the night clerk to open the safe, so they took the petty cash, about $60. I took $600.

Our gang liked to imitate tough actors like Richard Widmark as crazy Tommy Udo in *Kiss of Death*. In the movie, Udo pushed an old lady in a wheel chair down the stairs as he laughed that insane laugh of his. He may have been nuts, but Udo was a real sharp dresser in his black shirt, white tie and, of course, pearl-gray fedora.

In fact, we were always on the prowl for stuff to add to our image. Maxwell Street, our favorite place to shop, had these Italian Borsolino hats worn by all the Mafia guys. We spotted a hat we liked, snatched it and ran. Sometimes, cruising around in our fedoras and Borsolinos, one of the guys would see a squad car close by and whisper, "Hats." In a single motion, off came the hats. No sense inviting trouble.

The guy who had the least fear in our gang was Jack Bailey. One classic night me and Jack went joy riding in a stolen car. We passed a squad car going in the opposite direction. When the cops looked over, Jack gave them the finger. The squad car made a U, turned on their siren and the race was on.

I stared at Jack in disbelief. The goofball was doubled up laughing. "Are you nuts?" I said.

On our high-speed chase, Jack made an abrupt turn down an alley. Seconds later we plowed into a girder that held up the El tracks. Now on foot, we ran maybe 20 yards. I turned around just long enough to see the cops gaining on us. Jack got the bright idea to hide in one of the hollow girders. Following his lead, I hid in another girder. Lucky for us we were thin enough.

By the number of cops swarming the area, you'd think we'd robbed Fort Knox. It was amazing the police were on the scene so fast because, at the time, a squad car couldn't radio police headquarters for reinforcements. Police car radios could only receive messages. Headquarters used a broadcasting system to contact the squad cars working their beats. The cops had to locate one of the police call boxes, strategically scattered throughout the city, and phone headquarters. The phrase, "Calling all cars, calling all cars . . ." brought a sense of realism to cop-and-robber movies of the era.

The cops combed every inch of the area with their flashlights. How they failed to spot us, I'll never know. We sweated it out over four hours. As soon as they towed the car, we took off. Flipping the bird at the cops while driving a hot car earned Jack Bailey the nickname "Bedbug," meaning crazy. From then on, that's what we called him. As for me, I sure walked a lot straighter for the next few days.

There was only one person Jack the Bedbug was afraid of—his father. I found out how deep that fear ran. One day, soon after the police chase, Jack's face was swollen and discolored where his dad had beat the hell out of him for the umpteenth time. I couldn't stand to see Jack like that so I told him, "I'll get a couple of the guys and we'll teach your old man a lesson."

"No, no. Don't come around my house," Jack warned, shaking all over.

But Jack wasn't afraid of another living soul—not even Loreny Rodgers, the most violent man I ever met. Yeah, the same Loreny on whose account I nearly took a bullet in that elevator. It was odd Loreny being so violent, because he had a little better family life than the rest of us. Loreny even scared us guys, he was so mean.

Me, Loreny and Leroy were headed for the El one day when a man passing the other way with his wife accidentally bumped into Loreny. Without warning, Loreny punched the man in the head. When his wife tried to help the poor guy,

Loreny hauled off and hit her in the face with a brick. We kept our mouths shut when Loreny did stuff like that, but Jack the Bedbug would just laugh at Loreny, egging him on. It was sheer suicide.

One winter, when Loreny's arm was in a cast from some fight, Jack started to taunt him. "I bet when your arm's okay, I can whip you," he said in front of the whole gang, infuriating Loreny with his charming smile. If looks could kill, the white heat shooting out of Loreny's dark eyes would have seared everything in its path. We thought Jack was a goner right then. It finally dawned on Jack that he'd better take care of Loreny before Loreny killed him first. There wasn't a shadow of a doubt that Loreny would wipe out Bailey as easily as he'd swat a pesky fly.

Jack and I cooked up a plan. When we were sure Loreny wasn't home, we went over to his apartment building and climbed Loreny's snow-covered roof. Jack managed to loosen a cornerstone that we positioned directly above Loreny's front door. When Loreny came home, we were going to drop it on his head. The only catch was that the temperature was falling rapidly and the wind chill was doing a number on us.

We were up there over two hours and still no Loreny. My fingers and toes had lost all feeling. That was it. The cold won out. Lucky for us, Loreny's beef with Jack blew over, which meant Jack got to live.

Jack Bailey could have doubled for the movie star John Garfield. In fact, girls elbowed one another out of the way to get to him first. When it came to females, that guy could generate more magnetism than a fire-engine-red hot rod at an auto show. To add insult to injury, Jack was the only one of our bunch who could dance.

It was no surprise to anyone when Jack met Libby Periso, the most beautiful Italian girl I'd ever seen, at the Riverview Roller Rink on Belmont and Western. For years I'd been visiting the Riverview Amusement Park next door. Chicago's answer to Coney Island offered hours of stomach-churning fun on the world-famous "Bobs" rollercoaster, my favorite. Hair-pin turns, rattling gears and high speed made it appear deathly dangerous. In 1967 the Schmidts, owners of the park, finally closed Riverview due to failing attendance.

Libby lived nearby in an area known as "the Patch," the most notorious mob neighborhood in Chicago. The Patch spawned such organized crime figures as Sam Giancana and the old "Forty-two" gang. Libby's father, a likable Old World Italian, made friends with everyone in the Patch. So when Jack took Libby home, nobody messed with him.

Jack fixed me up with one of Libby's girlfriends, but I never had any special feelings for a girl until I laid eyes on Betty Lou Sabatka, a blond Polish beauty. I couldn't help but notice the traffic-stopping Betty. Fascinated, I watched her in her gray and pink skirt and matching pink sweater as she swirled around the Riverview Roller Rink in time to the music. Every pair of male eyes in the place was riveted on this platinum-blond Doris Day look-alike.

When the first strains of the "Skater's Waltz" belched from the huge live organ, I summoned my courage and sprang into action. After a slight hesitation, Betty smiled and took my outstretched hand. We skated together as if we'd been doing nothing else all our lives. We didn't talk much. Betty was a little shy and I was completely stunned; all self-confident male on the outside, mush on the inside.

I heard myself invite Betty to the Arcadia and her accept, but it seemed like two other people were talking. I remembered how mercilessly I had kidded Bailey when he told me how he felt about Libby. "Hey, Jack. You look like a love-sick calf." With a gulp, I realized it was me I was describing.

I escorted Betty home on the streetcar after a night of skating at the Arcadia. She lived on Western and Division, a long way from my place, but the time passed like the blink of an eye. I didn't want to leave so we sprawled on her stairs for hours, me spilling my guts out to her, talking about anything and everything. Normally, I couldn't sit still for five minutes. I was hooked. The chemistry between us was hard to explain. It got to me more than Betty's looks. The fact that I was a gang member didn't faze Betty in the least. She was convinced I was different. Betty's relatives gave her a lot of static about me. Like any girl in love, she ignored them.

During one long ride to visit Betty, I glanced over to study Jack's profile. Here's my best friend who's the spitting image of John Garfield and I'm crazy about a girl who could be Doris Day's twin, I thought. Look at me, just an Irish kid with good taste.

Within a few months Jack and Libby were married. Nobody would make odds on who was next. It was a sure thing.

Our wedding was no big deal. Preston Bradley, a Protestant minister, married us in a little chapel on the North Side. We figured we'd have a big bash in a Catholic Church with all the trimmings when we got the money for a real wedding. I found us a cheap, furnished apartment on Winthrop and Foster, not far from my mom's place. Here I was only seventeen, a married man. I guess that wasn't so surprising when I figured how much I'd already packed into my short life. With a wife to support, I needed extra cash. But us guys never went out for big money. Besides, we didn't have the brains to pull off an elaborate heist. If a place was deserted we'd empty the cash box, penny ante stuff. Everything operated on a whim. Our specialty—Disorganized Crime.

I'd do a lot of things, but killing innocent people wasn't one of them. If we robbed a bank, for instance, I'd have to be prepared to take out anyone who stood in our way. Of course the cops weren't mind readers. They didn't know my gun was only a prop. It put me in a dangerous position.

I learned just *how* dangerous a few months later when me and Jack Bailey stuck up a hotel. We didn't know the place was crawling with bureau cops who had our *modus operandi* down pat. The cops would rip a guy's head off if they got the urge, and there was no one to say, "Don't do that, fellas."

We walked in sporting our pearl-gray fedoras never smelling the set-up. Luckily, the detectives had their backs to the front door, minus their shot guns. Only a few minutes earlier the cops were hiding behind the front desk ready to blast us. We strolled by the lobby on our way to the cash register. One of the detectives did a double-take. "Don't move! Put your hands against the wall," he warned. They patted us down, took our guns, then beat and kicked us till we couldn't stand up. Every blow was punctuated with "We should kill you bums . . . we were laying for you dirty sons-of-bitches . . . now you hoodlums will rot in prison."

They hauled our battered bodies down to Shakespeare Station. Me and Jack were separated so we couldn't cook up any stories. For three days I got the third degree in the interrogation room. I lied that I was with Betty on the dates they were trying to nail me. I told them nothing. For that I took a lot of lumps. I figured they were doing the same thing to Bailey.

On the fourth day it was back to the interrogation room. This time the police ticked off the 17 hotels I robbed, waved a confession in front of my face and demanded to know who was with me. They told me each of my buddies confessed and I'd get off a lot easier, just like them, if I signed a confession. I didn't want to spend my next 20 years in prison. I'd be an old man by the time I got out. I figured the cop must have been telling the truth about the guys, otherwise how did he know all the facts? So I signed on the dotted line.

Jack couldn't hold out, but for a different reason. His father threatened to kill him if he didn't confess. Nothing was worth paying that high a price.

5

I told Father O'Brien, "I don't know why, I
just had to yank that kid out of the toilet."
Turned out, it was a stroke of luck.

O N JANUARY 23, 1951, a photo featuring eleven sheepish guys
handcuffed together bumped news of the Korean War right
off the front page of the *Chicago Tribune*. "Outer Seam Gang
Captured," read the headline in large, bold type. Next stop:
Cook County Jail.

I felt rotten when we pulled up to my temporary "home"
next to the Cook County Courthouse on Twenty-sixth and
California. Before you knew it, I was talking to the guy next to
me. He told me all kinds of interesting things about the place.
For instance, there's a maze of tunnels that connect the county
jail to the courthouse so the prisoners won't get any funny ideas
and try to make a break for it. Inmates destined for the electric
chair wait it out on death row in a separate wing. The chair was
a grim reminder of what a guy could expect if he wasn't lucky
enough to have a connected attorney.

When someone like me couldn't afford to get out on bond,
he'd sit it out in County. If a guy was convicted and sentenced
to less than a year, he was transferred to Bridewell Jail next to
County. Over a year, he'd go to a state penitentiary. Most guys
from my neighborhood said they'd rather do two years in a state
pen than a year at Bridewell on account of it being a filthy place
where you did tough time. I prayed I wouldn't be sent there.

While I waited for my trial date, I was assigned to G-1-11—
tier G, first floor, cell 11. My other rap partners were scattered
throughout the jail. It was considered too risky for members of a

gang to share the same tier. On my first day, guards escorted me to a large bullpen where maybe 40 inmates were milling around. There were four picnic tables in the room. The "playroom," as it was called, was where guys passed the time playing cards, eating meals, arm wrestling and so on. I was about to find out it wasn't all fun and games. At 9:00 p.m. sharp, guards opened the bullpen door that led to a long hallway where our one-man cells were located. It was lock-up till 6:00 a.m., then back to the bullpen.

That would be my routine for the next month and a half. It wasn't the Ritz, but it sure beat a lot of places. I shuddered to think what my fate would have been if I'd ended up in some rat-infested Panamanian jail—or worse.

Not more than 20 minutes after I was introduced to my new surroundings, one of the colored guys who "ran" the tier strolled over to my table. "Hey, man," he said leering at me. "Why don't you just give me those alligator shoes of yours? They look mighty fine." Without hesitating I took off my shoes and handed them over. The colored guy swaggered back to his table, tried on the shoes, discovered they were too small and set them on the bench next to him. His friends snickered and jabbed at each other.

I hardly noticed the dinner tray that was slapped down in front of me. Guys on kitchen detail shuffled out with the food. It arrived on the dumbwaiter that connected the kitchen, one floor below, to the bullpens on each floor. All the while, my blood was boiling. The better part of my first tasteless prison meal congealed in a pool of grease on my well-worn metal plate. I examined the smallest detail of a glob of gravy clinging to my spoon. Forks were forbidden in prison—too easy to make into a weapon.

By now all the guys in the room had split up into their usual groups. Satisfied with my gravy findings, I calmly carried my metal tray over to the colored guy's table, not giving a damn who was watching. The distinct sound of splintering bone echoed throughout the room as I cracked the colored guy's head open with my tray. He landed in a heap on top of uneaten lumps of beef and mashed potatoes, peas rolling every which way. Blood spurted from his head gash onto the gray cement floor. All eyes were riveted on me as I picked up my shoes and quietly took my place at my table.

By this time a guard heard the ruckus and looked in on the bullpen. Pretty soon 10 guards descended on the scene. They shouted commands, shoving us inmates against the wall. During the commotion, I caught a glimpse of other guards carting the colored guy off to the infirmary. Never did find out what happened to him. So much for my first day in Cook County Jail.

Nobody ratted on me. That was a good sign. Since no one squealed, the whole tier was put on "banned" which meant no cigarettes, candy or milk. There was a store on wheels where these things were for sale if you had the money. When you were on "banned," buying was prohibited.

Sundays in the prison chapel were the only time me and my rap partners were allowed to see one another. In hushed voices we'd talk about why the electric chair was right across the hall.

"Maybe it's so a guy can say his prayers before he dies," Leroy added glumly.

I told the guys about the time Joe, an inmate cleaning guy who had access to off-limits areas, let me sit in the chair. "I started to sweat just thinking about it," I whispered. "He buckled me in tight with these wide brown straps. I almost got sick when I imagined the jolts of electric current surging through my body." Nobody wanted to admit my story got to them, but their pale faces staring back at me said it all.

By the end of my first week I knew everyone in County. They were mostly guys like me from the North Side. My friend Joe, the one who let me sit in the electric chair, would palm me cigarettes that I'd share with the other inmates. This gave me a little respect with the guys who ran the tier, which meant they left me alone.

My time in jail could be summed up in one word: MONOTONY.

For a guy like me who lived every minute in the fast lane when most people were still looking for the on-ramp, life in jail was worse than boring. The smallest distraction in this joint was like manna from heaven. So imagine my surprise when Leroy actually paid me a visit one day. He pulled off this amazing stunt by riding the rickety dumbwaiter down from tier G-2, right above. Before the guards kicked him out, me and Leroy had time to exchange a couple of slightly exaggerated jail stories. Maybe Leroy wasn't manna from heaven, but the sight of his sweaty, wide grin as he crawled out of the dumbwaiter gave me a good laugh. For a few fleeting minutes I even forgot where I was.

After a while, I noticed there was a white guy on the tier named Matthews who had a thing against other white guys. Matthews refused to give a white guy a cigarette, but if a colored guy asked him, he fell all over himself to oblige. I knew his game, and I didn't like it.

Now there was a guard we called Crow on account of his blue-black hair, enormous beak-like nose, and jerky movements. All he needed was wings. Crow strutted around the galley doing bed check like a mother bird counting her chicks. First he'd check on me. Then he'd strut over to Matthews's cell next to mine and peer in. He hit the other cells one by one. Every night he performed his little ritual.

It was time to put my plan into action. I waited just long enough for Crow to cross to the other side of the tier then I yelled, "Hey, Crow—go fuck yourself!"

Crow darted back, his shiny hair bristling like ruffled feathers. "Who said that?" Crow shrieked into the dimly lit hall.

Catching Crow's eye, I nodded toward Matthews's cell as I motioned Crow over. When his small, greasy ear was just inches from my lips I whispered, "Let's fix him, Crow. The minute I call out to open Matthews's cell, do it. He'll think he's getting out on bond. Wait till he finds out it's a trick. I'll bet he won't be calling you anymore names."

Maybe twenty minutes passed then I shouted, "Knock down

15; Matthews going out on bail." The clanking of heavy steel jarred the silence. I smiled knowingly.

Matthews smirked when he passed my cell. He strode confidently down the aisle past the other cells, convinced he was minutes from freedom. As he walked by the colored guys, he shook his fist and rattled their bars. "I'm gonna' bang all your mothers and there ain't nothin' you can do about it," he threatened smugly. Now that he was getting out, Matthews didn't need to suck up to the colored guys who had all the juice. If he had a brain in his head, he would have realized he wouldn't be safe on the outside either. Word travels like lightening.

After two long minutes hysteric cries echoed down the tier. I laughed to myself knowing Matthews found out it was all a trick. I could hear him pleading with the guards to take him off the tier, dead certain the colored guys would kill him in the morning. Lucky for Matthews, he got his wish. That's the last I saw of him.

A couple of days later Sammy "the Rock," also known as "Hard Rock," showed up on our tier. He was a gang member from the Patch, in tight with the Outfit. The words "hard rock" described Sammy perfectly; a well-built, five-foot-eleven-inch block of pure muscle. I could tell he was the kind of guy you didn't want to mess with and I knew I'd never cross him. In spite of his tough exterior, his laid-back manner intrigued me. I noticed he kept a cool head, calm and quiet in the face of danger. The shades were mostly down on Sam's bottomless, dark eyes. He let you see only what he wanted you to see. Sammy had a habit of squeezing bottle caps in half with his strong, square hands. His odd smile when he bent those caps hinted at darker forces smoldering just beneath the surface. I came to realize that Sammy wore his wall-like exterior as a kind of invisible armor to ward off anyone who tried to get too close too him.

Me and Sam started to hang around together. In his cautious, deliberate way he taught me how to play chess. "It's one of the few games where you can't cheat," he told me. Playing chess helped make the time go by faster.

About a week after Sam showed up, some bad-ass from the South Side made a grand entrance on our tier. I guess he thought being in with the other colored guys gave him the power to throw his weight around. Sammy was getting ready to take on bad-ass when I stopped Sam. "Let me take care of this," I said, giving Sam a knowing wink.

My opportunity came a few days later when I caught bad-ass sleeping on top of one of the tables. A small curious audience, including Sammy, watched me carefully unwind a roll of toilet paper and drape it over the snoring form. I fumbled in my pocket, locating a pack of matches. "Voila!" I announced with all the gusto of a chef preparing a flaming dessert. I lit the paper. Jaws dropped, but nobody said a word.

Bad-ass woke up to the horrible realization that he was on fire. He rolled on the floor, arms flapping like a man possessed by evil spirits. The inmates went crazy with laughter until three guards broke up the little party. Two of the guards carried bad-ass out on a stretcher while the third guard interrogated everyone in the bullpen.

When he got to me I shook my head. "He must have fallen asleep with a cigarette," I volunteered. The white ash from the burned toilet paper left hardly a trace. Bad-ass recovered and was transferred to another tier. After that, me and Sam became inseparable.

Now that Sammy knew I had no fear of tough guys and could keep my mouth shut, he began to tell me bits and pieces about the inner workings of the Mafia. One day that knowledge would save my life. At first he told me unimportant stuff like how there were only two groups in Sam's neighborhood: Italians and everyone else. Later, he described how the levels in the Mafia worked. Suddenly his face would change, he'd remember I wasn't Italian, and up went the wall.

My worst experience in County Jail was when Betty visited me. What made it so unbearable was that, by strange design, the small visiting room had glass panels so anyone in the bullpen had an unobstructed view into the room. It reminded me of a Goldblatts display case. Of course, Betty's drop-dead looks attracted every male in the bullpen. I imagined how her slightest move agitated the sex-starved guys who lusted after her. These perverts didn't say anything to me but, from the sideways glances they threw my way, I knew they'd be masturbating to her image that night. It drove me crazy with jealousy.

My brother-in-law, the bookie, got me two famous Mafia "fix" lawyers, Bieber and Brodkin. We planned my defense in a second room attached to the bullpen. I looked forward to those meetings. They gave me hope. My lawyers told me the longer I was in jail, the easier it would be to get off light on account of the time I was already doing. But they warned me I'd be coming up before Judge Crowley, notorious for dealing out the stiffest sentences. A sign on his bench read: "The Man with the Gun Must Go!" Bieber and Brodkin sure as hell better do a convincing song and dance.

Luck turned my way when a young, green kid came on the tier a while later. He had tears in his eyes and shook all over. The kid never should have committed a crime because he couldn't take the heat—like when the bullies pretended the kid stole one of their combs. I watched them search the kid in the middle of the crowded bullpen. Naturally, they found what they were looking for. For his offense, the kid was ordered to stand in a filthy toilet in the bathroom while the bullies took turns urinating on him.

Until this moment I'd always minded my own business with stuff like this. I don't know what came over me this time. I grabbed the kid's arm and yanked him out of the toilet. Ignoring the looks of hatred boring into the back of my skull, I scolded the whimpering kid, "Don't let anyone do that to you!" Then I walked away.

This put me and Sammy in a very vulnerable position. If those bullies decided to get even, we'd be dead meat.

Puzzled, Sammy asked, "Why did you do that?"

"I really don't know," I shrugged.

It turned out that brash move worked in my favor. No sooner did I rescue that kid, than he marched straight downstairs to the chapel and told the priest, Father O'Brien, what I did. Father O'Brien wasn't your ordinary priest. He was monsignor of Blessed Sacrament Church whose diocese included the inmates of Cook County Jail and Bridewell Prison. It was a tough beat. When they sentenced a guy to die in the electric chair, Father O'Brien consoled him. He even had time to write a book called *Brass Knuckles* about the criminals he'd met.

Soon after the toilet incident, Father O'Brien summoned me to the lawyer's room. Judging by his reputation, I expected to find King Kong in a cassock. I was shocked to find myself face to face with Barry Fitzgerald's double, straight out of a Bowery Boys movie. This kindly little guy with unruly black hair and a leprechaun grin squinted up at me through an old-fashioned pair of square, wire-rimmed glasses. Impish dark eyes, illuminated by some deep source of amusement, peered quizzically into mine.

"Why did you care about the lad?" he inquired in a thick brogue.

I told Father O'Brien the same thing I told Sammy. "I don't know why I yanked the kid out of the toilet."

During our talk, it came out that me and Betty weren't married by the Catholic Church. "You see, my son," Father O'Brien said in his mild voice, adjusting the wire rims that he had absent-mindedly let slip down the small curve of his nose. "In the eyes of the Catholic Church, you're not married."

Here I was an armed robber and the Catholic Church thought it a worse sin that I wasn't properly married? I could hardly keep a straight face.

"If you really wish to repent, my boy, I must marry you before you go to prison." Naturally, I agreed. I needed all the help I could get.

Meanwhile, Sammy the Rock went to court on an assault charge. He was a juice collector for the Outfit, which meant he collected money owed to loan sharks. Since Sammy had mob protection, it was easy to figure out why the witness against him didn't show. Sammy was released.

The whole time I waited for my trial, I was obsessed with the thought of going to prison. Sleeplessness followed by fitful dreams dogged the endless nights. I wondered where I was gonna go next?

My day in court finally arrived—March 6, 1951—a day I'll never forget. Thanks to my lawyers and Father O'Brien, I was given five years probation for armed robbery and so was Bailey. It was unheard of to get off so easily, especially since we signed confessions. I guess it was a stroke of luck I pulled that kid out of the toilet. It probably didn't hurt that Judge Crowley had been Father O'Brien's student.

Leroy and Thor were indicted and arrested, but they weren't convicted. Me and Bailey never ratted on them and Leroy and Thor never actually signed confessions, so the police had nothing to hold them on. Besides, how could Judge Crowley justify sending them to prison when he gave us probation?

Judge Crowley assured us, "In case you young hoodlums get too cocky, if I ever see any of you in my court again, you'll serve five years to life. You can bet on it." I for one didn't want to test him.

Betty and my mother were waiting for me outside the courtroom. Betty's gray silk dress made my eyes feel good the way it clung to all the right places. Boy, she looked better than anything I could imagine in jail. That night I explored every inch of Betty's yielding warm flesh. Without any hurry I peeled the gray silk dress from her body, admiring her curves in the bureau mirror next to the bed I hadn't slept in for a long time. Never mind a few months—I'd endure years in prison for this.

Ten months later, in 1952, me and Betty had a little girl we

named Billita. Wow, my first kid. I worked for my brother-in-law
for a while, but he was a bookie. With Judge Crowley's words still
fresh in my memory and my parole officer breathing down my
neck, I had to keep my nose clean. I began to install aluminum
storm windows, which was a good job in the winter and unbearable in the summer heat, but the work was steady.

Before long I was hanging out with Bob Mauro for kicks.
When I met Bob at the pool hall he was already a decent card
mechanic. Like so many card cheats, Bob started out as a magician. Little by little he used the sleight-of-hand for something
that paid better—taking off card games. Hustling cards was
second nature to Bob. Few guys could match him. But, in a
pinch, Bob was out for himself. That loner mentality made Bob
unpopular with the other guys. It didn't bother me because we
made such a good team.

Sometimes after a decent score me and Bob would hit Rush
Street for dinner. They had great spaghetti on Division and
Rush, a mob place called Milano's. It's there I happened to run
into Sammy the Rock. Right away Sammy offered me money.
Refusing the large bills he shoved in my direction, I said, "Your
friendship is all I want Sammy. Thanks but no thanks." He told
me if I ever needed anything to look him up. I knew he meant it.
Every time I went to Milano's after that, someone mysteriously
picked up my tab.

While I installed storm windows by day and learned card
cheating at night, Leroy, Loreny and Sonny were convicted of
armed robbery. The first stop for them was Joliet Prison, then
on to Stateville Prison, a short ride from Joliet.

Sonny figured a way to escape. He went to Leroy and said,
"Listen, I'm breaking out tonight, do you want to come along?"
Leroy declined the offer but wished Sonny good luck. Later that
same night when the prison sirens started to whine, Leroy knew
Sonny had made it. What Leroy didn't know is that Sonny found
a car parked down the street from the prison, casually removed
the jumper cables, and drove off while the guys jumping it looked

on in amazement. He bumped and jerked along wondering what was wrong with the car. It had the new hydromatic drive, the forerunner of the automatic. When Sonny thought he was stepping on the clutch, he was actually hitting the brakes. The cops caught Sonny in Joliet twelve hours later. Those twelve hours of freedom cost Sonny another ten years in the slammer. He wound up doing a lot of time due to that incredible nerve of his. I guess he was what you'd call a habitual criminal: in the joint a lot more than he was out.

Guys who served time with Sonny said you couldn't break his spirit. If a guy got caught doing something bad, the guard would drag him before the captain. The guy would humble himself, remove his hat and beg for leniency. If the captain was in a good mood, he rewarded the inmate with a ticket that read "seven days in solitary," the most being thirty days. When it was Sonny's turn to take his punishment, he'd grin and toss his prison hat at the captain with a cheerful, "Fill it up." The captain would oblige with thirty days in solitary.

Sonny became known as a stand-up guy. He got a lot of respect from the other inmates but more important favors came from other quarters. Sonny's increasing power with the mob big shots in prison gave him a leg up toward a new occupation when he got out: hitman for the Mafia.

As for me, I kept doing my thing, installing storm windows and hustling card games. I heard about Jack Bailey's card games, but I made it a point to steer clear of them because Jack was getting into heavy drugs. I liked Jack, the Bedbug, but it disappointed me that he could do that stuff. Besides, you just can't trust anybody on dope.

On the North Side hard drugs weren't around in the 1950s. You could only buy heroin and cocaine off the colored guys who hung out at the black and white clubs on the South Side. The Club De Liza showcased great colored performers like Joe Williams and Louis Armstrong. The club catered openly to queers and dope dealers. If you had enough money, anything was possible in Chicago. Jack was irresistibly drawn to those clubs by the hot music whose rhythms overpowered him like an aphrodisiac. His new friends, the jive-talking, track-marked musicians, introduced Jack to another kind of high. Before long he was hooked on heroin.

One terrible Christmas Eve I found out how bad his addiction was. I arrived at Jack's, my arms loaded with presents for his kids. The whole family was in a turmoil. Libby was crying, the kids were crying and Jack was nowhere to be found. The first thought that ran through my head was that Jack was dead. The truth made me sick to my stomach. Through Libby's steady sobs, I pieced the story together. Jack had sold all the Christmas presents to buy heroin. Jack's life was snuffed out by heroin a few years later, after he'd lost everything, including his family. Like I said, you can't trust anyone on dope. To think I once envied that poor bastard.

Speaking of families, Mary my second daughter was born April 30, 1954, two years after Billita. Now that I had two beautiful kids and a wife, I needed more money to feed my growing brood. But where was I gonna get it?

6

"You can't con an honest person—they're not
motivated by greed—but you can cheat them."

B Y THIS TIME my Arcadia friends were either dead, doing time
or rolling in dough. Two of that last kind were Jerry Patten,
a quiet, brooding guy, and Chucky Douglas, short, red-haired
and Irish. Orphans had a better start in life than these two. One
time eight-year-old Chucky came home with his cheeks ruddy
from the winter air. He walked in to find his alcoholic mother
turning a trick. Chucky didn't stay home much. He hung around
with another clever guy from the neighborhood, Jerry Patten.
For most of his early life Jerry's wacky folks locked him in the
house. The authorities finally ordered Jerry's parents to send him
to school. On his first day of class, the teacher asked the kids to
draw a picture of where they lived. Jerry drew a house with no
doors or windows.

Eventually Jerry, the more frugal of the two, scrounged enough
cash to buy a nightclub in Lincoln Park West. The neighborhood
was so ritzy, people fed their dogs filet mignon. Chucky helped
Jerry run the place.

Around ten o'clock on a stormy Wednesday night, I decided to
pay the two a visit. I had no trouble finding The Vertigo. Yeah,
the atmosphere made me dizzy the minute I stepped inside.
Had it been a few years later, I might have seen Jimmy Stewart
making a play for Kim Novak. Pretty soon my eyes adjusted
to the dim light. I noticed cozy linen-draped tables with those
little lampshade-covered candles flickering over couples with
more than food on their minds. In the middle of the room, a
single spotlight illuminated a piano bar. A chocolate-skinned,

husky-voiced female in low-cut black velvet purred, "I wish you bluebirds in the spring . . ."

Betty would have loved this but I never took my beautiful wife anywhere—not that I took anyone else. There were a lot of reasons. Number one, I wanted Betty to stay home with the kids. Number two, I was so jealous I always got into a fight when she was with me, and number three, you couldn't talk business with your wife hanging around. Earlier that evening, I knew by the hurt expression on Betty's face she was dying to go with me, but didn't have the nerve to ask.

I answered her pleading look with the honesty of a guy who just failed a polygraph. "Aw, it's probably a lousy joint. Besides, this is strictly business."

I spotted Jerry and Chucky in their tailor-made suits, pockets bulging with money. They must have had some bankroll because half a dozen good looking girls hovered at close range.

"Hey, Chucky . . . Jerry. How's it going?"

"Whatta ya say, Bill? Long time, no see." Jerry pumped my hand like he was genuinely happy to see me while a curvy blonde made a perfect landing on his left arm.

In private, the required bullshitting out of the way, the two let me in on why they were so flush. Seems Chucky invented a scam called the "granny game." For years, until it was exposed and copied by others, it was a great money-maker.

"The fact is," Chucky explained, "you can't con an honest person—they're not motivated by greed—but you can cheat them."

"Yeah, count me in." I jumped at their offer to join them on the road the next week. This new scam intrigued me but, more important, I needed dough in the worst way.

Too early the following Monday we headed for Dayton, Ohio, in Jerry's new Cadillac with the white leather upholstery. As we cruised along Chucky gave me the lowdown.

"First thing we do when we get there is find the local library and pull up the month-old obituary columns in the newspaper. We pick the obits that are good prospects. You know, old codgers who left a widow."

Chucky grew as enthusiastic as a bloodhound hot on a rabbit's trail. "I phone the widow pretending it's her bank calling. More often than not she's alone and dying to talk to someone—anyone." Chuck's face turned beet red with excitement. "Without my saying a word, the old gal tells me who's home with her, how many grandkids she's got, and even how much money she has in the bank."

"Only one piece of information really matters, Bill," added Jerry with a smirk. "If the widow's loaded, the game is on."

Once we arrived in Dayton, it didn't take us more than an hour to find a "live one" by the name of Wilma. Lucky for us, Wilma and her husband were listed in the phone book. Wilma answered the phone on the first ring, at which point Chucky launched right into his speech. He discovered Wilma's husband left her $8,000. She trustingly passed this information on to Chucky who was "such a considerate young bank employee to worry about a lonely widow."

"I'll check into your account, just to be on the safe side, and call you back tomorrow with any news," Chuck reassured Wilma.

By the second phone call Chuck never let Wilma off the hook. He rang from a phone booth near her house. "It's what I suspected," he told Wilma. "One of the tellers is stealing from your account. But don't you worry, Wilma. You're covered by the FDIC. You want to catch this crook, don't you?"

"Yes!" she sobbed.

"The teller already took $2,000," Chuck explained. "That leaves $6,000 still in your account. We gotta protect it."

Now Chucky went into considerable detail describing the scoundrel. After that first phone call, we went to the bank and memorized the looks of an actual teller.

"Oh, you mean that silly old man with those horrid false teeth and the thin blond hair? I never would have thought . . ."

"This is strictly confidential," Chuck whispered into the phone now that he was sure Wilma was home alone. "An agent is on his way over to take you to the bank to cash your check for $6,000 so we'll have the evidence we need to nail the crooked teller."

Generous to a fault, Chuck and Jerry always left the widow a little something, in this case $2,000. The plan was for me, the agent, to drive Wilma to the bank, bring her home and take her "evidence." Jerry and Chucky would wait in the Cadillac down the block. If anything went wrong, I was supposed to take off.

I rang her doorbell. She hung up with Chuck and went to answer the front door. I flashed my phony badge at a tiny gray-haired lady in fuzzy slippers and a clean apron. Wilma beamed recognition. Jeez, she really did look like an innocent lamb being led to the slaughterhouse.

"I'm all set to take you to the bank," I smiled pleasantly. The rented car was parked outside.

This is a piece of cake, I was thinking. But as we headed for the door, Wilma looked up at me smiling kindly and said, "Have some of my home-made cookies and milk, son. You've been so good to me."

Uh oh. Suddenly it was my mother talking. I knew what we were doing was wrong, stealing from a sweet old widow. Terrible feelings started to well up but I managed to block them out. Wilma hummed a little tune to herself as she cashed her check. Carefully she folded the bills and put them in her best Sunday purse. I glanced over my shoulder. The teller's curious stare followed us all the way out of the bank. Did he suspect something?

On the way home my mind wouldn't stop. I was supposed to give Wilma a receipt for the money I took as evidence, and tell Wilma we'd contact her tomorrow. Naturally, we'd be long gone by then. I glanced up at a neatly stitched picture hanging just inside Wilma's front door that said, "God bless our happy home," then down to Wilma's innocent face. Her unblinking blue eyes hit me with the biggest load of trust I've ever seen.

"My dear boy, you saved me from losing my life's savings," she said offering me the bills.

That did it. "Keep your money for now," I said, pushing her hand away. "We don't need it today, Wilma."

There. It was done. I walked out minus the cash. I joined my two partners down the block, resigned to the abuse I was gonna take. "I just didn't have the heart to grab the old lady's money," I confessed.

You'd think I passed up the crown jewels the way they called me every name in the book—a moron, pathetic and much worse. When they were done with me, they threw me out on the street corner to "find my own fucking way back to Chicago."

I had exactly four dollars in my pocket so I called my sister. Good old Louise wired me the bus fare. During the long ride home I wondered, could I do anything right? Back in familiar surroundings, I decided to stick to what I did best—cheat at cards. There was one other thing I did pretty well. My third kid, a girl we named Betty Lou, arrived in 1955.

*The same familiar faces crowded into Lee's
day after day, night after night.
Bullshit flowed as freely as the liquor.*

A YEAR LATER, ME and Betty finally had a boy we named Tommy
after my brother who was a whiskey salesman earning good
money. Three girls and a boy. Not bad for a guy of twenty-five.

Maybe Tom came back a war hero, but he didn't earn any
medals in my book for refusing to help our poor mother. My
sister was the total opposite. Not only would Louise give you the
shirt off her back, she'd wash and press it then make sure there
were a few bucks tucked in the pocket. That was Louise.

Louise and her husband Lee weren't around much, so they made
me manager of Lee's Lounge around the corner from my mom's
place. The joint has stood there forever. From the sidewalk, it
looked like any other tavern in Chicago, just a plain, glass-fronted
brick building. Neatly painted window ads proclaimed, "I'm from
Milwaukee and I ought to know, it's draft-brewed Blatts Beer
wherever you go." "Hamms—from the land of sky-blue water."

The din from the smoke-filled bar hit you the minute you
stepped inside. When your eyes stopped watering, the pinball
machine against the wall grabbed your attention. Players wore
out their thumbs ringing up thousands of points. Ka-ching, ka-
ching, ka-ching. A red and green Wurlitzer glowed in the corner.
Inside its plastic skin mechanical guts ground away so black vinyl
records could churn out your Hit Parade favorites. Dino crooned,
"Dat's Amore" in the background while a quartet of working stiffs

wailed on about what went wrong in Korea. Wiseguys held court at the end of the jam-packed bar. Like most Italians, they had their own brand of body English—hands, all hands.

Once in a while a loser would slam his fedora on the bar screaming, "Arlington, shit! Why did I bet that long-shot in the seventh?"

"Hey, Louie," moaned another guy. "How come dames are so hard to figure?"

Cheap entertainment was as close as the sidewalk. An endless stream of colorful characters glided by the front window like they were on a concrete conveyer belt. "Wow! Will you get a load of that shape." Heads jerked to attention.

The same familiar faces crowded into Lee's day after day, night after night. Bullshit flowed as freely as the liquor. I guess it was no different from bars everywhere. I worked swing, put Bob Mauro in charge of the book in the basement, and made another guy from the neighborhood, Dick Kummer, the day bartender. When the place was hopping, Louise would come in to help. Everything went really good . . . for a while.

There happened to be a Manpower place around the corner that hired people by the day for minimum wage. They got mostly American Indians. The 15-cent beer drew the Indians into Lee's. The best time I can remember was the night every Indian in the joint was riveted on the TV movie *They Died With Their Boots On*. In the end, the Sioux wiped out Custer and all his men in the Battle of the Little Big Horn. As if on cue, the Indians in the bar let out an ear-splitting war whoop. You'd think they were part of a real massacre. This time it was the Indians one, the white man zip. What a shame the place couldn't always be so upbeat.

But good things never seem to last. The mob guys laid money all over the bar. A strong tip from Bob on a "sure thing" and out rolled fists full of green stuff. The Indians downed their cheap beer, silently watching the action. Loaded Indians and gangsters mix about as well as wives and hookers. Lee's was a powder keg waiting to explode. It didn't take long.

Just before noon on a busy Friday I got a phone call from Dick. "One mean son-of-a-bitch drunken Indian is wrecking the joint," Dick said in his raspy voice. "The guy's the size of a buffalo."

"Circle the wagons," I shouted into the phone. "I'm on my way."

In less than two minutes I was in the back door of Lee's. The place looked like a fucking war zone. If someone had told me a stampede of wild horses had just come through, I wouldn't have batted an eye. The casualties numbered about ten slightly inebriated, mostly intact customers. A hysterical fat lady lay sobbing in a jumble of overturned stools and broken glass, red dress thrown over her head to shield her from flying objects. I glanced to the right. Thank God, I sighed. At least the front window was still intact.

Goo dripped on what had been my clean, white shirt. I looked up in amazement to discover some kind of food, mashed potatoes and gravy I think, had found its way onto the ceiling. That's strange, I thought scratching my head. We don't serve food.

The cause of all the trouble, a six-foot-six-inch red-faced hell-raiser, bellowed threats at some little shit that I didn't recognize. My anger kicked in. At that moment I didn't care if the Indian was ten feet tall. Somehow I managed to grab the Indian's left arm. Dick struggled with his right one. We wrestled him out the front door and locked it. Within seconds, the Indian's massive shoe kicked in the glass door. I sprang through the shattered glass in hot pursuit. The Indian turned and ran.

I caught the creep in front of the Greek restaurant on the corner of Leland and Broadway. With at least 150 pounds to his advantage, this "raging bull" could have killed me in a heartbeat, but adrenaline coursed through me. I tackled the Indian from behind. The momentum sent us both flying to the pavement. Now a freaky thing happened. The Indian's head struck the cornerstone of the building on his way down. He hit with such force that his eye popped out of its socket. Here we were on the corner—horns honking, people shouting at the traffic cop who, by this time, had come over to investigate.

A bystander wagged his finger at me. "It was all his fault, officer. He deliberately shoved the Indian into the building. I saw it all."

I looked around, but no one came rushing to my defense. What happened to Dick? I shrugged as the handcuffs clicked into place. It didn't take long for an ambulance to arrive. As it pulled away from the curb with the Indian, I spotted Betty watching me from across the street. Tommy, the baby, was in her arms, the other three children clung to her skirt. Our eyes met. Funny how there's nothing to say at a time like this. Betty's face said volumes—the unasked questions, my broken promises that things would get better, her eyes brimming with tears.

I was held on an open charge to see if the Indian was going to live. He did, minus one eye. Two days later, my brother-in-law bailed me out of jail. I was charged with assault. By this time, I had witnesses who were willing to defend me and tell the real story. My case came up at Town Hall about a month or so later. The Indian blew his chances when he got into a violent argument with the judge. They dismissed the case and released me.

Soon after the Indian thing Leroy was out on parole and came around to see me. I introduced him to Betty's sister, Georgeanne. I didn't see much of Leroy, since he was always hanging around the Mist Lounge on Narraganset and Montrose, where Georgeanne worked as a dice girl. The Mist Lounge was Sam Giancana's hangout. Giancana, Chicago Outfit kingpin, got his start as a great wheel man under Tony Accardo. You could say his drive got him to the top.

Mugsy, one of the guys who allegedly murdered Marilyn Monroe, ran the Mist for the Outfit. Another mob heavyweight confirmed that sensational story years later. Mugsy and Leroy got chummy in the pen. Mugsy put Leroy in charge of the mob-run whorehouses on Mannheim Road once they got out. Funny thing about Leroy, he wasn't the smartest guy in the world, but he knew how to keep his mouth shut.

Loreny's parole came up a while later. He had a few stories to tell. Who should walk up to Loreny's prison cell one day but Mike Moretti, the maniac who almost killed me in the elevator. It so happened that Loreny had been cheating Moretti at cards and it got Moretti all steamed up. Moretti wanted to start something so Loreny would blow his parole. What Moretti didn't know was that Loreny had a concealed shiv he made out of a sharpened toothbrush. If Moretti made a move toward him, Loreny would stick him with the shiv. What a break. Maybe it was instinct, but Moretti never stepped inside the cell, so Loreny didn't have to kill him. While Loreny was telling me all this, I watched his face turn dark purple with rage. It made me shudder to think of these two pathological nut cases face to face.

Pretty soon me and Loreny were cheating a real bad bunch of guys at cards. These guys were going to be trouble with a capital T. I could feel it in my bones. One night just before we were going to play them at cards, Loreny shacked up with one of the neighborhood girls at the Leland Hotel. He boasted to the girl how he had to go "make some money."

Turned out we beat these guys for all they had. Wouldn't you know, the girl Loreny was with was in tight with these guys. The next day they knew the whole story. They demanded their money back or they'd kill us. We denied everything and accused them of being poor losers. They wouldn't have any of it. It looked like we were on the verge of a war. I knew the target for their revenge would be Lee's Lounge. But more important, my whole family was in danger. I couldn't take the chance of hurting them.

As I sat at the bar trying to think this thing out, in walked Jimmy LaFleur, one of the guys from our old Arcadia gang. I studied Jimmy, admiring his slim, athletic build and easy manner. Let's see, the last time I saw Jimmy, he was just released from prison and we were celebrating his marriage to Connie, a voluptuous long-legged blonde, his grammar school sweetheart. Boy, was that some party!

"So how's Connie?" I asked, expecting Jimmy to spout on about married bliss.

Jimmy's strained voice told a different story. "Connie landed a job as a Playboy bunny just after we got hitched. We were both excited about the extra cash that was coming in from Connie's tips," he explained. "Pretty soon the whole Playboy thing went to Connie's head."

Jimmy stared quietly into his drink as if the answers he was seeking were somehow written in the bottom of his glass.

"Instead of coming home, she'd hang around with that Rush Street crowd." Jimmy screwed up his face. "Damn Heffner's parties."

His haunted eyes locked onto mine. "Suddenly I wasn't good enough, Bill. Connie wanted a divorce. After a lot of arguing, I finally gave in to her."

Jimmy grimaced. "I still can't get over the fact that she's gone. . . . I'm going nuts. . . . I gotta get out of here. Everything in this town reminds me of Connie. I was thinking of going to the West Coast for a while. I always wanted to see Hollywood. Besides, I'm two payments late on my new '57 Chevy." Jimmy ran his fingers through his sun-streaked hair, pulled out a Camel, lit it with shaking hands and lapsed into silence.

As I watched Jimmy, an idea hit me. If I wasn't around, it would take the heat off my family. I smiled. "You know, Jimmy, a little trip could be the answer to both our problems."

8

When the dust had cleared, ambulances hauled
off the worthless rubbish. "Who's gonna
clean up the blood?" someone inquired.

EXACTLY ONE WEEK after me and Jimmy hit L.A. we came
dangerously close to running out of money. We were desperate for a score.

We devoured our breakfast bought with the change we had left in our pockets, grumbling that things couldn't get much worse. They did. Someone stole Jimmy's car while we were eating. Hell, maybe the thing was repo'd. Here we were trying to hustle and we didn't have any wheels. We were in deep shit. In a nearby park, we wracked our brains trying to figure out our next move. A burly guy in a white van pulled up and began painting a sign not 20 feet away. We didn't have anything better to do so we walked over and watched him.

First Jimmy helped the guy set up his ladder. Then, in his natural easy way, Jimmy pitched in and began handing things to this painter. Otto was his name. I studied Otto with his thick German accent, grunting for a paint brush or a tool he needed. He had these bushy black eyebrows that partially hid intelligent brown eyes. Once in a while he'd glance over at me. I knew he was wondering why I just sat there. Maybe Jimmy liked this kind of work, but my mind raced through other possibilities—like making a real score. I kept drawing blanks.

After a couple of hours Otto offered to take us both out for dinner. He wondered what we were doing in California and how we got into our predicament. He listened quietly to our story.

When we came to the part about being stuck there with no money, Otto said, "Jimmy, how'd you like to be my helper? You're good and I could use you. What do you say?"

Glancing my way, Jimmy stammered a little, embarrassed that Otto only wanted him. "Yeah," answered Jimmy. "I could sure use the money."

"Good," said Otto. "Then you can start tomorrow." At least one of us was making some dough, I thought glumly.

A few days later I was cooling my heels at the mob joint Sherry's Bar on Sunset Boulevard. My thoughts were interrupted as I sat alone nursing my coffee.

"Do you know that you're sitting just a few steps from the famous Schwab's Drugstore where Lana Turner was discovered drinking a soda?"

I knew who it was without looking up—a couple of characters from my old neighborhood by the name of Little Jack Little and Joe Levy, alias Jacob Ship. Joe opened the conversation in that signature voice of his. It was the sound gravel made rolling around in a cement mixer. Pock-marked Joe was as ugly as Little Jack was movie-star handsome.

"Oh yeah?" I answered, thrilled to run into a couple of familiar faces from back home.

The small talk didn't last long. In less time than it takes to pinch a wallet, these two seasoned con-artists invited me to join them for a night out on the town. Sounded good to me, and no one else was busting down my door.

A few hours later, Joe screeched to a halt in front of my motel. I could see my reflection in his shiny black Buick. Little Jack beamed me his 200-watt smile from the back seat. I'd followed Jack's advice and sported my whitest shirt and classiest necktie, mandatory dress code when you need to blend in with the evening crowd.

"After all," murmured Little Jack, "we don't want to call attention to ourselves."

I puzzled over what these two were cooking up as we cruised down Sunset Boulevard. The sun did its thing, exiting in typical movie-style splendor behind the Hollywood skyline, our cue to spring into action.

Later, back at my motel, my mind ran through the events of the last four hours. I unknotted my rumpled tie and sighed at the slumping image in the bathroom mirror. If only I'd known we were going to steal—not the dough, but the cash registers.

The first couple of hours we cased joints. "Our object," said Little Jack, "is to find out which stores have registers near the front door so we can be in and out fast."

"Yeah," growled Joe. He fished inside his pocket and came up with a thin plastic rectangle. "It ain't hard breakin' in. We just slide this piece of plastic inside the door lock and it opens quick and easy." (It was guys like these that created the huge market for dead-bolt locks.)

About eleven o'clock, when most businesses were closed, Joe dropped me and Little Jack off a half a block from our first job. Joe waited in the car for my signal. Seeing the coast was clear, we casually walked to the front door. Quietly, Little Jack let himself in with the plastic while I stood watch. If anyone noticed us, they might think we were customers checking to see if the place was open, or the owners themselves locking up.

When we had the register and were ready to leave, I brushed the back of my head—our signal for Joe to pick us up. He pulled up slowly. With the register balanced between us, we made a bee-line to the car and took off.

At $75 per cash register after we fenced the goods, I figured my lousy cut of $25 would scarcely pay my half of the motel bill for a few days. Four more nights I went along on these goofy capers. What else did I have going? Finally, I gave up, knowing something better had to come along.

One day after work I met Jimmy and Otto at a blue-collar

tavern around the corner from our motel. I decided to swallow my pride. "Hey, Otto," I said trying to sound as casual as I could. "Do you by any chance know where I could find a job?"

"What can you do?" Otto shot back.

"Well, I used to run a bar in Chicago . . ."

Otto winked at me. "Say no more. My best friend is just the guy you need to meet," he said throwing his paint-spattered arm across my shoulders. "In fact, we'll go there tonight." I had the feeling Jimmy had been doing some talking on my behalf.

Otto's friend owned The Tail of the Cock, a high-line restaurant and bar on La Cienega Boulevard. "Can you beat that," I mumbled, straining my neck toward the ceiling. There was a giant tree, leaves and all, growing right in the middle of the restaurant. This Tail of the Cock was swarming with producers, directors and famous movie stars. I couldn't help admiring what money can buy—stunning women in knockout gowns, pampered broads dripping with jewels. If I was single, I could have been tempted.

Otto introduced us. I could see I wasn't making too big a hit. The owner, a lacquer-haired Oriental in a silk Shantung suit, gave me a fishy-eyed look. Maybe he didn't give a shit about me, but anyone could see he really liked Otto. I was to start the following week. Otto even arranged for me to go to bartending school so I could learn how to make those fancy drinks with the little umbrellas in them, the kind that all the classy dames go for. What a guy, that Otto!

I figured it was time to call Betty and share the good news. After I got the hang of things I could go get her and the kids. Not only would I earn good money, it was a chance to make an honest living for a change—no more gangs and no more cash registers! My mom answered the phone. All excited, I told her my plans, but she didn't sound too happy. She didn't say much. I just had a gut feeling something wasn't right.

Later, when I finally got a hold of Betty, I poured my heart out to her.

"Fine," she said. "You stay there. I met a postman and I'm leaving you."

Her words didn't sink in at first. "But Betty," I pleaded. "This is just the beginning. You and the kids will love it out here. . . ." Faint crackling from the lousy phone reception hit my ear. Then dead air.

How could this happen? I didn't cheat on Betty and she knew it, I thought bitterly. We were married. I didn't die, she didn't die. It had to be the postman's fault. My blood boiled with anger and the sting of resentment bruised my ego.

Thanks to Otto I bought an airline ticket on the first flight to Chicago I could get, the following morning. Well, so much for the bartending job. I wasn't about to just roll over like an obedient dog and let my wife go off with some fucking postman.

The plane took off and made a wide swing over L.A. Below us the California sun glittered on palm tree-lined avenues. Turquoise swimming pools beckoned cool and inviting from their ritzy neighborhoods. Geez, the parties those people must have. I wondered if I'd return to this crazy city that seduced me before I knew what was happening. It was Las Vegas all over again.

When I walked in, my mom was baby-sitting. It was good to see her and the kids. If it was any other time I'd stay and talk with them, but this was different. Visions of my Betty with that postman blocked out all other thoughts. On the bus ride to Evanston where Betty worked, I wanted to hit someone, see them hurt.

The bowling alley jumped with company bowling teams and raucous guys out for a few beers after work. I spotted Betty right away. She was waiting on some smooth-talking young punk who was trying to impress his friends.

I walked straight up to her, threw her cocktail tray on the floor and said, "Get your stuff, we're going home." Her eyes looked like those of a frightened deer when you catch them in your headlights. She didn't utter a word.

The manager came over ready to start something, but I cut him short. My voice had a hard edge. "My wife doesn't work!" Then to Betty, "Let's get the fuck out of here." We rode the El home in silence.

The next day I got a gun, put on my hunting cap and went out to find this guy who would chase after a married woman with four kids. Stealing, beating people up—almost nothing bothered me. But what he was doing was worse than a sin.

I went down to the Evanston post office where the bastard worked. I had pumped my mom about him earlier. Most of the postal workers I talked to were afraid to say much, considering I was acting like a lunatic, but this one guy was sympathetic. He told me where I could find the son-of-a-bitch. He was living with his parents. The postman wasn't home, but that didn't bother me. Sooner or later I'd flush him out. Hunting season wasn't over yet.

I was going on about the postman at Lee's that night. In mid-sentence five of his friends stormed in to "teach me a lesson." This was a very bad move on their part. I watched from the sidelines while the home team crucified the visitors.

When the dust had cleared, ambulances hauled the worthless rubbish away. "Who's gonna clean up the blood?" someone inquired.

All five wanted to press charges, but they were terrified we'd kill them if they pointed us out. They were right to keep their mouths shut. The police were on our side. After all, these guys went out of their way looking for a fight. That was the truth. The cops decided the troublemakers got what they deserved—and their wallets were a little fatter for upholding justice.

The postman disappeared off the face of the earth. From that moment on, Betty became very cold toward me. She didn't laugh at my jokes anymore. I didn't give up, though. I'd find a way to win her love back, if it was the last thing I did.

I started searching in earnest for Sammy the Rock. Maybe Sam had a connection. Unpredictable Sammy. He'd turn up when you least expected to see him, but finding him was another matter. I searched all the mob hangouts I could think of, left my number—and waited. A few weeks later we met at Milano's. Sam was glad to see me but wondered what was up.

"I need a legit job, Sam, out west." I figured if I took Betty to live near her family, things might go better for us.

Sam nodded knowingly. "No promises, but I'll do what I can."

I cooled my heels a little longer. Every time the phone rang I jumped a foot in the air. Finally, it was Sam giving me the name of a business agent, Johnny Desmeier, at the Teamsters union hall over on Ashland Avenue. I was in luck. Johnny could use me. I got friendly with one of the drivers who taught me the basics of driving a rig. Pretty soon I went out on short jobs. I drove tractors that big trucking companies would lease. When I didn't know something, I winged it. I only wiped out one trailer when I misjudged the height of an overpass.

After a few months I was in good with most of the dispatchers. With an honest job under my belt, I felt better than I had in years. It was time to move Betty and the kids to the West Side. We leased a two-bedroom walkup in the same building where her sister, Georgeanne, lived on Taylor and Sacramento. Betty seemed happy. At least she never complained.

Now I heard through the grapevine that Sears and Roebuck's Fleet Maintenance Service was hiring drivers. The pay was great, benefits included. The company even had something called profit sharing. I put in for a job. The dispatcher there took a liking to me so I got lucky. Never seemed to have trouble getting a job, just keeping it. It was the best working for this outfit. Even wore a fancy uniform. No unloading on the longer hauls. The other drivers looked at me with envy when I told them where I worked.

Sometimes I'd drop off a load at one of the small warehouses on the way to my final destination, like Milwaukee. Fleet Maintenance gave me a "500" key so I could get inside the warehouse. It meant they trusted me. That was a new feeling, being trusted.

Boy, was I happy. I started to believe I could actually support a wife and four kids. I knew I had Sammy to thank for getting me started.

A month later the dispatcher told me the boss wanted to see me in his office. I closed the door quietly behind me, wondering why I was there. I knew he couldn't beef about my performance. The boss glanced up from a stack of papers on his desk and motioned to a chair. On his desk I spotted my employment file open to a particular page.

His words were like a slap in the face. "William, you forgot to tell us you're a convicted felon." There was nothing in his manner or voice to indicate that he was angry. It was more a sadness. He stretched out his hand. "I need your 500 key."

If I'd wanted to rob those warehouses, I sure didn't need a damn key. Picking a lock for me was as easy as breathing. Silently I reached in my pocket, took the key off my key ring and lobbed it over to him. What was there to say? My record said it all.

When I broke the news to Betty that night, I'll never forget what she told me. "Can't you do anything right?" Her words stung far worse than hearing I was fired. Maybe she was right. Maybe I couldn't do anything right?

The next day Betty took the kids and moved in with her mother. I let two or three weeks pass, then I paid Betty and the kids a visit at her mother's place. Betty wouldn't look me in the eye. She mumbled something that she was seeing a guy named Ray, a bricklayer, who didn't want me coming around. He said I was a bad influence on my kids. I reeled under the impact. By now I was resigned to the fact that Betty didn't want me, but the thought of not seeing my kids made me fume. That would never happen.

There was Betty just sitting at her mother's table, not saying a word. The kids were rough-housing behind her. I looked at Betty and thought, now I had a wife and four great kids, but I also had a felony conviction and a third grade education. With Betty popping out kids like wine bottle corks, it finally dawned on me. How was I going to support my growing family? I must have been crazy to think I could manage with a legit job.

In my world there wasn't any family planning. No one asked, "Are you using birth control?" It was more like, "Get rid of that broad." I guess in the back of my mind I always knew the truth. If I was on my own, I had a better shot at making the kind of money I needed. I was just one score away from a big bankroll.

Betty finally broke the silence. Mustering courage, she said the thing I dreaded to hear. "I want a divorce."

I knew what I was going to say, but the words stuck in my throat. My mouth was as dry as parchment. "Look," I finally told Betty. "I don't want a divorce, but if you want one, go get it. I won't stand in your way."

The next two months dragged by. The entire time was a blur. If I'd had a weakness for drinking, I'd have been an alcoholic by now. Then Betty called one weekend. Her voice sounded hard like metal. I couldn't get used to it.

"The divorce is final," she said, "and Ray and I got married. I don't want anything from you. Send the kids money when you can. Just stay away. We don't want any trouble."

She went on a while longer. I tried to listen to what she was saying, but all I could hear was the dull throbbing in my head. That was it. It was over, a done deal.

I just couldn't stand not seeing my kids, so about a week after Betty broke the news, I went over to Belmont and Western where she lived with this Ray Fester. I parked under a side window and honked my horn shouting for the kids to come down, praying they'd still want to see me. I waited impatiently. They sneaked up behind me giggling and threw their arms around me like a friendly boa constrictor. I swung them around all together as they hung on for dear life. What a feeling. Just then I was the richest man in the world.

When things quieted down a little, I told them I'd be gone for long periods of time. They were too young to understand everything, but their serious faces told me something was getting through. I made them promise to stick together. I tried to impress on their young minds that was their best shot in life, sticking together. I realized no one could break the bond we had—ever.

Once a week I called my mom for news of the kids. I'd pump her for the smallest detail about her brief visits. Sometimes that animal, Ray, wouldn't let my mom come over for fear that she might give me information he didn't want me have. God knows what that could be. Okay, maybe I could see why this guy might not want me around. But my mother. Everyone knew she was a saint.

A big change came over me when Betty divorced me. While I was married, I never once cheated on Betty. It wasn't my thing. Now I started to go out with women—lots of women.

Some guys started the Cosa Nostra in Sicily. It's
a secret society which means "Our Thing." Well,
it's about as secret as the Indianapolis 500.

IT WAS TIME for a change of scenery, so I went downtown and
got myself a basic, $25-a-week room at the Devonshire Hotel
at 15 East Ohio, where Bob Mauro was living. Next door to the
Devonshire was the Berkshire Hotel. These weren't your run-
of-the-mill hotels. They were the mob's Chicago headquarters. I
guess it took pull to stay there—pretty much by invitation only.
Bob's connections got me in.

On the first floor of the Devonshire, a coffee shop occupied
one side. Across from the coffee shop was a bar loaded with
prostitutes. The Berkshire resembled the Devonshire except, on
the left, it had an Italian restaurant called Valentino's, on the
right a bar loaded with prostitutes. A little guy, Davie Fuch,
made tough decisions as the doorman at Valentino's. If he didn't
know you or you weren't okayed by someone important, you
didn't get in, period.

It was Valentino's where the mob-run Rush Street nightclubs
like the Chez Paree, Mr. Kelly's and The Living Room quietly
dropped off the nights' receipts in brown paper bags. A few times
a week, the big shots in Cicero sent a runner for the dough.
You'd see Mafia guys rubbing elbows with famous movie stars
in Valentino's. Buddy Greco always hung around. His father-
in-law, Lou Goldman, ran the penthouse poker games at the
Devonshire. Valentino's never lacked for excitement.

Balding, round-shouldered Jimmy "the Monk" Allegretti ran the place for the mob. He was "Little Caesar" DiVarco's soldier. If you needed anything okayed, you went to Jimmy. He had the say about what went on at the two hotels. When Jimmy barked, all the dogs jumped. He left most of the barking to his underlings like Big Joe Arnold, his bodyguard-enforcer-collector. The last table in the narrow, well-lit Valentino's was permanently reserved for Jimmy and Joe to conduct business.

When I was growing up, there was talk everywhere about the Outfit. That was the name for organized crime in Chicago, but nobody seemed to know exactly what it was. As long as I can remember, us guys heard about a bunch of gangsters who supposedly ran the city with the help of the upstanding Chicago Police. I knew Sammy the Rock was with the Outfit, but other than the few scraps he told me, organized crime remained a mystery—until now.

It would be impossible not to hear things living in the middle of "mob country." I learned that the Outfit, syndicate, mob, Mafia were some of the names given to organized crime. It all started when a bunch of guys in Sicily got together and called themselves the *Cosa Nostra*. Then they migrated to the United States. *Cosa Nostra* is a secret organization that means "Our Thing." Well it's about as secret as the Indianapolis 500. If you were Italian and served a "made" member of the organization, after a few years they might let you become a member too. You'd go through the secret ceremony of *omertà* where you'd swear that the Mafia came before everything, even your own family. Then you were a made guy. That meant you were part of a privileged gang that could kill on a whim. But you couldn't tell just anyone. They had to be made guys just like you or guys who were part of your crew. It was all hush-hush.

If you weren't lucky enough to be Italian, then you formed a sort of "marriage" to a mob member. You were considered an "associate," like Bugsy Siegel. Other countries had organized crime, too, but the Mafia was by far the most powerful. Funny how the FBI's top dog, J. Edgar Hoover, continued to deny there was any such thing as the Mafia when the evidence of its existence cropped up everywhere.

Personally, I don't understand how the mob could attract even three members. When you consider that you have to kill whoever they say and fork over most of your money to them. Then, if you're stupid enough to screw up on an assignment, they slowly torture you before mercifully allowing you to die. I can't see what the big draw is? The guys in our gang always had loyalty to one another, but no one was boss. None of us could stomach the Mafia's rules. We called our own shots.

Bob Mauro stayed at the Devonshire because he had a job with the *Illinois Sport News*, the mob's wire service also know as the Green Sheet. Tom Kelly, a big ruddy-faced Irishman and a friend of Bob's father, operated the Green Sheet for the Outfit. Tom, highly regarded in betting circles, never threw his considerable weight around. He started Bob out as a driver delivering the Green Sheet to newsstands around the city.

I was "that Irish kid," Bob's friend, so I was okayed to stay at the Devonshire, too. We could hang out at the hotels as long as we didn't cheat. Boy, were we tempted to take off some of the big poker games in the Devonshire's penthouse—until Lou Goldman, who ran the room, warned us, "Your first mistake will be your last." Translation: You fuck with us—you're dead. We took his words to heart. Me and Bob continued to cheat at cards, but never on our home turf. Then we'd go to Arlington or Hawthorne racetracks and blow our winnings.

If we needed "paper" (marked cards) or "tees" (loaded dice) we didn't have far to go. KC Card Company, where all the cheats got their stuff, was just a few blocks away on Wabash. KC had a mailing list of over 40,000 from the U.S. and 25 different countries. Not all of them were cheats. Magicians needed marked cards and other trick stuff for their acts.

It wasn't long after I moved into the Devonshire that a persistent ringing woke me out of a deep sleep. It was my phone. I checked the clock. Two minutes to 12:00. Who was crazy enough to call before noon?

The voice on the other end grumbled, "Are you gonna sleep all day, you bum? There's a bunch of bad-looking characters down here in the coffee shop. I'm scared they're gonna hurt me so you better hurry up."

I detected muffled laughter. It finally clicked. The voice belonged to Buddy LaRue, one of the guys from my old neighborhood.

We bullshitted while I downed some eggs, toast and much needed coffee. Buddy suggested we take a walk around the block.

Now that we were out of hearing range, Buddy opened up. "Listen, Billy," he confided, "I just got a tip that a jeweler who lives on Marine Drive keeps a lot of gold in his apartment. I even know where he hides the stuff." Buddy's eyes glowed like emeralds.

"There's only one problem. Me and my partner need one more guy to distract the doorman while we grab the goods. Whatta ya think?"

This was right down my alley. Besides, I was running low on cash. If I didn't make a score soon, I couldn't pay the rent. The image of Joe Arnold, the enforcer, made up my mind. "Okay," I said. Let's take a ride and look it over."

We circled the block where the jeweler lived, a swanky apartment building near the lake. Out of the corner of my eye I spotted trouble. Oh shit, I thought. That's a bureau cop car and they want me to pull over.

"Haven't I seen you guys before?"

The taller of the two plainclothes detectives gave me the third degree. The interrogator, a hulking giant with dark curly hair and a broad, unsmiling mouth, kept at me while the other blondish guy searched my car. It was clean. I was ready to tell the nervy cop he was violating my civil rights, but something about his looks made me bite my tongue. Two bear-like paws gripped the door beneath my open window. I could feel these unblinking, black marble eyes bore a hole right into my brain. I was convinced he could read my most secret thoughts. Jeez, he looked more like a killer than the guys at the Devonshire. I switched tactics, turning on my best behavior and the cops decided to let us go.

"I've got a bad feeling about this so count me out," I told Buddy reluctantly on the way back. He smirked and nodded.

A month later I read in the *Chicago Trib* about a jeweler on Marine Drive who was robbed to the tune of $70,000 in gold and precious stones. How about that. I missed out on one big score. Still, I wasn't sorry. That bureau cop set off all my alarm bells. Pulling a job was hard enough when you didn't have some lunatic mind-reading cop breathing down your neck. I couldn't shake those eyes. The next time I encountered them, the circumstances would be shockingly different.

A lot of goofy things went on around the neighborhood. Living there certainly had its perks. Every morning a guy who worked for city hall would systematically collect all the parking tickets on the cars in front of the two hotels and have them fixed. In the summer Handsome Joe, a four-foot-tall ex-fighter with his nose plastered all over his face, drove a carload of strippers out to Calumet City to turn some tricks. Unlike Chicago, the bars there were open to prostitution. It was sort of a shopping center for hookers. Prostitutes who hung around the hotels had a funny kind of morality. After a hard day's work, it was common for a girl to sit down with some of the guys at Valentino's. When it was closing time, she'd announce, "Okay, who wants to spend the night with me?" We were family so it wasn't like going to bed with a john. The flip of a coin decided who got lucky.

Within a two-block radius of the hotels you'd see more characters than all the rest of Chicago combined. On the corner opposite the hotels was the Front Page, a mob bar run by a guy whose name was Tony Montana. No kidding. That was his real name. Across the street was the Shrine Temple. Never could figure out how a legit joint like the Shrine Temple wound up in that neighborhood.

Make no mistake. There was a dark side to living in the heart of mob territory. Me and Bob were in Valentino's one night eating dinner. The place was packed. Conducting business at his usual table was Jimmy Allegretti. Marshall Caifano, alias Johnny Marshall, sat across from Jimmy. Among other things, Caifano burned down the El Rancho Vegas and whacked bunches of people on mob orders when he fronted for the Outfit in Las Vegas.

Another unsavory character at the table was "Milwaukee Phil" Alderisio, one of the most feared of all syndicate enforcers. Alderisio directed a crew of cat-burglars on Chicago's Gold Coast district. He liked to keep a low profile and lived in a posh apartment smack dab in the middle of the folks he robbed, but his real job was murder.

Rounding out the foursome was film star Marie "the Body" McDonald. She was so obsessed with Outfit guys, she'd do anything they wanted—the more dangerous the better.

An incident started when Marie said something smart to Caifano. He jumped up and called her all sorts of filthy names. So outraged was Caifano that he unzipped his fly and ordered Marie to suck his dick on the spot. Fearing for her life, she obliged. No one, and I mean no one, in Valentino's dared to look at them. You could hear a pin drop.

In the 50s and 60s the Outfit ran all the famous Chicago nightclubs plus every jukebox in the city and surrounding suburbs. The mob also controlled the International Alliance of Theatrical Stage Employees and Motion Picture Operators. The Outfit turned the screws on anyone they pleased, including actresses like Marie McDonald. When you played in the mob's playground, you played by their rules.

I loved to play practical jokes, but one sort of backfired. Me and Bob were sitting in the dark, smoke-filled bar at the Devonshire with a guy named Dick "the Ape." He had so much hair, he'd give the "gorilla man" in the side show a run for his money.

Well, this sappy singer we nicknamed "the goon" was torturing the patrons with his rendition of "Autumn Leaves." He also mangled a few other tunes so badly, I didn't recognize a single one.

The goon kept his tips in a tin cup on top of his piano. Me and Dick decided to have a little fun so we tied a black thread to a ten dollar bill. We made a big deal of putting it in his cup. Flattered by our generous tip, the goon smiled and thanked us. When he wasn't looking, we quickly pulled the ten spot out of the cup, back to where we were sitting. The customers laughed but the goon didn't catch on. Every time we repeated our little joke, the house went wild. Finally, on a break the goon peered into his cup. No money. I thought the crowd would go nuts. The goon went straight to Jimmy Allegretti.

Me and Dick were called on the carpet. Jimmy told us if we couldn't behave, we'd have to move out. I could tell Jimmy wasn't really sore, but he had to keep peace around the place. What the hell. Me and Bob itched to hit the road anyway. Marks were getting harder and harder to find.

The life we led wasn't for the wannabes. People who cheat at cards come in two categories—amateurs and professionals. There's a big difference. The amateur holds a regular job—could even be a family man. Somehow he learns a little about marked cards, maybe decides to cheat his friends around the kitchen table. Pros cheat full time. It's a different world from the amateur—always on the move. Like a burglar needs accurate information to pull a robbery, a professional card cheat needs "bird dogs" or scouts to find out where the action is. Real pros spend years, day in and day out, practicing sleight-of-hand. Most prefer this method over marked cards because, with marked cards, the risk of discovery is too great. To insiders, the professional con man is known as a "crossroader." That described me and Bob to a T. We were a couple of carefree young crossroaders, hell-bent on having the time of our lives.

10

This Cadillac passed us swerving all over the place.
Sure enough, the driver plowed right into a palm tree.

ME AND BOB worked our way through the racetracks from the Windy City to balmy Miami Beach. We rode in style— Bob's 1958 red and white Ford convertible. It didn't take long to see that the tracks gave us the best odds to fatten our bankroll. Bob, being good at making a line and lousy at picking winners, came up with a clever angle. Our story was that we were laying off money for the big Chicago bookies. We were betting on a "sure thing." Suckers bit and we hauled them in.

When we arrived in Miami, we checked into the Lido Hotel on South Collins. The Lido, a beachfront hotel, fit our limited budget because it was in South Beach, a slowly decaying area loaded with cheap hotels and apartments. We discovered a well-known crossroader's joint, Wolfie's Restaurant, only a block away. It was common to run into other crossroaders. Sooner or later they all hit the same cities, worked the same joints and developed a code all their own. For instance, if a crossroader on the way out of a restaurant told you, "The lamb stew is awfully good." That meant the check was easy to beat.

While me and Bob were waiting for a table at Wolfie's, who should we run into but two of the best crossroaders in the business, Sye Furlong, better know as Billy Morgan, and Vern Andrews.

This pair of con artists was so accomplished, they no longer needed the money. They were in it strictly for the thrill.

Billy, a dapper card man, operated out of the Fremont Hotel in Las Vegas. Dice were "hayseed" Vern's specialty. When he wasn't on the road, he hung around his ranch in Eagle River, Wisconsin. Hundreds of suckers, who had underestimated Vern on account of his appearance, traded their cards for a lottery ticket that promised better odds. I laughed to myself as I studied this oddly matched twosome.

"Hey, Bob," said Billy. "The last time I saw you was at the Sheridan Rec Pool Hall in Chicago. What brings you guys to Miami?"

Billy's dark hair was neatly combed. He was decked out in a crisp linen suit. The diamond stick-pin poking out of his under-stated silk tie glinted in the light. Billy looked as slick as a newly minted silver dollar. I noticed Billy wore his gold pinkie ring with a polished back—the same one he always used as a shiner to read the down cards he dealt.

"We're checking out the tracks," said Bob, giving Billy a wink.

The square-looking, porky Vern—thumbs hooked in his suspenders—watched the action quietly. It would be easy to blow this guy off until you noticed that his shrewd eyes missed nothing.

"How's the action around here?" I asked Billy.

"That depends on how good at cards you guys got," he answered, only half serious. With that, Billy whipped a deck of cards out of his pocket and had me and Bob check it out. "Anything wrong with these cards?" he asked.

Me and Bob examined the cards, looked at each other then at Billy. "They're okay."

"Are you sure?" Billy asked again. "Make sure you study them closely."

We took our time checking out the cards just as he asked. Shaking our heads, me and Bob answered, "Yeah, we're sure they're okay."

Billy went through a series of complicated cut procedures then, voila! On top of the deck was the ace of spades—king, queen, jack and ten—all spades. The only way I knew how to accomplish this move was using what's called a "stripper" deck.

Strippers are cards that have been shaved along the edges to have a different feel from the others in the deck. It makes the cards curve slightly outward so they're easier to pull out. Me and Bob took turns with the cards but couldn't feel anything odd.

Billy shuffled the cards back into the deck. "Here," he said. "Now you try it."

No luck. We couldn't do shit.

A broad smile played across Billy's deadpan face. Leaning close, he let us in on a fascinating story. "Years ago," he began, "I got into a beef with this guy who had the absolute gall to shoot me in the buttocks. As you might imagine, I had a lot of time to kill lying on my stomach. I was bored out of my skull so I decided to try a little experiment.

"I took a brand new pack of cards and an emery board. I picked out a group of cards and filed each one exactly fourteen times in the middle of the two long edges. Then I filed all the cards in the deck seven times the same way. This made the deck slightly concave, just the opposite of a normal stripper deck.

"Now I trained my fingers to feel the difference in the cards." Billy let out a wild laugh. "My backside healed a whole lot faster than I learned the trick I just showed you."

Billy's invention became known as the "concave stripper." Only the best card cheats have the patience to master the moves, which take years of constant practice. Once magicians discovered the concave stripper, they began to include it in their acts. We practiced for months but could never get the hang of the concave stripper, so me and Bob used ordinary stripper decks when we needed them.

Years later I learned through the grapevine that Billy was the victim of a mob hit. Apparently, while in a card game in Las Vegas, he got a little too clever with a Mafia big-shot and won the game but at a costly price—his life.

Me and Bob went to work at the track. It was horseracing during the day and the dog tracks at night. Hialeah had a bunch of flamingos that made the grassy park in the center of the track their home. Like clockwork, when it was time for the seventh race, the flamingos took flight in one big pink cloud. It was a tradition. One day me and Bob were at Hialeah and I was losing my shirt. Just then the birds did their thing. "Those ain't flamingos," I cracked. "They're greenbacks with wings."

Before long, we added the Kingston Yacht Club to our routine. It was a small joint on the Intracoastal Waterway with mediocre traffic, but me and Bob got to like the characters who hung out there. Martha Raye and Rocky Graziano were regulars.

Before we knew it, Christmas had rolled around. Business was off on account of the holiday. Even though me and Bob were short on cash, we knew at least twenty restaurants where the lamb stew was great. Even better, Santa was about to deliver an unexpected present.

Around 3:00 a.m. on that mild Christmas morning, me and Bob were driving down Alton Road. A Cadillac passed us swerving all over the place. We followed the car for a few miles. Sure enough, the driver plowed right into a palm tree. We pulled up behind him and I went over to check the guy out. He was drunk as a skunk and, lucky for us, all alone.

"Are you okay?" I asked, giving his car the once-over. The guy was so out of it, I could see the tweety birds circling above his head. No response.

"Show me your driver's license," I ordered, hoping he'd think I was a cop. It worked because he promptly pulled out his wallet. Pay dirt. My eyes feasted on three crisp $100 bills. It was like waving a juicy T-bone in front of a starving man. I tossed the empty billfold into his back seat and me and Bob made a hasty retreat. Now Christmas wouldn't be so bad after all.

The dead week after Christmas, Miami was like a graveyard. Me and Bob had some time to kill before things got back to normal. We'd never seen Key West so we drove across the rickety old Seven-Mile Bridge to what we thought would be a tropical paradise. To borrow a famous Bette Davis line, "What a dump." Key West was nothing but a few claptrap wood-frame buildings and a crummy dock. We were about to turn around and go back when Bob pointed to a sign: "Plane ride to Cuba: $10." Me and Bob looked at one another. Next stop, Cuba.

Havana was so beautiful, I had to pinch myself to make sure I wasn't dreaming. Giggling, brown-skinned school girls offered us brightly colored flowers, horns honked, musky cigar smoke mingled with the humid air. Cubanos danced and plucked guitars under the setting sun as me and Bob weaved our way along the Malecon outside our hotel, the Nacional.

Outdoor cafes with their striped canopies jammed the sidewalks. Tanned beauties waved at us as they downed their rum-laced *mojitos*, a Cuban mint julep that packs a double whammy. Now this was a tropical paradise. You could keep your Key West. How bad could this place be? Gorgeous, young women would spend the night with you for only twenty dollars.

First we hit the Hotel Nacional's casino. I thought I was right back at the Devonshire.

Wherever you turned, there was some Mafia guy puffing on a Cuban cigar. It looked like a mob convention or something. Me and Bob bumped into a couple of Outfit guys we knew from Ohio Street. Pretty soon they were teaching us a little about Cuban history—stuff you don't find in too many school books.

It seems years earlier Meyer Lansky had gotten chummy with Cuba's thug dictator, Fulgencio Batista. Lansky attended an important mob meeting in Havana in '46 to decide the fate of Bugsy Siegel, who had a nasty habit of skimming construction funds from the Flamingo and the show place was loosing money big time. Apparently Lansky pleaded to spare Bugsy, but it was a no go. Bugsy had been stashing away the mob's money in a secret Swiss account and that was just too much for the mob to swallow.

Shortly after that meeting Bugsy met his end at the home of his girlfriend, Virginia Hill, who was conveniently out of the country. The incredibly skilled marksman, allegedly Gussie Alex, shot Bugsy's eye clear across the room. Strongy Ferraro was the other alleged hitman, as well as a point man from New York, Frankie Carbo. Whether it was Cuba, Chicago, New Orleans or some other mob-infested city, these same alleged killers' names popped up time after time.

Batista legalized gambling in Cuba, aided and abetted by his not so silent partner, organized crime. Casinos sprung up like mushrooms all over Havana in the forties and fifties. The city was dubbed the "Latin Las Vegas." Rumors flew around that Batista's take from Lansky's casinos was as much as 30 percent of the millions Lansky held. Besides the Hotel Nacional's casino, the Montmartre Club, another Lansky hot-spot, shelled out big money to Batista. Casinos weren't Batista's only source of power. He already had attracted plenty of U.S. businessmen by throwing them choice construction contracts the way a poker cheat deals winning hands to his agents.

Geez, I thought. The mob's everywhere. Even when you leave the United States you run into the same guys.

It was a New Year's I'm not likely to forget. Me and Bob had picked up a couple of shapely señoritas. They took us to their hotel somewhere in Old Havana near the Avenida del Puerto. On the way over, I checked out the neighborhood. I think Havana had more monuments than bars, if that's possible. There seemed to be a statue of some guy on a horse every few feet.

All night long the streets echoed with constant gunfire and explosions. "Boy," I remarked to Bob and the girls. "If I didn't know it was New Year's Eve, I'd swear there was a war going on out there." Everyone laughed.

The first day of the New Year, 1959, started out peaceful enough. Me, Bob and the girls were having a quiet breakfast when in stormed three bearded guys wearing these funny olive-green berets. They shoved their filthy machine guns in our faces and shot rapid-fire questions at us in Spanish. I was about to tell them I was an American citizen and had rights, but one of the girls covered my mouth with her hand. She explained in hushed tones that Fidel Castro, a communist, took over the country last night and these were his men. Batista had skipped to Miami in a plane. Can you beat that? There was a civil war going on last night and we didn't even know it!

When the soldiers found out we were the "filthy American pigs," they got very angry and punched us around. It didn't help matters that we were with their women. I guess we should have considered ourselves damn lucky to get out of the country alive, minus our money. They loaded us on a truck with other Americans, put us on a boat and, in about three hours, we were back in that dump, Key West. Seeing as we didn't have a peso to our names and Bob's car was running on fumes, we needed a bankroll quick.

"Now what?" I asked Bob, but before he had a chance to answer, I spotted a broken-down motel across the road. A hand-painted sign in the window read, "Desk clerk wanted."

I had a plan so I marched right in. The place was so ancient, the Bibles in the rooms were probably carved out of stone. No sooner did I ask about the job, than the mangy-looking manager offered it to me. Being the off-season—and in this place it was always the off-season—the guy must have been desperate. He looked like he hadn't slept in about two weeks.

My job was simple enough. I was supposed to hang around all night and in the morning do the wake-up calls to the guests. (One person wanted a 5:30 call, another at 6:00.) Sure I would. About 2:00 a.m., I grabbed the petty cash. Bob was waiting outside in the car. Me and Bob filled the gas tank and high-tailed it back to Miami.

Our luck held. We ran into an easy mark killing time by our hotel pool, a mooch only too happy to play us a friendly little game of gin rummy. The next morning me and Bob hit the road $200 richer. We heard the Fairgrounds Race Track in New Orleans was gearing up for its winter season and Mardi Gras was just around the corner, so we made tracks for "The Big Easy."

A few days later we arrived in New Orleans but again our pockets were nearly empty. If we didn't find us a bigger bankroll, we might as well forget about making a killing at the track. Opportunity was about to knock. Me and Bob inched our way down Bourbon Street. The bumper-to-bumper traffic gave us a chance to take in the sights. Lush green plants spilled like waterfalls over black, wrought-iron railings. A colored guy stopped his sweeping to admire Bob's car. "Hello, baby," he greeted us in his friendly Southern drawl.

Just then a familiar voice rang out. "Hey, Bob!" It was Dino, a Greek bartender from the Devonshire.

Dino jumped in Bob's back seat, yacking about old times on Ohio Street. He looked pretty good with the sun hitting his black curly hair—until you noticed the good-looking head was attached to this short, dumpy body.

Dino directed us to an address off Canal Street in the heart of the French Quarter. Dixieland Jazz floated from every other doorway. Lazy, seductive rhythms drew the hungry and thirsty into the bars and restaurants packed with more of the same, only luckier because they had a table. Patrons guzzled Hurricanes at the famous Pat O'Brien's and devoured the spicy shrimp that arrived on steaming platters piled almost a foot-high.

"DINO's." The bar's neon-red sign flashed off and on invitingly. So far things looked promising. The French Quarter was obviously the place to be. Once inside, I quickly adjusted to the dim light sifting through the smoky bar. My eyes hit on a perfect target—the blue-eyed, blond barmaid. What a shape I thought, filing her vital statistics away for future consideration. From the cool, "no-vacancy" stare she gave me, I decided this filly would need a little encouragement. I better find me a carrot.

Dino took us to a table where we could talk. "So what brings you guys to New Orleans?" Dino asked the question casually enough, but the gleam in his eye gave me the impression he was ripe for our scam.

Me and Bob went straight into our act. "We're down here laying off money on a sure thing for the wire service," said Bob. I motioned toward my waist like I was wearing a money belt.

Dino nodded his head and grinned knowingly. I could already see his brain racking up the dollar signs.

"We're gonna check into the Roosevelt," I said. "So I expect you'll be seeing a lot of us."

The Roosevelt was a classy hotel not far away. We figured Dino's greed would kick in any minute now. It did.

"Come on you guys, you can tell me," Dino pleaded. "I promise I'll keep my mouth shut. What's the sure thing?" Me and Bob smiled mysteriously.

Now Dino insisted we stay at his house as his guests. He wouldn't take no for an answer. It was hard to keep a straight face at a time like this, but we managed.

We lived like kings—free meals, free phone calls and free rent. If that wasn't enough, when we ate at a fancy restaurant, Dino picked up the check. Every day when we returned to Dino's Bar after a hard day at the track, Dino would grill us. "Was today the day of the cinch?" We refused to talk other than to tell him we had to check with our nameless informant. It drove Dino nuts.

One night that carrot appeared unexpectedly. Me and Bob were sitting at a table. I couldn't help but notice the barmaid kept glancing over and I nearly fell off my chair when she flashed me a big smile. "Hey, Bob," I said. "Is that barmaid coming on to me?"

"Could be," he said. "You know she thinks we're Mafia guys. Last night I heard Dino tell someone he thought for sure I was a made guy and you were my hitman." Bob almost choked on the words he was laughing so hard. "Your barmaid overheard the whole thing and she seemed very impressed."

The next day Bob asked, "What's that tune you keep whistling?"

"Back in the Saddle Again," I answered.

Now Dino was getting very antsy. Our little holiday was going on two weeks and I could see Dino wouldn't be put off much longer. This "sure thing" was costing Dino a shitload of money.

The very next day Bob handicapped a two-year-old. The horse should have gone off at eight to one, but Bob knew the public would bet it down to even money. Our horse won by a mile. We bet $20 on the horse and took home $40. Better yet, Dino won $4,000! Bob was so excited, he began to think maybe he could pick a winner. "Don't quit your day job," I told him. "Let's just count ourselves lucky."

That night Dino got loaded. Four grand was a substantial amount of cash. "Hey, you two," he slurred. "Get me another winner like that one. Whatta ya say?"

About 3:00 a.m., while Dino snored away, we sneaked into his room. His pants still lay on the floor where Dino had dropped them. I fished inside the left front pocket, located the four grand and took the pants and all. Seeing as we were getting a little homesick, we pointed the car toward Chicago.

On the way out of town I asked Bob, "Why did it take you so long to leave Dino's room?"

"Oh, I wanted to leave Dino a note."

"What did it say?"

"Dino, we took your pants to the cleaners."

11

To describe a G-string—it wasn't much more than
a few bits of dental floss attached to a microscopic
triangle that more or less covered the privates.

NOTHING HAD CHANGED at the Devonshire—same guys bullshitting about the same stuff. I was killing time with Jimmy
Allegretti in Valentino's.

Out of the blue Jimmy asked me, "Do you want a job?"

I popped right back with "Sure" before I knew what he
was going to say. I figured if Jimmy had an offer, I better take
advantage of it. Besides, I was broke. Hustling gave you a lot of
freedom, but a steady job meant you could count on a regular
paycheck.

Jimmy explained the deal. "I want you to meet a guy named
Big Joe Smith at the Crossroads, a strip joint over on Van Buren
and State. It's next to Minsky's. Big Joe's the manager and he's
looking for a bartender. I think you'd fit in. Whatta ya say?" I
nodded.

You had to have an alliance with the Outfit to work in one of
their places. I guess Jimmy thought I was trustworthy. Jimmy
was the first to hear what went on at the mob joints and the
Crossroads was one of the biggest money-makers in Chicago.
Curly Fishman fronted it for the Outfit. Curly and his brother
Bill also ran a bookmaking operation on the third floor. It was all
part of Gus Alex's domain, the booming downtown First Ward.
The Outfit took a big chunk of the profits from the Crossroads—
50 percent from upstairs and 50 percent from downstairs. Further
south on State Street you'd run into Louie Argo's places and other
Greek-run, small-scale strip joints. They were all under Gussie

Alex's control, the guy who continued to reap benefits from his alleged role in Bugsy Siegel's murder.

The job sounded interesting, but I didn't know much about strip joints. I once heard some guys call them "bust out" joints because that's how a sucker would leave—busted.

In fact, when I was about eight years old, me and Sonny Clark were climbing roofs across from the Wilson El Station. Right below us was a strip joint called the Silver Palms, owned by Ross Miller, the father of one-time governor of Nevada, Bob Miller. We sneaked down an enclosed area and peeked through the window. What an education that was. There were women prancing around on stage wearing a couple of pasties, these sparkly round things, which barely covered their nipples.

As if nearly naked breasts weren't enough to arouse a young kid, I almost came in my pants when I saw my first G-string. To describe a G-string—it wasn't much more than a few bits of dental floss attached to a microscopic triangle that more or less covered the privates. Maybe glue really kept the tiny G-string in place because it seemed like the least little wiggle would cause it to fall down. That was part of the excitement—praying the G-string would fall down. After that peep show I'd go over and over what I saw. It gave me hours of hot material to fuel my sexual fantasies. I've been a street kid all my life so I thought I knew everything there was to know about the hustles. Turns out my education was just beginning.

The Crossroads was a monster of a place, maybe half a block across. The long bar could easily seat 75 people. It paralleled the enormous stage. In the daytime the Crossroads was a high-class restaurant with matching high-class prices. It catered to the white-collar crowd. Once night fell and the lights went way down, out strutted the girls. Twenty-eight stunning strippers bumped and grinded their way into the erotic daydreams of the guys who ogled them. No doubt about it. Female flesh was on sale and it didn't come cheap.

While a stripper peeled off her satin gloves and gown under

the spotlight, shady acts took place in the inky depths. Bar girls, or B-girls as they were called, played the touchy-feely game, enticing suckers to lay down their cash for overpriced drinks. Sex was the unspoken promise. Most of the strippers worked the floor when they weren't on stage. That's where the real dough was made. I was about to get the inside scoop on the Crossroads con. The anticipation made me edgy and excited.

Big Joe Smith didn't need any makeup to play Frankenstein. This six-foot-three-inch crude-talking giant with the pockmarked face and heavy-lidded eyes was a dead-ringer for Boris Karloff. I could see Joe didn't waste time with small talk so I kept my intro short.

"Jimmy A sent me."

He looked me over, grunted and motioned to this little Greek bartender, Spiro, to join us. Joe left Spiro to show me the ropes.

Spiro seemed eager to get down to business. "Okay, here's the spit glasses." He noticed my questioning look. "They ain't nothing more than tall, frosted glasses with a few ice cubes thrown in," he said in a raspy-voiced whisper.

"Here's what you do if a girl approaches a customer. You give her a few minutes, walk over and pour two shots of this watered down booze into two shot glasses." He pointed to one of the bottles behind the bar. "Instead of drinking hers, the girl spits it into the spit glass. The mark thinks it's a water chaser. If the mark won't give you four dollars, take one shot away, but leave the other shot and spit glass and try to get two bucks.

"Now if the mark wants to take the girl to a booth in the back, he has to buy a bottle of champagne which is nothing more than seltzer and Rhine wine. You collect $26 plus a two dollar tip."

By now the oily little Greek was wound up. I could see he got real satisfaction out of teaching the fine art of hustling suckers.

"If a customer don't want to spend any money," Spiro continued, "then you treat him to a free shot of 100-proof vodka and sometimes 500-proof grain alcohol. Of course he don't know it.

And if a guy thinks he's gonna nurse a beer all night, you pour him a boilermaker. That's a shot of alcohol in a beer." Spiro gave me a toothy grin minus a couple of teeth. "It don't take long for a customer to loosen up."

Spiro reached under the bar and brought out some other props. "These colored swizzle sticks here go into the spit glasses. They get the girls their commission. A white stick represents one dollar, a red stick $10 and a green stick $25.

"At the end of the night the sticks are added up," explained Spiro, "and each girl gets 15 percent of her total take. If the girls don't turn in at least $500 worth of sticks, they're fired. But it ain't unusual for a good mixer to turn in $5,000 worth of sticks in a single night."

Spiro's watery eyes glanced over to make sure I was taking all this in. I wished he'd move back a little. His heavy cologne was making me sick. Instead he leaned closer like he didn't want anyone to overhear what he was saying. I couldn't figure why, because nobody was within earshot. I guess mob guys were always on the lookout.

Spiro told me the idea was to dump a guy after he'd gone bust. It worked like this. A girl would say, "Listen, honey, you wait for me out back." She'd ask for a bottle of champagne to go, the bartender would wrap it in a brown paper bag, and the mooch would wait for her out back. He'd think the girl was going to join him after the place closed. Of course, she never did. Most of the time he didn't have enough to pay for the bottle so she'd say, "Oh, that's all right, honey. I'll take care of it."

"Near closing on any given night," Spiro continued, "you'd see four or five guys each holding a brown paper bag, pacing back and forth outside the rear door. The girls would beat it out another exit. Funny how all the mooches fell for this line. It just goes to show what I call the POP principle, or the Power of Pussy." Spiro doubled over laughing.

"Any guy who had the nerve to come back and try to start a fight, got beat up. But most of the suckers were married so they sure as hell didn't want it to get around that they were taken to the cleaners by a hooker."

I thanked Spiro. Happy to breathe again, I reported back to Big Joe Smith. "You start at 7:00 tomorrow night. Be here at 6:30 sharp," he warned.

"Okay," I answered.

"Get the fuck out of here," he barked. That was just the way he talked, no frills.

Strip joints had a reputation for attracting trouble. That didn't bother Vince Eli, the emcee and bouncer at the Crossroads, one bit. Vince knew his way around the ring. It didn't hurt that he'd been Rocky Marciano's sparing partner. During the years they were on the road together, Rocky negotiated scores of fights for Vince. The map-of-Italy face combined with a brick-shithouse body scared the crap out of guys. But Vince didn't need an edge. He was a great fighter in his own right. Vince may have looked like a stone killer, underneath he was a softy. That's why me and him hit it off. Besides, Vince was a very funny guy. Come to think of it, Vince was the only guy I knew who could make Big Joe Smith laugh.

Joe called me and Vince to the back room one day. We were running low on the house champagne so we had to mix up some more. Vince glanced around the room taking in the empty champagne bottles, corks, funnels, Rhine wine and seltzer. He scratched his head, turned to Joe and said, "Isn't this illegal?"

Joe laughed so hard, he almost knocked over a case of wine. "That's a riot, kid. Hey, this kid's got a real sense of humor. If you think that's the worst thing that goes on in this town, you're lucky."

My first couple of weeks at the Crossroads were an eye-opener. I noticed that when Vince asked troublemakers to leave, sometimes they'd want to duke it out in the alley. This was the cue for Joe Jambaroni, "Little Joe Jam" for short, to hit the guy over the head with his blackjack. By the time I could lend a hand, the whole thing was usually over.

Joe Jam was a made guy and precinct captain who served under First Ward alderman and mob guy, John D'Arco. Joe was the Outfit's on-site muscle. He made sure the mob got its cut and nobody made trouble. If I had any doubts about the syndicate running Chicago, D'Arco and Jamboroni's "dual" job descriptions made everything as clear as double-distilled gin.

Something a little different happened one night. A colored guy came in, which was pretty rare. There were strong feelings against colored at this time, but if they behaved, we let them spend their money. Business was business. Our rule was that a colored guy could buy a drink for himself, but never for the girls. The girls flirted brazenly with every other customer but ignored him. The guy flipped out.

"What's wrong with me?" he yelled. "I'm not good enough?"

Joe Jam quietly walked up and whacked him in the back of the head with his blackjack, but the guy refused to go down. Instead, his bony hands went straight for Joe Jam's throat. All hell broke loose. I jumped over the bar and grabbed the bastard by the collar. Vince charged him like a mad bull. Out of the corner of my eye, I caught sight of Big Joe looming in the background. Then everything went black.

The next thing I knew, my face was inches away from the most incredible cleavage. This platinum blond stripper in her skimpy costume was mopping my forehead with a cold towel. Everyone in the joint just stood there gawking.

"What the hell hit me?" I mumbled still groggy. My head felt like a punching bag.

In the confusion, the blackjack had connected with my thick skull by mistake. Vince beat the colored guy senseless and deposited him out in the street like a piece of dead meat. I smiled up at Vince with genuine gratitude, but my warm feelings were cut short.

"Whatta ya' need, a wake up call? Get to work you bum! And that goes for the rest of you, too." Big Joe Smith had everyone scrambling back to their battle stations.

Vince had his share of inconveniences. One night this tough guy approached Vince at the door. "I wanna see Big Joe Smith," he demanded.

Vince countered. "What's it to you?"

The guy repeated that he had to see Joe. Vince was getting annoyed so he finally told the guy, "I'm Big Joe Smith. Whatta ya want?"

Catching Vince unawares, the guy punched him so hard, Vince landed in the hot dog stand. Everything went flying—hot dogs, buns, relish, mustard—you name it. Vince chased the guy into the alley, but no luck. He was gone.

It was awful quiet when Vince walked in. "From now on," he announced. "The only name I answer to is Vince Eli."

Every strip joint had a mob guy like Joe Jam whose job it was to keep the undesirables out and the conventioneers in, the guys with a hard-on and money to spend. The joints had an agreement with the cabbies. For every customer a cab driver brought to the club, he got a commission. It was three dollars a head at the Crossroads. Other joints paid roughly the same amount. "Line loading," as it was called in the biz, made some guys a good buck.

One of the best line loaders was none other than Bob Mauro. He didn't own a cab, but when he needed cash, he'd borrow a cab for an hour or so while the driver was in the Devonshire coffee shop. Bob headed straight for the Silver Frolics down the street to pick up a bunch of convention guys. "How did you make out?" Bob would ask them, pretending he didn't know the answer.

"No good," they'd say.

"Well, that's because you went to the wrong place. At the Crossroads, the girls will leave with you. Jump in and I'll take you there."

As soon as Bob dropped off one cab-load of guys, another group piled in. He used the same story except he changed the name of the strip joint. Back and forth Bob shuttled guys for maybe an hour. Then Bob returned the cab with enough money to play the horses the next day.

Nothing in my job description prepared me for what followed. Myra, a wild redheaded hostess—that's a girl who mixed but didn't strip—needed a favor. It so happened that Joe Louis, the ex-heavyweight champ, was her boyfriend.

After work one night Myra asked if I'd drop her off at Killer Johnson's, a nightclub on the South Side named after the famous boxer who owned it. Killer didn't come by his nickname helping old ladies cross the street. The joint was on Sixty-third and Cottage Grove in the heart of the toughest colored section in Chicago. Myra was supposed to meet Joe there.

I thought to myself, I might as well step in front of a train. A white guy like me sure as hell didn't stroll into a joint with all these colored fighters and live to tell about it. They'd kill me just so there would be one less white guy, even if I was doing Myra a favor. I'd seen the bloody remains of too many like me who had made the mistake of straying into colored territory.

"Are you crazy?" I said. "You'll be reading my obituary tomorrow."

"Don't worry," she laughed. "Nobody's gonna lay a hand on you."

She insisted I walk her in. I sweated a little but acted like it was no big deal. I was saying good night to Myra thinking I might get out alive, when I felt these heavy weights clamp down on my shoulders. I froze. I couldn't have moved anyway. Invisible hands spun me around. They were attached to none other than Joe Louis himself.

"Hey, man, thanks a lot for driving Myra all the way down here. Let me get you a drink."

Can you beat that? Joe was a perfect gentleman and nobody bothered me. I took some real kidding after that incident. Let 'em laugh, I thought. At least I'm alive to talk about it.

A few months later Vince was offered a job at the Showboat, a smaller strip joint on the corner of Balbo and State. His long-time friend, Nervous Joe Sauro, co-managed the place. Me and Vince hit it off so well, I asked to transfer to the Showboat. I got my wish. The Crossroads may have been all business, but the Showboat was just the opposite—fun and games, which suited me to a T. Once inside the Showboat, you disappeared into a black hole. It was so dark that if your sister was working there you'd never know it. What a cover to fleece suckers!

Nervous Joe, whose name described him perfectly, and his partner Irv, a calm quiet guy, ran the place from a booth by the front door. Every time a customer came in, Joe would shine his flashlight on the guy's feet to see if he was a cop. Black patrolman's shoes and white socks were a dead giveaway. Joe wouldn't let a girl hustle a guy when he spotted that combination. If a cop wasn't on the payroll, he could make trouble.

On the left, an oblong bar seated about sixteen. Directly behind the bar, one of six to ten strippers paraded down the narrow runway in front of the stage. It was the usual scene. Footlights bathed the girls in a kaleidoscope of colors. Scratchy phonograph music, with its bump and grind rhythm, played backup.

Vince warmed up the house with his familiar one-liners. "Remember, the difference between a dog and a fox . . . is about six drinks." Laughter. Next he'd introduce the dancers, "Here's a girl no bigger than your hand and a lot more fun." More laughter. Then he'd slap on a record and find a strategic spot where he could catch the action. Once in a while a record would stick. Vince would rush back and lift the needle before the mood was ruined. Sometimes he had to break up a fight—not the customers' but a couple of brash, name-calling strippers—each laying claim to the same record.

I eased into my bartending routine. With my back to the stage, I watched the customers whistle and hoot. When business was slow, I turned around and leered a little myself.

One of the dancers, a smart-mouthed leggy brunette named Tamara, was going with Frank Laporte, a Mafia capo. In fact, Tamara had a kid by him. Frank ran the syndicate operations from Calumet City to Kankakee. He was strictly bad news. Tamara started kidding around with me. She was a sexy babe, so it didn't take much to get me going. I'd drive her home to Calumet City and spend the night. Only one problem: Tamara was a primadonna. If she said jump, I better ask, "How high?"

Vince took me aside when the place was empty. "Are you nuts? You're messing with Frank Laporte's property. If he finds out you're screwing around with Tamara, I'm gonna have to scrape what's left of you off the sidewalk."

Since he put it that way, I was only too happy to oblige. I sure didn't need any problems. But the more I tried to steer clear of this dame, the more she came on to me. I guess I should have been flattered, but my good health seemed more important.

I was wiping down the bar after a busy night. I looked up. A very drunk Tamara swayed just inches from my face. "Come on, honey. Take me home," she pleaded.

"I've got other plans," I told her coolly.

Tamara's mood turned nasty. She slapped me in the face. I slapped her back. She called Frank and told him I hit her. Suddenly I was in a shit-load of trouble. Luckily, Vince and Irv came to my rescue. They set Frank straight on what really happened. Frank said three words, "Fire the bitch." Everyone breathed a huge sigh of relief, especially me.

I couldn't seem to stay out of trouble when women were around, and they were always around. One of the strippers, I think her name was Sandra, was hitting up all the guys in the joint for a donation. It was my turn.

"How about buying some raffle tickets? It's for a good cause, the Chicago Police Association. They're gonna raffle off a new car."

"Naw," I joked. "I don't need a police car."

Turned out Sandra lived with this wise-ass detective we called JK who tried to push his weight around at police headquarters on Eleventh and State. He wasn't too pleased with my snappy response to Sandra, so he dug through the records looking for dirt. When he turned up my felony conviction, JK decided to pay me a little visit. Tootsie, a smooth-talking gypsy, covered the bar while smug JK and me slid into a booth. JK leaned over. His dull gray eyes never blinked.

"Listen, asshole. I know all about your felony. I can make it really rough for you. As a matter of fact, I own you, you son-of-a-bitch."

JK went into all the things he could do to me if I didn't cooperate, like ripping my head off on the spot. I wanted to laugh, but thought that wouldn't go over too big with JK. Cops, especially tough-talking ones, didn't scare me.

Vince had been watching the whole thing. After JK left the booth, Vince moved into the seat across from me. "What was that all about?"

When I relayed what happened, Vince turned scarlet with anger. I thought he was going to pop a blood vessel.

On his way out, JK had collared Irv. Irv frowned over something JK told him and shook his head from side to side. Vince announced the next girl and then walked over to the two, automatically clenching his enormous fists.

Ignoring Irv, Vince hunched over the table and looked JK squarely in the eye. "It's nice you being a cop and going out with one of the girls here. You know it ain't allowed. On top of that, you're threatening one of our bartenders because he's got a felony."

"Do you know who you're taking to?" JK spat the words in Vince's face.

Vince kept his cool. Towering over the puny JK, he stood up emphasizing every word as if he was chewing out some kid. "I don't have a felony conviction you lousy little shit, so if you don't like the way I'm talking, take off that gun and we'll step outside."

Irv hadn't uttered a peep, but now he piped in. "Don't worry, JK. I'll hold your gun."

Well, JK decided to stay put and he didn't come in so often after that. When he did, he minded his own business. Irv had plenty of juice if he wanted to get JK transferred to the South Side, but that would never happen. JK would have wound up in the hospital first.

12

She used her body the way
a politician uses promises.

THE SHOWBOAT WAS in for fireworks when they booked a strip-tease dancer named Kitty Carr, the Baby Doll of Burlesque. This four-foot-eleven Sicilian bombshell with the great body was as hot-tempered as a female tiger protecting her kill. Raven-haired, muscular, and exotic looking, Kitty took the Showboat and me by storm. It was no use my trying to stay away from her even if I wanted to. The mutual attraction grabbed us the minute we set eyes on one another. That was it.

Kitty called the Devonshire home, like everyone who worked at the Showboat. She drove back with me in the wee hours after work. Pretty soon our toothbrushes were laying side by side in the room we shared on the fourteenth floor. I scrounged Kitty a phony birth certificate and social security card, all under her mother's maiden name, Rosso. The IDs stated her age as eighteen, but she was much younger.

Most of the time trying to get Kitty to talk was like prying open an oyster. The rough "pearls" of her hard life came tumbling out in reluctant strings. I didn't learn the most important part till later—much later.

Born and raised in Montreal, Kitty idolized her Sicilian uncle on her mother's side. Her father was a Scot who followed the family tradition of hard-drinking. Both of Kitty's brainy brothers graduated from McGill University. Black sheep Kitty hated school. Instead, she hung around with her mob-connected uncle who owned a flashy nightclub in Montreal. The excitement ground to a halt when the uncle whacked some waiter, caught with his hand in the till. Rumor had it the uncle beat it to New York where he had Mafia contacts. No one in the family heard from him again.

Kitty, restless and lonely, took up with a guy who got her pregnant. Her parents wouldn't budge. They made their wayward daughter give up her baby girl for adoption. It wasn't until years later that I realized just how hard it hit Kitty. In fact, giving her baby away affected nearly everything Kitty did.

There was nothing to keep Kitty in Montreal any longer so she answered a newspaper ad on a whim. It read: "Exotic dancer wanted. Apply in person." The ad gave an address across the border in Hurley, Wisconsin. So the nervy fifteen-year-old hitched a ride to the little town of Hurley. She landed the glamorous-sounding job as striptease artist and Kitty Carr, the Baby Doll of Burlesque, was born. The owner of the strip joint took the young, pretty girl under his wing. He taught her the right moves, bought her some sexy gowns. Her career was on a roll.

Pat De Carlo, theatrical agent and part-time bartender at the Berkshire, booked Kitty into the Showboat. In fact, Pat was also Vince Eli's agent. Pat and Vince worked the burlesque circuit that grew out of vaudeville.

It was 1960 and burlesque was starting to loose its luster. In a few more years the Go-Go craze would hit the country. Sexy girls in hot pants and white vinyl Go-Go boots would wig out in wire cages, dancing to a new beat. For the time being, plenty of guys still preferred the old tease.

As for Kitty, nobody put anything over on her. She learned early on that a guy would promise a girl the moon. Once he got what he wanted, she was history. Kitty found out that if she strung guys along, she could manipulate them to her advantage. Control was the name of the game. Kitty used her body the way a politician uses promises.

Things went swell at the Showboat until one night this convention guy sat down and ordered a beer. The drinks were two dollars. When I examined the bills at the cash register under the light, I realized I had a "sleeper." In the blackness, the guy pulled out a dollar bill and a $100 bill by mistake. I rang up two dollars and put both bills where the dollar bills go. I was now $99 up. When the next order came around, I'd palm a dollar bill from the customer, put it in the register and take the $100 for myself.

Just then a vice cop in the back booth yelled, "Don't anyone move." Another vice cop seated at the bar stood up and three more cops stormed in the front door ordering Nervous Joe to turn on the lights. I had no time to make the switch. They pinched me, Joe and the vice cop's "date" along with the waitress who served them. A raid was no big deal. We usually left our IDs in the car and gave the cops phony names in case something like this happened.

Joe noticed me glumly staring into space. "You look like you're gonna die," he said. "Relax, we'll be out before you know it."

"Yeah, yeah," I answered, not daring to tell Joe the cash register was up $99. Not only would I lose my job (mob guys have no sense of humor), Kitty would dump me. What rotten luck.

The next night I went to work figuring I'd get the axe. Hell with it. I saved a nice bankroll so let 'em fire me.

When I walked in, Joe was telling Irv what I looked like in jail. "Speak of the devil. Boy, Irv," Joe said slapping me on the back. "You should have seen this guy last night. He was the exact shade of a stiff on a slab."

Irv flashed me this shit-eating grin. I knew then that Irv beat Joe for the $99. I whistled as I drove Kitty home that night. I still had my job. I was lucky this wasn't the Crossroads. They would have canned me on the spot.

It dawned on me I could be jobless without warning. Forget about working in the mob-run strip joints. I'd have to leave town. A week later I bought a new Pontiac Bonneville convertible while I still had a regular paycheck coming in. My mom co-signed the note. I built a secret compartment on the driver's side under the floorboard. I always carried a gun and, as a felon, I needed a place to stash it.

It was a slow Sunday night at the Showboat—no conventions in town. Nervous Joe told Tootsie to watch the bar for a while.

"What's up?" I asked Joe when he called me into his office.

"I'm very good at gin rummy," Joe announced. "Suppose me and you play Hollywood for a penny a point?"

"Okay," I said reluctantly. But I was thinking I didn't want to cheat him too bad, since he was my boss.

In about an hour I was up $20. I told Joe, "It's time I went back to the bar, don't you think?"

"One more game, double or nothing," Joe offered me the deck.

Most guys in my situation never cheat, but it just wasn't in me to do that. I was powerless to stop the con even at crucial times like this. You can imagine the problems it caused.

Before I knew it, he owed me $40 . . . then $80.

I was getting like Joe's name, nervous. "This is ridiculous," I said hoping he'd call it quits. "You could end up owing me thousands before we're through."

"Okay," said Joe. "You're fired." He took the deck and threw it up in the air. It was comical the way cards rained down on our heads, but no one was laughing.

Kitty cornered me on the way out. "What's wrong?" she demanded, reading the resigned look on my face.

I told her the news. She went crazy.

"Why that son-of-a-bitch! I quit." Typical Kitty, loyal to a fault.

Kitty tossed her gowns in my back seat. Now we were both out of work. With my car payments, we went down fast. Pretty soon we owed rent, too, but all we had was the change in our pockets.

We sat in our room trying to brainstorm. We were so hungry, our stomachs sang a duet. I dialed room service and ordered one cheeseburger. Kitty elbowed me in the ribs. I knew she was hungry, but I ignored her. I had a plan. A young kid brought the sandwich. As he walked toward the door, I hid the cheeseburger and called him back.

"There's no meat in here," I said showing him the empty bun.

He looked puzzled. "I guess somebody must have dropped it. I'll be right back."

A while later in he waltzed with another cheeseburger. Now *that* was broke.

Kitty stepped in to save our necks. She called her agent Pat De Carlo, who booked Kitty for three weeks at the Gay 90s, a strip joint in Cleveland, Ohio. What a brilliant move buying the car, I thought. At least we had wheels.

I didn't look forward to what I had to do next—ask Joe Arnold for a loan so we had a bankroll for the Cleveland trip. He advanced me $300, which meant I had to pay $30 a week interest till the entire loan was paid off. That's the way juice loans work.

One last problem loomed over us. Me and Kitty still owed $150 for rent, but I had another idea. I rang for room service and in walked the same goofy kid.

I told the kid, "I'll give you $20 if you take Kitty's gowns out the back way."

"The manager will know I did it, and he'll fire me."

"Okay," I said. "This is how I'll take care of that."

I tied our bed sheets together and explained I was gonna throw the "rope" out the window pretending that's how we left. The kid fell for it. He never noticed the sheets only reached to the twelfth floor.

While Kitty dazzled them with her body language at the Gay 90s, I dazzled them with my card mechanics on Short Vincent Street off West Third. There was a place called Celebrity Ribs where all the wiseguys and entertainers hung out. I felt right at home. I made a few good scores, which meant we both went home with money in our pockets.

Joe Arnold got his $300 including interest. What I didn't know was that Kitty had borrowed $100 on her own from Joe. I guess Joe asked her to pay up and she ignored him. That night in Valentino's he grabbed me by the collar and spun me around. "I'm going upstairs and throw that fucking old lady of yours out the window. Who does she think she is ignoring me?"

"Hey," I said trying to smooth things over. "I'll give you the money. How much does she owe you?" Instead of accepting my offer, Joe started to walk away swearing.

"What's the problem?" Jimmy had heard Joe beefing and came over to check things out.

When Jimmy found out about Kitty, he shook his head in disgust. "For starters, you know better than to loan money to a broad." Jimmy paused for a minute as if he was weighing something in his mind. He looked up at the ugly giant, Joe. "And there's gotta be something in Kitty's past that makes her fearless . . . which means you can't get to her with your threats." Jimmy's steady gaze never wavered. While Joe tried to figure out what Jimmy had just told him, the monk turned to me.

"Okay. Give Joe the hundred Kitty borrowed and forget about the juice."

Nothing more was said. Now it was time to settle our rent.

Mr. Monroe the manager grinned. "You're old room plus your old bill are waiting for you." I guess things were pretty slow and our little con with the sheets struck him as funny. Nervous Joe apologized for firing me and offered me my old job back.

I said, "Okay, under one condition—no gin rummy."

Kitty got a gig down the street at the Club Rouge on Randolph. At least we didn't have to look at another cheeseburger for a while. It just goes to show, you need money to make money even when you're stealing.

The past month had been a picnic compared to what happened next. Kitty got pregnant. I never felt for a second it was anyone's but mine. Kitty was young and vain, so the fatter she got, the quicker that volcanic temper of hers erupted.

Soon after we found out about Kitty, two new girls came aboard the Showboat. Shirley was the girlfriend of Phil Muscanero, a made guy who ran the notorious La Flame Club in Calumet City. Jeannie, a tall, buxom blonde, belonged to the La Flame Club manager, Jackie Doll. Phil, being a high rung on the Mafia ladder, owned 100 percent of the club. Instead of giving a piece of the place to someone else, Phil kept every dime for himself. He was too cheap to share the profits.

The La Flame Club was one of a three-block string of smaller mob-owned joints that ran all the way to the state line at Hammond. Across the street was another famous mob hangout, John's Pizzeria. Those dagos sure love their pasta. The clubs wielded a lot more power than the Chicago clip joints because the Outfit had Calumet City sewn up tight, including the mayor, the chief of police—everyone who had pull.

If you were a guy in Calumet City looking to get laid, you were in deep shit. When the hookers couldn't get a mark to spend his money, they drugged him and took what they wanted. These joints had one thing in common—trick rooms. After the price was settled, a girl led the john to a specially equipped room. He hung his clothes on a wall hook. Once they were going at it, hot and heavy, the wall underneath the hook opened from the other side. This allowed an accomplice to search the guy's pockets.

Well, the good news was Shirley and Jeannie made a big score using the trick room. The bad news was the guy they robbed was a state senator. Phil made a call to Nervous Joe who agreed the girls could lay low at the Showboat till things cooled down. Like everyone who worked at the Showboat, the two new girls roomed at the Devonshire. It got real cozy.

Several things sparked up my life. Actually, the spark was more like a raging forest fire. It was inevitable that I'd meet Phil

Muscanero through the girls. This tall, thin guy, who seemed endlessly distracted by who knows what, took to my easygoing ways. Before long, he invited me and Kitty to his house in Calumet City for dinner. I was a little surprised, seeing as how I wasn't a mob guy. We brought Shirley along which made everything convenient.

Dinner at Phil's turned into a weekly thing. Phil always made his special *pasta e olio*. Pleased with himself, Phil would announce, "This meal only cost me five cents to make."

I could see it coming. Kitty was in one of her moods.

The minute Phil obliged us with his usual remark, she piped in. "Not spaghetti again! Next time I'm going to buy us some steaks."

Every face in the room froze in a fake smile except Kitty's. If Sam Giancana himself rubbed Kitty the wrong way, she would hold nothing back. This was no exception. Phil rushed us through dinner. Suddenly he had to meet a guy. I waited for the bomb to drop, but Phil acted like everything was okay. We left right after the meal.

On the ride home all you could hear was the humming of the motor. I didn't feel like stirring up a hornet's nest any worse than it already was and I was in no mood for an argument. Our problem was simple. Kitty needed to control everyone and I wouldn't let anyone control me.

The roof fell in the next day at work. Phil was so enraged, I thought he was gonna have one of his goons take me out. I never showed any fear, but Phil's searing look could have grilled a porterhouse steak in two seconds.

His pinched lips barely moved. It struck me that Phil had watched one too many gangster movies when he said, "Kitty steps foot in Calumet City again, she's dead."

Later I broke the news to Kitty. Her response, "Fuck the cheap bastard."

Now all hell broke loose. Jackie Doll, Phil's hot-headed manager, accused me of having an affair with his girlfriend, Jeannie.

He was absolutely right. We'd been screwing around for some time. The flophouse above the Showboat was just that, a convenient place to crash on a limited budget. I finagled a key to a hotel room whenever I wanted. I sneaked out through a secret panel that connected the Showboat's basement to a stairway in the hotel.

Twice a week I secretly passed Jeannie the key. "If I'm not up there in half an hour, start without me," I whispered. She never did.

Kitty and Jackie Doll showed up at odd times trying to nail us. Only one person knew for sure what was going on—Vince Eli. As soon as the coast was clear, Vince's weird sense of humor kicked in. He chuckled, scratched his head, grabbed the mike and announced, "Slick Willie gets away with it again." No one caught the meaning except for me and Jeannie. Vince repeated the phrase so often that people started to call me "Slick" or "Slick Willie" without knowing why. The name stuck. Everyone thinks it's because I'm a card hustler.

Apparently Jackie was so upset, even without proof he was planning to have me worked over by a couple of Calumet City boys. Now *two* mob guys wanted to do me great bodily harm on account of a woman.

Jimmy Allegretti got wind of Jackie's grumblings. He told Jackie to forget it. Jimmy's exact words were, "He may be an asshole like you say, but he's *my* asshole."

I could hardly keep a straight face. It dawned on me that mob guys got their best material from Hollywood.

Driving to the Devonshire late one night, me and Kitty got into a horrible argument. I think this one was about my screwing around with Jeannie, but who could keep track? Our fights were getting so violent, they were off the Richter scale. It didn't help matters that we both had short fuses, and now Kitty went crazy if I so much as blinked.

I barely had the door open to our hotel room when Kitty stormed over to the trunk where she kept her four or five gowns. Each gown was worth around two grand. A new car cost six grand. There was no stopping this very pregnant, Sicilian fireball. Adrenaline must have charged her with super-human strength, because she picked up the trunk and heaved it out our fourteenth floor window as if it was nothing more than a bag of dirty laundry. Holy shit!

Some neighbor swore he saw a body fly past his room and called the cops. Any call to the Devonshire was automatically given to O.C.D., Organized Crime Division. The first cop through our door was Mike Secoya, one of the guys from Montrose and Broadway, my old neighborhood. He took one look at me and whispered, "Not you! Get the hell out of here. I'll take care of this."

I went down and salvaged Kitty's gowns. The trunk had splintered into a million pieces when it hit a parked car.

The next day some of the boys told me in no uncertain terms, "You and that nutty broad need to find another place to live. Jimmy insists."

We moved to the LaSalle Towers, furnished efficiency apartments on Division and LaSalle. I bought Kitty a TV to calm her nerves, no small order. We waited.

June 17, 1961, I got a call at the Showboat from Kitty to come home. It was time. All the way to the hospital Kitty fumed. I planned to wait, but Kitty said she didn't need me. The head nurse hastily scribbled the number to the Corner House Restaurant where I decided to sit it out. I felt about as useful as a counterfeit ace in a poker game. But who should I bump into at the Corner House but my friend, Vince, stuffing his face. Later we sat on the curb killing time. Throughout the warm, humid night we gulped down strong coffee, anxiously waiting for news.

The sun already looked like an egg, sunny-side-up, when an excited busboy rushed over. "Hey Slick, you have a girl." I went home and slept like a baby.

The next few months were a whirlwind of making the rounds with our pride and joy, Katherine Mary Hanner. The arguments disappeared now that we had Kathy to think about. Both of us realized our gallivanting from city to city was a lousy way to raise a kid and we weren't going to change any time soon. It was decided Kathy would stay with Kitty's family in Montreal till she was a little older. At least we agreed on something.

It was the week after Christmas, 1961. The months dragged by and good scores were getting scarce. Business at the Showboat was about as lively as a morgue. Time to hit the road. Me and Bob were bullshitting with some guys in Milano's. Horse racing season was gearing up in the South, the perfect time to hit New Orleans.

One of the mustaches, an old Mafia guy named Libby Nunzio, broke in. "When you guys get to New Orleans, if you bump into Joe Poretto, tell him I said hello."

Mafia guys never talked straight, just like politicians. What he meant was, I like you guys so I'm okaying you with Joe, a top lieutenant of Mafia boss, Carlos Marcello. What a break for us. With Kitty due back from Canada at any time, I had to get my stuff out of the LaSalle Towers before she returned or she'd want to come along. Once in a while I needed to be on my own.

I jockeyed my Bonneville convertible out of city traffic and onto the open road. Me and Bob were still laughing about Dino and the four grand. Wonder what loonies we'd meet this time around?

The jockey's agent grinned broadly and ran
down to the winner's circle. That's when the stuff
took effect—in front of thousands of people.

JOE PORETTO MANAGED the Town and Country Motel, a typical
Mafia joint, meaning mob guys oozed out of the woodwork.
Since Joe was in charge of the Marcello crime family's horse
racing interests, the motel's Airline Highway location couldn't
be better. Jefferson Downs, a bush track featuring night racing,
was no more than a few furlongs away. As if that didn't keep him
busy enough, Joe also ran the Nola Wire Service for the mob.
Me and Bob introduced ourselves to Joe and tossed some names
around so he could check us out. One false step on our part, and
we'd leave the Big Easy in a cement-lined coffin.

Being in New Orleans was like *déjà vu* all over again—Fair-
grounds Racetrack during the day, Jefferson Downs at night.
Once in a while Joe gave us $50 to bet for him at Jefferson Downs
and maybe I'd add $10 of my own. Joe never lost, but they were
always short prices.

Now we made a contact that was going to lead to a crazy
situation. Joe introduced us to Don Stone, Carlos Marcello's
bodyguard. I had a hard time concentrating when I looked at
Don because he had a glass eye that didn't focus. I didn't know
if I should look at his right eye or his left one. I decided to
middle it.

To say that Marcello, also known as "The Little Big Man," ran the city was like saying God wields a little clout. He owned everyone in the state of Louisiana and way beyond. Carlos Marcello was the undisputed crime boss in New Orleans since 1947. The U.S. government tried to deport Marcello, but had trouble deciding where to send him, since his country of origin was never established. Attorney General Bobby Kennedy finally ordered federal agents to escort Marcello to Guatemala, stating that was Marcello's country of origin. Within weeks Marcello was back in the U.S., through his connections. Some say Marcello was responsible for the deaths of JFK and RFK on account of Bobby kicking Marcello out of the country. The jury's still out on that one.

This Marcello was hard to figure. You'd think with all these guys trying to wipe out the "top banana," Marcello would hire an army of bodyguards. But one night he asked me to give him a lift to Metairie, an outlying area, where Marcello wanted to visit one of his crap games. It was just the two of us—no goons.

We turned off a country road overgrown with thick bayou grass on either side. There was a rundown shack with a bright light over the door, nothing else. Marcello eased his squat frame out of the passenger side. As I opened my door, I spotted it—the thing I dreaded most in the whole world—a slithering snake the size of the Mississippi River. Boy, how I hate snakes. If there was a million dollars together with a snake in a sack and all I had to do was grab the money and the million would be mine, I'd say, "No thanks."

I quickly slammed my door and yelled as casually as I could, "If you don't mind, I think I'll just wait here."

Carlos saw the snake and laughed his ass off. "Go on home," he said in his coarse Southern accent, choking through his tears. "I'll get a ride back."

That was Marcello. No guns, no bodyguards. You'd think the guy didn't have an enemy in the world.

✸

Don Stone ran a strip joint called the Moulin Rouge on Canal Street across from the Jung, a fancy old Southern hotel. When he wasn't tied up with business, Don would hit the track with me and Bob. One loudmouthed jockey's agent was getting to be a real nuisance. He pestered Don to bet his jockey's horses.

"I swear, if that asshole so much as looks at me again, I'm gonna break his legs," Don fumed.

"Hold off for a while," I said. "I've got a better idea,"

Me and Bob had a contact out of Memphis, Tennessee, who could get us this white powder they use for large animals. You dissolve a pinch of the stuff in a small bottle of water. It may be colorless and tasteless, but it sure packs a wallop. A drink laced with a few drops of this ipecac, a powerful horse laxative, worked its magic in just 15 minutes. The guy drinking it better be standing in a bathtub because there was no warning. We used it when we were hustling a game and a sucker was knocking us. One sip of the potent ipecac cocktail and the chump disappeared for good, probably died from embarrassment.

A few days later me, Bob and Don were watching the races from the jockey club. Sure enough the jockey's agent, obnoxious as ever, sat down next to us. I distracted the shmuck while Bob put a few drops of the ipecac potion in his glass. Smiling like the moron he was, he downed his entire drink. Wouldn't you know, his horse came in first. The agent grinned broadly and ran down to the winners circle. That's when the stuff took effect—in front of thousands of people. Word of the incident spread like a brush fire. The agent never showed his face at any of the racetracks again.

Don liked the way we took care of the jockey's agent, but he wasn't too happy with his manager at another joint Don ran, the Texas Lounge, a short distance from the Moulin Rouge. He asked if I wanted to manage it for him, offering a 20 percent guarantee of the take. I agreed.

The Texas Lounge had the usual B-girls and prostitutes, but instead of male bartenders, sexy barmaids added a spicy twist. I taught the barmaids the fine art of using a "whip cup." That's a heavy leather cup that has its inner surface polished for use in combination with "gaffed dice." Gaffed means the dice have been altered to come up favoring certain numbers when they're "whipped" out of the smooth cup.

"Let the marks run up a tab," I instructed my all-female crew. "Then shake them for the tab, double or nothing. Of course, the house always wins." I watched the girls to make sure they mastered the technique.

"Here, honey. Let me show you how it works." I took the cup from a voluptuous redhead having trouble with the whipping action. The rookies learned fast and I was eager to help.

"Now if a girl goes to a table with a customer, the guy has to buy her at least $10 worth of drinks," I added.

I could see the girls approved of the new rules. It meant they had more chances to make a score, plus I knew it would improve the house's take by a huge margin. The place really started to go. Everything was strictly on the up-and-up as far as me and Bob were concerned. We could hustle for ourselves if we handed over 80 percent to the mob. What a joke.

It was already March 1962. Who should walk in but Kitty gloating over how she tracked me down. She was booked into a club on Bourbon Street called Madame Francine's operated by mob big-shot Jerome Conforte. Conforte went on to become boxing commissioner of Louisiana. Thanks to Carlos Marcello, the state reeked with corruption. As long as the kickbacks were meaty, nobody high up beefed about the stench.

Kitty moved in with me and Bob. True to form, her tantrums grew like the angry black clouds that loomed over the city. When the outbursts came too close for comfort, Bob retreated to Chicago. He didn't have storm insurance.

Through a hooker named Joanie who worked at the Texas Lounge, I met her suave boyfriend, a Lucchese Family mobster named George Romi. A real dapper Dan, this George cut quite a figure with his pencil thin mustache and full head of silver hair. George had an eye for the ladies and the ladies had an eye for George.

Everything was going good, maybe too good. I hung around with Don Stone, George Romi and a safe cracker named Chuck Mintz. It was hard not to like this big, ruddy-faced farm kid who happened to be married to Jerome Conforte's sister. I built up a sizable bankroll as Chuck's lookout on a number of burglaries, so I started spiffing up the apartment. Me and Kitty were all set to bring Kathy to live with us.

It all began to turn sour when Chuck got a tip from a guy running booze to Jackson, Mississippi, a dry state. There were places out in the boondocks that sold illegal hooch. They smuggled booze from New Orleans in cars specially fitted with heavy-duty springs, so when the back seat was removed to stash the bootleg cases, the car wouldn't ride too low. No need to tip off the state cops. They'd want too big a cut.

One day the guy running the booze confided to Chuck, "There's a bootleg joint on this deserted road outside of Jackson. I know they keep as much as ten grand there on the weekend. It would be a cinch to take the place off."

That did it. Me and Chuck drove to Jackson with the informant. After he told us where they stashed the money, we put him up in a motel, stole a car and headed back to pick up the dough. This is gonna be a piece of cake, I thought, already counting my chickens!

There was only one guy manning the shed when Chuck drove up to this window. At gunpoint Chuck ordered the attendant to hand over the fishing tackle box with the money. No sooner were the words out of Chuck's mouth, than bullets started zinging all around us. From what I could tell, they came from a farmhouse about a hundred yards away. The guy must have signaled whoever was in the house. I answered the barrage with five rounds of my own. Chuck screeched away. A couple of good shots shattered the car windows, but luckily missed us. Another bullet took out the rear tire.

We ditched the car a quarter of a mile down the road. With the nearby woods as a cover and Chuck, a sure-footed country boy, leading the way, we made good time through the thick brush. I jogged along uneasily on account of all those snakes I was dead certain were eager to pounce on me. I heard somewhere that snakes had a mysterious way of smelling fear. Naturally, I was the guy they'd go for.

Chuck thought that was the funniest damn thing he ever heard. "Just shuffle your feet and they'll run away," he laughed.

Fifteen hours later we made it back to the motel. Our informant seemed relieved to see us.

"You guys took so long, I thought they caught you," he said. He was probably the guy who tipped off the bootleggers.

Back in New Orleans, George Romi pumped us about the job. "Did you have a good trip?" he asked.

"The best time I ever had," I answered.

George reported regularly to his New York Mafia family. He told them he was having a little trouble collecting from a guy who owed them money. The family sent out the goon squad to teach this welsher a lesson.

A few days after the call, George walked into the Texas Lounge with these two wiseguys. They stood out like a pair of matched bookends with their New York accents. George asked to borrow my car. Without a second thought I tossed him the keys.

Six, maybe seven hours later, I wondered where George was with my car. Not long after that, in they waltzed. One of the goons told me they had a little problem but nothing serious. I blew it off. I knew better than to ask questions.

The next day one of the girls ran into the office all excited. "I think you better have a look," she said. "Some cops are snooping around your car."

"Is there anything wrong, officer?" I asked one of the cops searching my Bonneville.

Ignoring the question he said, "Is this your car?"

"Yes."

"Okay. Stand against the wall. You're under arrest."

He patted me down and then handcuffed me. But I needed some answers.

"Wait a minute. Why are you arresting me?"

"For starters, assault and kidnapping."

They hauled me down to police headquarters and locked me up without booking me. It didn't make sense. The next morning the cops took me to some hospital. There was a guy in really bad shape lying in this hospital bed, his face swollen and lacerated, arms in casts. He took a long look at me trying to focus.

"No. That ain't one of them," he whispered.

Then it was back to the police station where I was taken to see Superintendent Joe Giarusso, every inch an Italian with his jet-black wavy hair and olive complexion. The only problem was that he talked like he had a mouth full of hominy grits. I expected *Serpico* but out came *Gone with the Wind*.

Giarusso offered me a chair in the interrogation room. "Okay," he sighed, perching on the corner of the table like a vulture sizing up his next meal. "You didn't do this thing, but you know who did." He smiled a little, testing the waters to see if a touch of Southern charm would help.

"If you tell me the whole story, I'll let you go." He flashed one of those high-beam smiles, the kind politicians save for special occasions.

"Well, about 4:00 in the afternoon," I said, pretending to be confused, "one of the customers said he wanted a po' boy sandwich. I told the guy I had a taste for one too and threw him the keys to my car. Now it was going on midnight and the guy wasn't back. Naturally, I was worried. Just as I was ready to call the police, he turned up and gave me back my car keys. The guy had a story about some girl and said he was sorry, he should have called. My car was okay so I dropped the whole thing."

Giarusso listened tight-lipped up to this point. Irritated, he said, "What's the guy's name?"

"I don't know," I answered.

"What did he look like?" Giarusso was getting steamed.

I gave him the description of some guy from my old neighborhood in Chicago.

That was it. Giarusso blew his top. "You Yankee son-of-a-bitch! You mean to tell me you gave a complete stranger the keys to a new Bonneville convertible to go get a couple of sandwiches and he was gone for almost eight hours?"

Giarusso stuck his head out the door. "Lock him up!"

I found myself in a crowded cell with the city's great unwashed. The place overflowed with bugs by the thousands. Next to snakes, the things I hated most in the world were creepy-crawlies. There were so many of the little bastards, I think I spotted the bones of one of their human victims lying in the corner. Don't worry, I reassured myself. They can only hold you 72 hours without charging you with a crime. Then I remembered this was the Deep South and it was 1962. Down here, they could hold some poor Yankee son-of-a-bitch until he rotted if they felt like it.

To make matters worse, Kitty didn't know where I was because they kept moving me from one jail to another. They called it giving a guy the "round-robin." The cops pulled this tactic when they had nothing to hold you on and wanted to keep your whereabouts secret. It was crucial I get word to Kitty. I had no intention of living out the rest of my days in some bug-infested hole. Giarusso agreed to see me when I told a guard I was ready to talk.

"Now look," I lied. "I honestly don't know the name of the guy who took my car, but I know where he hangs out. It's a bar called The Ship. Take me there and I'll point him out when he walks in." Giarusso fell for it. If I could slip a message to my friend Al, the bartender, he could get word to Kitty.

That night two detectives escorted me to The Ship. I felt like a human mouse trap. While I sipped my coffee at one end of the bar chatting with the bartender, the cops followed my every move from the other end. I was waiting for the right opportunity. It came in the form of a knockout redhead bumming a light off one of the cops. Nobody noticed the secret note inside a match cover I palmed to Al.

Four hours later, the detectives decided my guy wasn't going to show.

"Don't worry," I told them outside. "He'll be there tomorrow for sure. How about getting a bite to eat before we head back to jail? I'm starving."

The following night we were manning our battle stations aboard The Ship when in walked Giarusso. He politely asked me to, "Please step outside."

"Sure," I said. "I don't have anything better to do."

In the parking lot Giarusso was all smiles.

"Did you have a nice dinner yesterday?"

"Yes, thank you."

Still smiling he threw his arm around my shoulder. "Well, if you thought that was good, tonight we're taking you for a gourmet dinner at the Roosevelt . . . you Yankee son-of-a-bitch!"

Giarusso shoved me against the wall, handcuffed me and threw me in the back seat of his squad car. My ass was back in jail before I could say po' boy sandwich. I prayed Kitty had gotten word. Geez, they'd been holding me for five days.

On the sixth day, I was debating between green or brown bugs for my prison wallpaper. Some cop yelled, "Hanner, you're leaving."

They told me I was "paroled." I never heard of a guy going out on parole without being charged with a crime, but I wasn't about to argue. It was over. I was free. The detectives searched my car but never found my stash. What a lucky break. If they'd discovered my .38-snubnose, me being a felon, I'd be picking cotton in some prison farm—probably Angola, the worst state pen in the whole country.

I went straight home and told Kitty what happened. This was one of those occasions when Kitty's hardheadedness paid off. It saved my tail. We decided I'd pick her up at Madame Francine's when she got off work at 4:00 a.m., then hash things over.

At 3:45 I was cooling my heels outside Madame Francine's waiting for Kitty, wondering where I'd be without that nutty broad. Who should walk up to my car window but my good buddy, Superintendent Giarusso.

"Get out," he ordered. I could see there was no more Mr. Nice Guy.

"Stand against the wall and show some ID."

"Not again." I tossed him my wallet.

He shook me down. "You are damn lucky to get out of jail, Hanner," he said in the most menacing Southern drawl I've ever heard. "But if you don't leave town within 24 hours, you'll find your Yankee ass right back in there." He tossed my ID on the ground and took off.

I broke the news to Kitty on the way home. "So, now what?" she asked.

"Don't worry. First thing tomorrow, I'm going to see Joe Poretto at the Town and Country and straighten this thing out."

I sounded a lot more confident than I was feeling, but I wasn't about to share my doubts. Kitty had a knack of nailing me with my screwups.

We weren't home 10 minutes when there was a knock on the door. Oh no, I thought, not Giarusso again? But it was George Romi, decked out in an Italian designer suit.

"Thanks for keeping your mouth shut with the cops." He smiled his charming smile while he told me and Kitty how they used my car to rough the guy up, which I'd already figured out. George's thugs would collect from the welsher when he got out of the hospital. By then he'd probably be more willing to cough up what he owed.

"Well, that's great," I said. "But Giarusso just made it clear that if I don't leave town by tomorrow, I'm history."

"Sorry. It's out of my hands." George threw me a sympathetic look. "I'm taking Joanie to Chicago in a couple of days to work for Pat Atkins. Pat runs a high-class call girl operation, so if things don't turn out here, I can get you in action."

The next day I told Joe Poretto where things stood.

"If it was anyone other than Giarusso, we could take care of it," Joe sighed, taking a big puff on his cigar. "We give Giarusso a wide berth. He has too much juice."

Poretto stubbed out his Cuban cigar. "If I know Joe Giarusso," he laughed. "You probably could have saved yourself a lot of agony by offering him a few bucks."

I gave Poretto my most innocent look. "Taking a bribe? But that would have screwed up his career, wouldn't it?"

Joanie would take Rhonda under her wing and give her some pointers—buy her smart clothes, show her how to apply makeup, teach her how to give a blowjob.

IT WAS JUNE. We'd missed the lousy Chicago weather. Me and Kitty checked into the Maryland Hotel on Rush Street. George Romi was staying there with Joanie, who earned top dollar as a highly paid call girl for Pat Atkins. Pat, with her mannish business clothes and snobbish ways, had no time for poor guys like me. But boy, could she smell a fat wallet a mile away. Her client list bulged with judges, politicians, and Chicago's most powerful.

Bob Mauro was playing ma and pa with a young runaway, a real looker named Rhonda. Bob latched onto the seventeen-year-old when a married cab driver Rhonda was living with ditched her. Bob wanted to turn Rhonda out, but he didn't know the first thing about pimping and Rhonda had no clue what being "turned out" meant. They were about to learn.

Joanie, George's young bubbly girlfriend, was bisexual. But when it came to guys, Joanie was no slouch. She knew how to press all the right buttons. George let her do her thing and she knew better than to ask questions when he went out on "business." It was the perfect trade off.

The minute I introduced Rhonda and Bob to George and Joanie, Joanie took one look at the shy newcomer and got a hard-on. George was smart. He could see that under the lousy Goldblatts dress and heavy-handed makeup, Rhonda showed real promise.

He asked her, "What do you like to do, dear?"

"Well, I like to cook," She said.

George promptly pulled out a wad of bills. "Here Bob," he said. "Get yourself a place with a kitchen at the LaSalle Towers and make Rhonda feel good." Sly old George knew that if Rhonda was happy, she'd be more likely to respond to a little coaching.

Before the evening was over, it was decided that Joanie would take Rhonda under her wing and give her some pointers—buy her smart clothes, show her how to apply makeup, teach her how to give a blow job. When Rhonda was ready, Joanie would introduce her to Pat Atkins. I could swear Joanie was already licking her lips at the thought of a little one-on-one.

The following week I asked Bob how things were going with Rhonda. After he stopped laughing, he described his conversation with the "hooker in training," as he called Rhonda.

Rhonda sat Bob down like she had the most earth-shaking news. In hushed tones, she told him, "Joanie said that sometimes guys would want to watch two girls make love, you know—eat one another."

Rhonda was confused. She asked Joanie how that would work and Joanie told her, "Well, you form the number sixty-nine and fake it. The john can't really see what's going on because our legs are in the way, so when you're supposed to be licking me, you put your hand there and lick it instead. It's just acting. After a while, the whole thing gets to be a snap. Here, I'll show you."

Now Rhonda got real quiet for a minute. She gave Bob a sort of odd look. "The strangest thing happened," she said. "I did just like Joanie told me—you know, licked my hand. But Joanie didn't lick her *hand*. . . ."

Bob could hardly continue, he was so doubled over with laughter. Then he turned serious. "You know, at first I was afraid Rhonda would get to like Joanie better than me. Then I said nah, maybe some other broad, but not Rhonda. She's too straight.

"The best part is the homework," Bob quipped. Joanie told Rhonda that ninety percent of the customers are old geezers who had trouble getting a hard-on so you had to suck them almost till they came. Otherwise, you'd be at it forever. Joanie sent Rhonda home to practice on Bob.

"Well," I asked Bob. "How's she doing?"

Bob didn't really answer. Instead, his eyes kind of glazed over and a funny grin spread across his face. I think that meant she was doing pretty good.

Groomed to the hilt, Rhonda knew how to suck and she knew how to lick. Armed with her new bag of tricks, Rhonda went to meet the formidable Pat Atkins. Within a few weeks, the rookie was making serious money. Turned out Rhonda was a natural. The more homework Rhonda brought home, the bigger Bob's grin.

Meanwhile, Kitty's agent booked her into a place she worked many times, the Club Rouge on Randolph. She stripped at the Brass Rail down the street until Louie Tornabeni, the manager, advised all the girls to take their gowns home. Later that same night the Brass Rail burned to the ground. "He must have been psychic," Kitty laughed.

Strip joints in every city in the country put their unique twist on the same timeworn formula—smoky, pitch-black bar, spotlit stage, tired one-liners, scratchy bump-and-grind records, strippers peeling off skin-tight gowns, plus the usual cast of backup characters. Any moron with half an imagination could figure out the rest. That was Kitty's world where she could be queen. She said the rush it gave her was like great sex.

Kitty and I had one of our rare talks instead of a shouting match one night. "So Pat Atkins has all this pull," said Kitty arching her brow. "Is the mob behind her?"

"As far as I can tell, Pat has no organized crime connections," I said. "It's got me stumped"

"If Pat doesn't owe the Outfit," Kitty observed, "can you imagine how much she's holding?"

Kitty paused. She was onto something. I could see the wheels turning in her head. "I'm going to work for this Pat . . . for a while."

I studied Kitty's face, realizing her cool-headed manner turned me on. If Kitty knew the power she had, she might tame down those temper-tantrums.

Kitty's voice broke the silence. "I'm taking Pat Atkins's business away from her," she remarked as casually as if she was ordering chopped liver.

With Joanie, Rhonda and now Kitty working for Pat, it was only a matter of time before we took off Pat's operation. I tried to find out who Pat's juice was while Kitty cased Pat Atkins's apartment searching for her contact list. Whenever Pat's girls were busted, they beat the rap in court. The million-dollar question was how?

"Mad" Sam DeStefano, a violent mob guy who years later was allegedly taken out by Tony Spilotro in Sam's own garage, needed to teach someone on Mannheim Road a lesson. George didn't waste any time carrying out orders, seeing as Sam called the shots. George asked me along for the ride.

The next day I drove me and George to meet an Outfit guy from Melrose Park. When we pulled up, the guy asked me to pop the trunk. In the rearview mirror I watched him place two sledge hammers in the trunk. Then he slid into the back seat without saying a word.

We arrived at our destination, an isolated spot, just off Mannheim Road. George and the mob guy grabbed the sledge hammers and went to work on a brand new Lincoln Continental. The registration was still in the window. The way they totaled that car, you'd think they were slamming for dollars at an amusement park. I almost cried. I spotted a state trooper about a quarter of a mile down the road. Uh-oh. I'm gonna hear his siren any second, I thought. But the trooper just sat there. I couldn't figure it. On the way back, I casually mentioned the state cop, wondering why we didn't get pinched.

"Relax," said the Melrose Park guy. "He was looking out for us."

When it came to hooking, Rhonda had caught on quickly but Bob was hopeless as a pimp. George laughingly called him a "mule pimp." That was a term colored guys used to refer to a pimp who worked harder than the woman he was turning out.

I warned Bob for the hundredth time, "Never drop Rhonda off to meet her trick and never wait for her in your car. They're gonna grab you."

Bob was stubborn. He stuck to Rhonda like mayo on a ham and cheese sandwich. One night it backfired on him. As usual, Bob waited in his car while Rhonda did a john upstairs. Bob didn't realize there were a couple of vice cops up there busting Rhonda until they came down and busted him, too. Selling your body was only a misdemeanor, but pimping was a felony. To make things worse, vice cops hated pimps. The cops were all set to take the pair down to Eleventh and State and book them when Bob began to wise up.

"Can't I take care of this?" he asked. Bob cleared his throat. It was a nervous habit that popped up when he was bullshitting someone. He was always clearing his throat.

"Look, I have $1,000 but not on me."

The two cops exchanged glances. One of them said, "Who do you know that'll okay you?"

"Jimmy Allegretti," said Bob, knowing the Monk wielded a lot of clout.

"Okay. Let's get to a phone booth and you call him. If he agrees, it's a go."

Allegretti loaned Bob the grand, but there was a price. If Bob failed to pay Allegretti the entire amount plus interest by the next day, Bob would be pushing up daisies. Besides that, Bob owed Allegretti a big favor. Bob could be ordered to hit some-one, and the mob didn't take no for an answer. Those were the

Mafia's rules. They do you a favor, you do them a favor. After the pinch, Bob let Rhonda take care of her own business. The guy was catching on.

It was only a matter of days before Kitty discovered Pat's books squirreled away in a hollowed-out table. The rest was easy. I chose a night when her place was dark. Armed with a complete layout of Pat's apartment, I picked her lock, found the table without any trouble and pinched her books. Kitty, Joanie and Rhonda wasted no time leasing an apartment near the top floor in one of those fancy glass high-rises on Marine Drive and Diversey. Before long business was so strong, the girls had to recruit a couple of part-timers.

It never failed. Whenever things were going good, tragedy hit. I got a call from Louise that my mother had a stroke. She was in a bad way. I was so numb I almost didn't catch the name of the hospital. It was on Marine Drive, not far from the girls' apartment. Suddenly my world had caved in.

I sat in a dark corner of the stuffy hospital room watching the unconscious figure lying so peacefully in the bed. A million thoughts darted through my mind. All the things my mother did for me over the years came flooding back, but one incident really stood out. I was a skinny little kid of about five when me and my mother found some guy, cut up and bleeding, sprawled in our hallway. He looked like he was going to say something, then he died.

We watched the ambulance take away the body. I asked her in that innocent voice of the very young, "Mom, how come God didn't save him?"

I remember her tone was soft and comforting as she took my small hand. "That's why God sent you, son."

Boy, was she wrong. Or maybe my mother was trying to tell me something else? How funny, I thought watching the clock on the wall tick away the hours. I'm spending more time with my mother than I have in the last twenty years and she doesn't even know it. That burden of guilt would follow me always. Soon after my visit she died. I still talk to her every day.

My rotten luck was on a roll. One of the prostitutes Kitty hired got busted. Instead of getting off easy, like our smart-ass lawyers assured us, the girl was slapped with a huge fine. Kitty tried to tell me she smelled a rat, but I was too distracted by my mother's death to think straight. Kitty was right. Like an idiot, I had greatly underestimated Pat Atkins's power. Pat didn't need the mob. She probably had every fucking politician in the state in her little black book. And those boys played rough when they thought the public might catch them with their pants down, especially with a hooker. Turned out crafty Pat kept a duplicate client list. She carried on her business as usual, watching to see where the original books would pop up—not that it was any big surprise when a couple of loyal clients told Pat they were hustled by her ex-employees.

That Friday started out like any other. Me and Bob were on our way to the track, but Bob had to see Rhonda about something first. Still in a fog, I followed Bob up to the girls apartment. He finished and we waited for the elevator to go down. The doors opened and who should brush past us but two detectives. They were cops all right. Even though I wasn't hitting on all six cylinders, I could still smell a cop at a hundred paces. We were already in the elevator when the detectives did a double take. They lunged for me and Bob, but it was too late. The door had closed.

That did it. I snapped out of my daze like a water-drenched fighter nearly down for the count. Good thing we parked in the resident garage in the basement. I spotted a third cop guarding the front door as we sped by.

I called Kitty from a nearby restaurant. She answered on the second ring. "There are two detectives here wrecking the apartment!" she screamed in her all too familiar ear-splitting style.

For a change Kitty's rage wasn't aimed at me. I congratulated myself. Finding humor even in a pile of shit was my specialty and I was back in top form.

I heard muffled voices in the background, then Kitty again. "They want to know who I'm talking to."

"Tell them you're talking to your lawyer, "I said. "I'll see you at home."

Later that night the six of us—me and Kitty, Bob and Rhonda, George and Joanie—held a pow-wow. We laughed, convinced everything would die down if we laid low for a couple of weeks. The next day me and Bob headed for Ohio Street. We didn't get more than a block from our apartment when a detective bureau cop pulled us over—not a good sign. His men searched the trunk and came up empty-handed. He let us go, but the message was loud and clear. It was too dangerous for us to roam the streets of Chicago.

We paid a visit to Casa Madrid, a restaurant on Twenty-fifth and Lake Street in Melrose Park. It was headquarters for Rocco "Rocky" DeGrazia, who ran the West Side for the Outfit. Rocky started out overseeing Capone's drug, loan-sharking and gambling interests, then rose fast in the ranks of Sam Giancana's organization. Rocky was as ambitious as an assistant D.A. Casa Madrid's legitimate restaurant fronted one of the biggest bookmaking joints on the West Side, hidden in a maze of rooms below. If there was a raid, a special tunnel made escape easy. It came up in a pool hall on Lake Street, about three-quarters of a mile away.

With the cops trailing us like bloodhounds, it was time to break up our little pimp and prostitute operation. George and Joanie headed west where Joanie knew yet another madam in Hollywood. I had to hand it to Joanie. She sure got around. For the next few weeks, me and Bob laid low. It was Casa Madrid during the day, home at night like good boys. We were so hot, we could have triggered the second Chicago Fire without striking a match. The timing was perfect for a Canadian holiday, meaning

Bob and Rhonda didn't want to wind up in jail any more than me and Kitty. It was a good excuse to visit Kathy in Montreal.

Me and Bob killed time taking in the sites of *la belle* Montreal. There were only a few places worth visiting. The Blue Bonnets Race Track featured harness racing at night. After the track we stopped by Ben's Smoked Meat Restaurant. Smoked meat is what Canadian's call corned beef. Somehow, it tasted better north of the border. During the day, we scrounged a little card action on postcard-perfect St. Catherine Street near our hotel, the Queen Elizabeth.

I walked into our hotel room to find Kitty in a nasty mood. "What's up?" I asked, hoping I wasn't the cause. She came right out with what was eating her.

"I saw my brother Eddie today and told him I want to try to find my daughter, Amy."

"Yeah," I said. "So what did he say?"

"He told me to forget about trying to find her. She probably has her own life now and doesn't want to be bothered. Can you believe that?"

"That's probably a smart idea, Kitty," I offered, trying to soothe things over.

By the look on Kitty's face, I expected her to pick up the glass from the table and throw it at me, but she retreated into the bathroom and slammed the door. Suddenly it dawned on me. We weren't lovers. We were sparring partners.

That night the four of us ate dinner in our hotel's ritzy restaurant. We dressed to the hilt. I sported a brand new tailor-made gabardine beige suit. It set me back a couple of C-notes but, what the hell, it made me feel good.

When the food arrived, nothing seemed right with Kitty's meal. The harder the waiter tried to fix things, the more upset she got. She sounded like a steam engine ready to blow. Now people were beginning to stare. Bob and Rhonda were smart. They made a hasty exit. I tried to calm Kitty down but it was no use. She thought I was taking the waiter's side. I glanced around the room seeing that all eyes were focused on our petty drama.

"So!" screamed Kitty. "You think the waiter's doing a good job? Here, you can have this."

I shielded myself with both arms, but the steaming plate of spaghetti marinara hit my spotless jacket dead center, trickling onto my neatly creased pants. I reached in my pocket and threw some money on the table, making excuses to the waiter. It's a good thing I left immediately. If I'd hesitated a second longer, the next day's headline would have read: *Man Strangles Woman in Restaurant!!*

I tore off what was once a beautiful suit and tossed the mess in the trash can of our hotel room. Why did Kitty pull stuff like this and why did I put up with it? If it wasn't for Kathy, I'd have left Kitty long ago. Who was I trying to fool? I must have had other reasons for staying. I guess Kitty's parents forcing her to give up her baby had more of an impact on Kitty than I thought, but I was no good at figuring out motives. Kitty was far from boring, I rationalized. And how could I leave her when she shadowed me from city to city?

One thing was clear—something other than love or our daughter bound me to Kitty. I felt as helpless as a moth on a one-way trip to a light bulb.

New Years Eve, 1963, we returned to Chicago, relieved to be back in familiar surroundings. We moved into our old digs, the LaSalle Towers, and immediately fell into our regular routine.

It was so jammed at the Devonshire coffee shop one morning, me and Bob had a hard time finding seats. Vince waved us over from the counter.

He raised his dark, bushy eyebrows. That meant Vince was excited about something. "Well," he announced, treating us to an overly wide grin. "I've decided to try my luck in Hollywood. I think I've got a good shot at landing acting jobs out there."

I sized up this big teddy-bear friend of mine who looked and sounded more like a gangster than ninety percent of the mob guys we knew. If Vince got a break with the right parts, he'd be dynamite.

"Here's George Romi's phone number," he said scribbling on a scrap of paper. "George and Joanie are renting a fabulous house in L.A. If you guys want a change of scenery . . ."

We were interrupted by the entrance of this comical, paranoid little Jewish guy, Louie the Jeweler. Louie was only about five feet tall, but he seemed even shorter on account of the fact that he tried to disappear. Louie was obsessed that someone would steal his merchandise, so he kept as low a profile as possible. Vince was the only person Louie trusted. Since they both lived in the Alexander Hotel, they worked out an agreement. Vince let Louie use his apartment to entertain hookers. Crazy Louie was convinced the hookers would rob him if he took them to his place. In exchange, Louie arranged for Vince to get laid.

This particular day Louie had a rare beauty—a sapphire and diamond ring he wanted to peddle. He popped open the velvet box and the guy sitting next to him promptly grabbed it, took a look and passed it to the next guy. That guy did the same thing and on down the counter. Louie scurried after the ring like a protective mother following her child.

When the ring got to me, I opened the box, tried the ring on my pinkie and sent the box on its way back—empty. Louie was so busy answering questions, he put the box in his coat pocket without opening it. Now I'd have something to sell at the track tomorrow.

The jangling phone jolted me out of a coma around dawn the next morning. Only one person would dare to ring that early. It was Vince bidding me a final goodbye.

By the way, Vince said, "Louie wants to know who stole his ring. Any ideas?"

"Have a nice trip," I answered.

One of the cabbies kidded George.
"You and your friends didn't have anything to do
with the Sinatra, Jr., kidnapping by any chance?"

THE SAME OLD grind was turning me and Kitty into zombies.
We decided it was California or bust. Our plans were to meet
Bob and Rhonda at the Stardust Casino in Las Vegas. From there
the four of us would head for L.A. and hang out with George
and Joanie for a while, see Vince, catch some action.

It was November 22, 1963. Packed and ready to go, I reached
over to turn off the TV when the stunning news flashed on
the screen: *President Kennedy has been shot. . . .* The gruesome
nightmare got worse. It turned out JFK was already dead. They
were holding Lee Harvey Oswald, some lousy Commie, for the
murder.

We drove out of town in silence. It felt like a damned Communist, no less, had killed someone in the family. Shock swept the
entire country, eventually turning into a kind of mass mourning.
Everything screeched to a halt. Me and Kitty walked into a diner
and all eyes were glued to the TV, including ours.

"You know," I remarked to Kitty. "We stand a pretty good
chance of being nuked before we reach Las Vegas." I wasn't
kidding.

Three days later I changed my mind. Jack Ruby (Rubenstein)
shot and killed Oswald in a police station. The shooting was
captured on live TV. The minute I heard Ruby's name, I knew
what happened. It was common knowledge around most Mafia

guys that Ruby ran a mob-owned strip joint in Dallas. The assassination had to be a Mafia setup. It made me sick at heart when I realized organized crime was responsible for whacking the President of the United States. If it was any consolation, now we didn't have to worry about the atom bomb. The truth was a lot closer to home.

Booming Las Vegas was a far cry from the last time I saw it as a skinny, seventeen-year-old Air Force private. Wow! The Stardust, Desert Inn, Riviera seemed to materialize out of thin air the way a magician pulls a rabbit out of a hat. Las Vegas was really something. Instead of water, this man-made oasis thrived on cash-flow.

We hooked up with Bob and Rhonda, and Bob showed me around the Stardust. I spotted a number of Chicago guys dealing blackjack. There was "Wheels," a get-away driver from Cicero, and other characters from Milano's and Valentino's. On one hand, it was good to see all the familiar faces. On the other hand, I remembered JFK's murder. Many of these guys would whack their own mothers on mob orders. This time I was happy to be an outsider.

There was no doubt who ran the Stardust. Just four years earlier, the mob took over this glitzy "grind joint," a house that relied on low-limit play and lots of traffic, to grind out its profit. If all these Chicago guys could get jobs, maybe I could, too. Hey, what about Jack Ross?

Jack owned a piece of the Frontier Casino on the Strip. Me and Bob met Jack in Chicago a while back. Nick Guerra, a Mafia enforcer everyone called "Mousey," bragged to Jack what outstanding card mechanics me and Bob were.

"Here's my number," Jack said, promptly producing his card. "You guys look me up if you ever get to Las Vegas. I can definitely use your talents."

I still had Jack's business card, so I gave him a call. His

directions led me to a sprawling ranch house. The Desert Inn Golf Course was Jack's backyard. I showed him some of my moves, like dealing seconds. He seemed impressed enough to offer me a job. I thanked Jack and told him I'd like to think about it. The reason Jack wanted guys like me is because the mob-run casinos needed "bust out" dealers who were skilled card cheats. If a customer was on a roll, the bust out dealer made sure the winning streak came to a sudden end. Come to think of it, all the dealers were men. It wasn't till Lefty Rosenthal entered the scene in the '70s that he hired women dealers at the Stardust. I think Shirley Vancuchie was the first.

Later I told Bob about Jack Ross's offer. "Just think of the money me and you could take off if we worked for Ross," I said, chomping at the bit.

"Are you crazy?" Bob said. "These guys I was just with warned me that if you want to stay alive in this town, you don't do anything on your own. A shallow grave in the desert doesn't sound too great right now."

"Well, if all we get to keep are a few measly tokes, it ain't worth it," I sighed.

The next day I wandered into the poker room. I got an earful from one of the off-duty dealers. Seems a guy had to be nuts if he got suckered into playing poker in Las Vegas. In the low limit games, they hired dealers on the basis of how many chips they could snatch from the pot without the customers catching on. Every card room posts what percentage the dealer takes for the house, maybe 15 percent. He drops it down a slot in the middle of the table. It's called the rake and that's how a casino takes its cut. Anything more than what's posted is strictly illegal skim, but that didn't stop anyone at the Stardust or the other mob-run casinos.

For instance, if a guy won a $60 pot, a good dealer would snatch $30 for the house. A player was lucky to break even. And in the high-limit games, all the dealers were accomplished card mechanics, which meant they had a license to steal—for the house, of course. The eye-in-the-sky, a guy pacing a catwalk above the pit, watched them do their job.

The minute we hit L.A., we called George from Schwabs Drugstore on Sunset Boulevard. Sherry's Bar, where I connected years ago with Joe Levy and Little Jack Little, still attracted the mob set a few doors down. Sherry's was a popular joint back in the '40s when Mickey Cohen, Bugsy Siegel's gunman, took a few bullets outside the famous bar. Johnny Stompanato, Lana Turner's gangster boyfriend, worked for Cohen until Stompanato was knifed to death by Turner's daughter, Cheryl. After the trial, Cohen was so disgusted by Lana Turner's testimony, he allegedly said, "It's the first time I ever saw a man convicted of his own murder."

George snagged a showplace fit for a movie star. He rented the bi-level in the Hollywood Hills from mobster John Dragna, who ruled Southern California. The house was situated above the famous sign that spelled out HOLLYWOOD in giant letters. I whistled as I took in the panoramic view from George's massive picture window. True to form, Joanie hooked up with a madam who operated a call girl service just up the road from George's. God knows what George was up to. I didn't ask.

The next day us four newcomers rented a two-bedroom apartment down the hill from George's place, then Joanie introduced Kitty to her madam. Before long Kitty was up to her old tricks—new ones, to be exact. Rhonda waited patiently for Bob's go-ahead to work for Joanie's madam. Bob had Rhonda so brainwashed, if he snapped his fingers, she would have turned back into a virgin.

It was time to look up Vince. "Life dealt me a good hand so far," Vince chuckled, obviously pleased with himself. He acted like he owned the joint as he led me around the *Bonanza* set, pausing every few feet to greet cast and crew. It was clear Vince was a welcome character down at the old Ponderosa. Vince beamed like a spotlight when he told me about the hoodlum boss he portrayed in a national Jack-in-the-Box commercial. How about that? Vince was finally cashing in on his tough-guy looks. The residuals from that one spot's four-year run netted him big bucks.

L.A. began to grow on me and Kitty so we decided to stick around. I scouted for something more permanent while Kitty brought home the bacon.

I fished out the dog-eared phone number of my old friend Jimmy LaFleur. Jimmy had stayed in L.A. since our first wacky adventure many years ago. Maybe Jimmy still had an in at the Tail of the Cock? Me and Vince took a ride over to Jimmy's place, a loft in Redondo Beach. One look at potbellied, drugged-out Jimmy, and my visions of his getting me any kind of job I might actually want went straight out the window. The slender athlete had turned into a sitting Buddha.

We weren't there more than a minute when lecherous Vince descended on the two sexy girls giggling in the corner, a couple of Jimmy's customers. Jimmy sent all three to "go play" in the bedroom.

Jimmy ushered me into another room overflowing with pot plants growing under artificial lights. "Besides the shit I grow here," he said lighting a joint, "I get pills from a chemist friend. There's room for you if you want in," offered Jimmy, grinning in his easy way.

There was a long pause. "Otto died a number of years ago. After that, I didn't much care what I did so I fell into drug dealing. It's easy money." Jimmy stared off in the distance.

"Ever since Connie took her life . . ." The sentence trailed off.

I watched my sad friend. Jimmy never seemed to recover from the Connie thing. She committed suicide after dope ruined her career as a Playboy bunny.

"Thanks, Jimmy. I'm doing okay," I lied. The memory of Jack

Bailey's downfall was etched painfully in my memory, and Jimmy wasn't far behind him.

A couple of Hell's Angels types decked out in black leather and chains came and went. The place was a fucking zoo. Vince finally put in an appearance direct from the bedroom. He became a regular guest at Jimmy's.

Then there was Bob. The guy began to worry me and George with his paranoia. Bob was convinced we were being tailed. But when I asked him why, all he came up with were vague answers. A few days earlier, we were hanging around on Sunset Boulevard.

Bob nudged me. "That guy against the wall over there is reading a newspaper and it's nighttime. How can he see? I bet he's tailing us."

"Why would someone follow us? We ain't important enough," I reminded him. Bob just shrugged.

But goofy Bob was so spooked, that night he packed his car. By morning, Bob and Rhonda were on their way to Florida. Later that same night, Joanie and Kitty booked George's house for the evening. They were expecting a couple of johns. Me and George were about to make ourselves scarce when I overheard Joanie trying to call the madam to make sure she set up the two johns. Something seemed to be wrong with the phone line. Joanie couldn't get through.

Speeding down the hill to a favorite pizza place, me and George rehashed the whole Bob thing. Bob was always uneasy about something, but this time he really lost it. George told me that a few days ago he was joking around with the cab drivers on Sunset Boulevard across from a high-class nightclub. The cabbies knew the dirt around town almost before it happened. They moonlighted as stool pigeons for the LAPD, but that didn't faze George. He had nothing to hide.

One of the cabbies kidded George. "You and your friends

didn't have anything to do with the Sinatra, Jr., kidnapping by any chance?"

"If we had ransom money, smart-ass, we wouldn't be pimping now would we?" George countered.

The Sinatra thing exploded about the time we hit L.A. Frank Sinatra, Jr., was allegedly kidnapped, then released after Sinatra, Sr., parted with a significant amount of cash. The town buzzed with cops trailing the kidnappers. The media talked about nothing else. I couldn't understand all the fuss. Then I remembered it concerned the Chairman of the Board.

Then things took an interesting twist. Just for the hell of it, George decided on a different route down the hill. Instead of turning left on Mulholland Drive, George turned right. Here's what happened minutes after we left George's house. The Vice Squad, disguised as the two johns, arrested Kitty and Joanie on a "conspiracy to corrupt public morals" charge, a felony. But the police were after bigger fish.

A couple of hours after me and George left the house, George called Joanie to see if the coast was clear. A guy answered. George asked to speak to Joanie. The guy wanted to take a message. George smelled a rat and hung up.

The next day George called his mob-connected bondsman. who told George the girls were arrested, but he'd bail them out. Seeing as how George's house and my apartment were being watched, me and George rented a dumpy two-bedroom in a seedy part of town. We got the shock of our lives when we met up with the girls.

A fuming Kitty described her ordeal. "Can you believe the fucking cop asked me why I got mad when Joanie patted me on the ass? Imagine! They were watching us the whole time. The cops had George's house under surveillance for weeks complete with infra-red cameras and illegal wire-taps. They tried to trick me into confessing what you were up to, and here's the kicker." Kitty took a deep breath. "They honestly think you guys had something to do with the Sinatra, Jr., kidnapping."

I fell off my chair. George looked like he'd been shot.

As we pieced things together, it became clear the cops were only using the girls, hoping to pinch me and George on info the cops received from the cabbies. With our Illinois plates and my felony conviction the LAPD, and now the FBI, believed we were with the Chicago Outfit.

Kitty's anger reached the boiling point. "They threatened to arrest you for the Mann Act if I didn't talk. Naturally I told them what they could do to themselves."

I found the situation incredibly funny. "I guess Bob wasn't so paranoid after all," I laughed.

When Bob and Rhonda disappeared, the FBI figured we were the kidnappers. The cops who were working with the FBI staked out our usual route that night, but since we'd taken an alternate road, they grabbed the girls hoping to get to us. We decided to carry on like nothing was wrong. It was up to the authorities to prove we were involved. For some reason, neither the FBI nor the cops made a move.

I had a little job to do. I sneaked back to George's house after dark and found where I'd stashed my Beretta. I heaved it as hard as I could over the HOLLYWOOD sign. What a shame to throw away a perfectly good gun but, as a convicted felon, I couldn't risk being caught with it.

A few weeks went by and still no action. It was Christmas Eve. Kitty and I went to the opening of *Around the World in 80 Days*. It was appearing in that new wide-screen Cinerama and all seats were reserved. During the balloon scene, the usher asked the guy next to Kitty to leave. He was in the wrong seat. The guy who took his place might as well have worn a sign saying: "I'm a cop." This jerk was practically in Kitty's lap trying to overhear our conversation. She moved away. The cop moved closer. He was like an annoying piece of dog shit that clings stubbornly to the bottom of your shoe.

An hour of playing games with this moron was getting on my nerves. I told Kitty, "Let's get out of here."

On the way down the aisle, another cop got up from the rear of the theater and walked ahead of us, Kitty's new friend taking up the rear. They arrested me in the lobby for "conspiracy to corrupt public morals." It's a lame charge they throw at you when they have nothing concrete. No big surprise. They read me my rights and escorted me down to police headquarters.

The cops bombarded me with questions like, "How did you get to L.A.? What are you doing in L.A.?" and "Do you want to make a statement?"

"Yes, I'd like to make a statement," I answered calmly. "Get me a lawyer."

I found out they had already booked George. They escorted me to a bullpen with other prisoners, not much different from the one in Cook County Jail. About fifteen minutes later, in walked a cop impersonating a prisoner. If they'd just realize you can't disguise a cop, it would save a lot of trouble. I let him go through his getting-to-know-you/I-wanna-be-your-friend routine. Then I calmly told him, "If you want to sit here and try to bullshit me that's okay with me, but I don't have a choice. I'm stuck here." I lay down and went to sleep. When I woke up, the cop was gone.

The D.A. refused to prosecute us for lack of evidence and they let me and George out on bond. The girls went to court. Money had to change hands to be convicted of prostitution. There was no evidence so their case was thrown out. The real story went something like this. After spending a shitload of tax-payer money trying to nail us, the police realized the only thing they could pin on us was pandering. The upstanding careers of too many VIPs were on the line—regulars of Joanie and Kitty's madam. It was Pat Atkins all over again. To bust us would be unthinkable. A trial was out of the question. The only thing to do with us low-lives was kick us out of town.

The police chief wailed on and on. We were "a menace to the upstanding citizens of Los Angeles." I wondered if upstanding citizens included big shots with a yen for prostitutes? Since we cost him so much grief, the chief was hell-bent on getting his money's worth.

When he ran out of insults, I offered my condolences. "I'm sorry we didn't kidnap the Sinatra kid, take over the movie industry or rob a bank," I apologized. "If I'd known all the trouble you guys went through . . ."

"Get the fuck out of here before I shoot you." The police chief raised up out of his chair like he had every intention of making good on his threat, but I was already halfway out the door. Just to make sure we didn't try anything funny, we had a police escort all the way to Arizona—the girls in one car, me and George in the other. I felt very safe.

George and Joanie split to New York. Me and Kitty tossed around a few ideas. Miami sounded good, but first it was time to see our baby Kathy in Montreal. "Oh, please, God," I prayed. "No more spaghetti with red sauce."

PART TWO

Miami
1964–1970

16

The story about the wooden leg and the hooker, Temple
Drake, still makes the rounds and it's entirely true.

FIRST STOP IN the Sunshine State—West Palm Beach. Kitty's
agent got her two weeks at some high-line club. She was
doing okay but I was so bored, I almost went to look for real
work. Lots of old money hung out in West Palm Beach. Only
problem was the sidewalks rolled up after sundown. It was like
trying to work a graveyard. Besides, how can you con a stiff?

We decided to head further south to Miami for some live
action. Almost overnight Kitty was booked into the Five O'Clock
Club in Miami Beach. It was next to the crossroaders joint,
Wolfie's Restaurant on 21st and Collins, the one me and Bob
visited years earlier.

Martha Raye owned the small burlesque theater, with a troupe
of only eight to ten strippers. More often than not, the funny
lady with the rubber face held court in the club's bar trading
wisecracks with her pal, Rocky Graziano. It reminded me of
the old days when they hung out at the Kingston Yacht Club.
Some guy observed that Graziano liked broads with big mouths
and wide behinds.

Me and Kitty took turns watching three-year-old Kathy. Our
life was a crazy mixture—half "Father Knows Best" and half
Guys and Dolls.

It wasn't long before I ran into Bob and Rhonda at our regular stomping grounds, the Hialeah Race Track. All Rhonda
could talk about was a famous restaurant and bar called the
Bonfire on the 79th Street Causeway. "The place is overrun with

millionaires," Rhonda gushed. "I think the toilet paper is made out of $100 bills."

I'd heard of the place. Every week some Middle East oil baron parked his yacht in Miami determined to drop a few thou at the Bonfire's Western-style bar. If the bar had a sign, it would have read, "Classy booze and classy broads served upon request." A friendly little Jewish guy, "Radio" Weiner, a bona fide character, owned the Bonfire. Radio gave Tony, his maitre d', carte blanche when it came to which hookers could hustle the bar, strictly girls with personality and pizzazz. Rhonda fit the bill. Pretty soon she made a bundle off rich suckers itching for a lay.

There's an interesting Bonfire story that's still making the rounds, and it's entirely true. It so happened that this maitre d', Tony, had a wooden leg. Now if Tony let a girl work the bar, she always made big money. In exchange for his generosity, he figured the girl owed him a little something. So when he asked the girl to come over to his place for "special favors," she obliged, except for one rebel—I think she was a redhead at the time—by the name of Temple Drake. Temple was a dancer friend of Kitty's who hustled the Bonfire when she was in the mood. She was the kind of girl who could pick and choose. Three words described Temple: Tall, good-looking, aggressive.

"If I'm coming over to your place, it's strictly business," Temple warned Tony.

"Okay," he said, "but you ain't gonna' charge me what you charge those other guys?"

"No, I'll only charge you fifty dollars."

Afterwards they cooled down in Tony's black satin-sheeted bed, cigarettes lit, iced Scotch in hand. Temple arched an eyebrow. "Where's my fifty dollars?

"Oh, I thought you were kidding," Tony answered taking a long drag. "You know, if you give me a hard time, I won't let you work the bar any more."

With that, Temple threw on her Rita Hayworth evening gown and stormed out. On the way, she noticed Tony's wooden leg propped by the front door, grabbed it and kept walking. When Tony realized Temple had stole his leg, he was filled with panic. He called all over Miami Springs frantically looking for Temple Drake.

A few nights later, Temple was trolling for a live one at the Traveler's Lounge, a notorious mob hangout. I was there with Bob scouting around for some loose change.

The minute I spotted Temple I took her aside. "Hey, Tony's going nuts. He said he's gotta talk to you."

A faint smile smoothed Temple's sensual red mouth. Carefully stubbing out her cigarette, she walked to the nearest phone and dialed Tony's number. Only one ring and Tony's strained voice could be heard, a couple of notches higher than usual.

"Look, I need my leg so I can go to work."

"You're not getting the leg till I have my fifty bucks," she told him, calmly checking her dress in the mirror.

"You'll get the fifty bucks when you bring me my leg," answered Tony.

"No," Temple insisted. "I'll hand over the leg when you bring me the money."

"How am I going to get there?" Tony whined.

"Crawl, you son-of-a-bitch!"

Half an hour later a cab driver walked into the bar. A wooden leg and fifty dollars exchanged hands.

Me and Bob hit the track on a regular basis and hung out at the Travelers for the weekly poker game, but we needed more action. We found just the place. On Collins Avenue, right on the beach, the incomparable Fontainebleau Hotel with its stately palms glistened like a cool jewel unfazed by the shirt-drenching Miami sun. The *Miami Herald* kept tabs on the celebs headlining in the hotel's opulent show room: *"Fontainebleau—Ol' Blue Eyes sells out another long engagement."* The Fontainebleau attracted the wallet-bulging jet set, but mostly rich Jews on their yearly pilgrimage from Chicago and New York. It's no wonder the house specialty was lox and bagels.

Happy Hour found me and Bob busy conning marks—guys looking for a little card action—in the hotel's trendy Poodle Lounge. But we weren't fussy. We took advantage of anything that cruised our way like the Latin gigolos who hustled the loaded, bored broads—meaning loaded as in money. I had a lot in common with the husbands of those wealthy women. The only difference was our *modus operandi*. With me it was at a fancy watering hole while the husband fleeced his sucker, some shmuck in a Brooks Brothers suit, inside a cushy office. The Poodle Lounge reminded me of a tiny ocean where the smallest fish were eaten by the bigger fish that were snapped up by the biggest fish. I figured you had to hook 'em before someone else did.

One very crowded happy hour I met a friendly old guy, a perfect mark, but Bob had gone off somewhere. The guy was a retired judge with dough to burn. While I sized him up, I was thinking there's a lot of different ways to pluck a chicken. Maybe I should invite him for a friendly game of cards even without Bob? Wouldn't you know, the guy beat me to the punch.

In a warm, friendly voice the judge urged me to have dinner at his condo in Ft. Lauderdale with him and his wife. He wouldn't take no for an answer. That was a switch. I accepted and he gave me his address. I picked up a bottle of wine on the way. I was thinking, maybe I should take along a deck of cards? Nah, that would have looked funny.

A few hours later, my new black Bonneville turned up a winding drive. The judge's condo was easy to spot, a multi-level thing with its own private beach. What a spread! Sea air filled my nostrils, but I detected another familiar scent—the smell of money.

The old guy greeted me like I was his long lost brother. I gave the wine to his wife, a petite blonde who could have been a cheerleader at one of those Ivy League schools where they talk like their jaws are wired shut. She was all smiles. Her short white dress showed off a deep, even tan on a toned-to-perfection body. I half expected her to pull out her pom-poms and give me a cheer. They offered me a seat and we bullshitted for maybe fifteen minutes. We watched the breakers hit the rocks through the massive picture window. I should have realized the waves pounding the rocks were a warning.

Pretty soon Pom-poms excused herself to open the wine. In an instant she was back. All pouty, she turned to me and cooed, "I can't get the cork out. Can you help me?"

In the kitchen I noticed there was no way in hell she was gonna cook dinner. The room was bare. Nothing, not even a can of tuna. When she brushed against me with her ripe breasts, it dawned on me that I was the one about to be cooked.

Back in the living room the judge, friendly as ever, asked if I'd like to see some family photos.

"Sure," I said, wondering what was up. "That would be very nice."

Pasted neatly in a scrapbook were vivid color prints of the judge, his wife and some other guy, all buck-naked. My face got redder by the minute as I looked at the three of them in surprisingly sexy poses. If I tried that stuff I'd probably dislocate something. Everyone in the photos was smiling like they were on a picnic. Well, I was a normal young guy, which meant if a strong wind blew, I got a hard-on. This really did it.

The judge asked me point blank, "Do you want my wife?"

"If you don't mind . . ." I stammered, trying not to be rude.

We scrambled for the bedroom like trained circus dogs on command. Bow wow! Clothes flew off our bodies so fast it must have looked like a silent movie with the action speeded up. Pretty soon me and miss cheerleader were in bed getting it on. I was on top not thinking much about anything other than what I was doing.

Suddenly, I felt these hands on my balls. I knew they weren't her hands because they were around my neck. I hit the ceiling. Before I landed, my wadded up clothes were in my arms and

I was out the front door. I laid down a lot of rubber, putting as much distance as possible between me and those perverts. What's wrong with them, I thought? Can't they just screw like normal people?

When I saw Bob the next day I asked him, "Do you want a wild broad?" He nodded his head yes, so I gave him a slip of paper. "Here, call this number." He never told me how it turned out.

An Italian burglar from Boston by the name of Jimmy Garafalo sat down at the Travelers Lounge poker game one night. Jimmy was the happiest guy I ever met. I bet if someone told Jimmy that he just lost the Trifecta by a hair, he'd die laughing. We pulled a few important burglaries together which fattened my bankroll considerably.

By this time Rhonda had introduced Kitty to the Bonfire, so now we were bringing in plenty of cash, enough to hire a nanny to watch Kathy. Rhonda, still under Bob's spell, forked over every penny to him. Bob steered clear of us guys when he was with Rhonda. We kidded one another that he avoided us because he didn't want Rhonda to find out he never received the Congressional Medal of Honor. I knew better than to pull that macho stuff on Kitty.

Who should I bump into at the Travelers but my boyhood chum, Jack Kearns, now a fireman in Miami. Jack had developed into a lean and tan athletic type. He didn't have movie star good looks but, chances are, he could have charmed the pants off most females. Jack moved with a restless energy, the kind that attracted women hungry for sun, surf and sex. His father, the famous Doc Kearns, died a year earlier. As we talked about old times, we ran down to the Fifth Street Gym to look at a couple of fighters. The Dundee brothers, Chris and Angelo, well-respected promoter/trainers throughout the boxing world, tightly ran the place.

Angelo, the younger of the two, was a great cut-man and

trainer, having worked with guys like Carmen Basileo and Willie Pastrano. Muhammad Ali and Sugar Ray Leonard came along years later. Angelo was head trainer at the gym. Older brother Chris promoted some 300 fighters from 1928 to the mid-1960s. Midget Wolgast, Ken Overlin and Ezzard Charles won titles under him. The Dundee brothers weren't always named Dundee. Years earlier in Philadelphia, a third brother fought under the name of Joe Dundee, adopted from the famous fighter, Johnny Dundee, who Joe admired. Chris liked Johnny Dundee, too, so what else could Angelo do but go with the flow?

Jimmy Ellis, the heavyweight champ, was punching the heavy bag when we walked in. Jack and Jimmy exchanged a few friendly words. It was clear Jack had stayed in touch with the boxing scene. Jack went on about how he'd managed an unknown fighter, Jeffrey Davis, renamed Jefferson Davis by Jack's father, Doc. Shrewd Doc Kearns claimed the fighter was a direct descendant of the famous Confederate president. The name-switch did the trick. It aroused the interest of a gullible boxing public.

While we watched a promising young fighter pound the shit out of his sparring partner, Jack told me who was an easy mark and who to avoid at the gym. Jack had no use for my kind of con. He had his own talents—the gift of gab, for example—exactly like his old man.

Me and Jack started to pal around together, just like the old days, except now we were big boys with grown-up appetites. Aside from women, Jack's hobby (with Jack it was more of an obsession) was diving to old wrecks searching for sunken treasure. The Florida Keys were filthy with shipwrecks from the time when pirates still roamed the Caribbean. Jack was an expert diver, with or without a tank of air strapped to his back, a real daredevil. I was Jack's match when it came to taking risks so it wasn't long before I picked up the basics of diving. We spent hour after hour exploring the multicolored reefs bursting with tropical sea critters. In spite of all the fun, I couldn't keep my mind from wandering to my favorite subject—rich suckers.

Miami was a con artist's feast, if you knew where to find the action. I studied the city's layout. It was crucial to making a score. The Miami Beach Dog Track bordered the south end of Collins Avenue. Nearby stood the world-famous restaurant, Joe's Stone Crab. Joe had such a way with his crabs, he converted loyal meat-and-potatoes diehards into shellfish fanatics. It all started in 1913 when Joe Weiss opened a small lunch counter on the beach, minus the stone crabs. That was before anyone knew you could eat the mouth-watering crustaceans. Just for the hell of it, Joe decided to cook up a batch for his friends. The rest is history.

If you traveled north on Collins you hit a bunch of rundown hotels with old Jewish people living in them. Whenever the ambulance sirens whined, about every ten minutes, odds were another old guy from one of those ancient hotels was having a heart attack. Cardiologists grew rich on the steady business.

Still further north on Collins, the Fontainebleau Hotel and its neighbor the Eden Roc competed with one another like a couple of glamour girls vying for attention. New condos all along the beach slowly but steadily gobbled up sprawling millionaires' estates. Miami was growing like a hungry teenager and real estate was getting pricey.

The heart of the city revolved around the Cuban section on Flagler Street in downtown Miami, with its Latin rhythms, Cuban spices and tropical colors that were so hot they scorched your eyeballs. It was on Flagler and LeJeune that me and Kitty rented a penthouse apartment. I loved the place. Sometimes on a humid summer night I'd come home to the strains of hot Salsa dance music drifting up from the restaurant around the corner. It made me long to be back in Havana wrapped in the arms of some warm señorita. The best thing about the apartment—it was minutes away from the Travelers Lounge. I could drive there in nothing flat to relieve a mark of his money.

Out of the blue, I got a call from my ex, Betty. She was all business, cut-and-dry. I felt a twinge when I remembered how Betty's voice used to sound—soft, really soft. Seemed my oldest

Wilson & Kenmore Ave.
Chicago
late 1940s

Montrose Harbor
Chicago Skyline
late 1940s

Frankie Laine
(autographed photo)

El Rancho Vegas
April 3, 1941

Bob Thor, Loreny Rodgers & Slick
Chicago 1955

Slick and ten rap partners handcuffed together at Shakespeare Police Station, Jan 23, 1951

Slick & Bob Mauro
Juarez, Mexico
1962

Lucchese soldier George Romi
(far right)
1960s

Betty Hanner & Slick
Penthouse apt.
Flagler & LeJeune
Miami, late 1960s

Slick gaming card
Las Vegas Metro Police Dept.
circa 1985

Loren "Loreny" Rodgers
(far right)

Chicken Ranch menu cover
Pahrump, NV
1982

Slick gaming card
Mississippi Gaming Commission
circa 1990

Slick, Casino Executive
Date unknown

daughter, Billita, was hanging around with a rough crowd and me and Betty decided Billita would spend the summer with me and Kathy. During those months I bonded closely with my two kids. Not a soul knew how much I missed my family. When it came time for Billita to return home, I took Kathy along so she could meet her sisters and brother. I was relieved they all clicked. Now I had more family memories to keep me going.

Things were so good that after one big score, me and Jimmy Garafalo opened a motorcycle rental business on Tamiami Trail. We hit on the name Cycle A-Go-Go since the Bosa Nova and Go-Go dancing were all the craze. The legit business made a perfect front for our illegal operation. Besides, it gave us something to do between burglaries. Our 150cc Hondas and Yamahas were in constant demand, especially in-season. Vacationers at the big hotels on the beach jumped at the cheap mode of transportation.

It was one of those typical, lazy sunny days. Me and Jim were hanging around the cycle shop in our flip-flops and shorts waiting for an order. Just then the phone rang. A regular customer needed a bike right away. Me and Jim each grabbed a cycle so we had a way to get back.

On the freeway we started to rev up our engines. Jimmy gave me one of his goofy faces and the race was on. We were neck-and-neck for a while. The breeze whipping my face felt cool and exhilarating. Then I watched in horror as the front fender on Jim's Honda shook loose. Within seconds it had wedged against his front tire. Jim flew off the bike like a giant slingshot had propelled him through the air. We were going so fast, it took me nearly a quarter mile to stop. I was afraid what I'd find. A still breathing Jimmy was nearly skinned alive, his clothes shredded right off his bloody pulp of a body.

When I saw the shape Jimmy was in at the hospital, a shudder ran through me. If I'd grabbed Jim's bike instead of mine . . . Jolly Jim. For once he wasn't laughing. Jimmy's wife waited silently outside his hospital room, a shattered look marring her pretty face. I handed her my key to Cycle-A-Go-Go. "Sell everything and keep any money from the sale," I said, placing the key in her hand. Tears rolled down her cheeks, but she said nothing. That was the end of me and motorcycles.

It didn't matter where you went in the 1960s; Miami's streets teemed with the New York Mafia's five ruling families and their thugs. Every once in a while you'd see some Chicago guys, but not often. The Chicago and New York mobs detested one another. Neither one could stomach playing second fiddle to the other. They co-operated just enough to get things done.

I met Michele "Mike" Miranda, head of New York's Lucchese Family, at the Newport Hotel on 163rd and Collins. He liked to hang out there when he was in town, which was often. The balding old man with the bushy eyebrows talked like he was just a regular guy, but that was hardly the case. Miranda had been a key figure in the mob's Havana Conference in 1946, the one where Bugsy had gotten the thumbs down. Miranda also attended the Apalachin Mafia meeting in 1957, at the farmhouse that the FBI raided. Every *mafioso* who was anybody showed up. Mike Miranda had enough power to light up Miami, but no single Mafia family ran the city.

One night during the regular poker game in Miami Springs, I met an ugly character by the name of Lucio, a Lucchese Family soldier. As I studied Lucio, my mind raced back to those old "Movietone" newsreels. During WWII theaters featured them regularly. That's how we got our news before they invented TV.

Why, this guy was the spitting image of the dictator, Benito Mussolini. There was the famous square jaw, same stocky body and even the grand gestures. The only difference was Lucio's head wasn't shaved. The uncanny resemblance sent a chill up my spine. The funny thing was that, after I got to know Lucio a little, he actually played up the similarities. He ranted on how Mussolini was such a great statesman. Puffing up his chest, Lucio spouted

Mussolini's exact words. "I would rather live one day as a lion than a hundred years as a lamb." Maybe he talked big but Lucio couldn't play poker worth a shit. In fact, I don't remember him ever winning.

I found out Lucio wasn't such a bad guy and we sort of struck up a friendship. It's funny me getting friendly with Lucio because I tried to steer clear of the New York mob. When you were around them, violence was never far off. Common sense should have told me I was making a big mistake, but when had I ever showed much common sense?

17

If Joe needed the card, Bob tugged hard on
the line and the white towel popped up behind
Joe's head, like a ghost floating in midair.

ONE AFTERNOON ME and Bob were hustling the Poodle Lounge.
We ran into a real sucker with a ton of money begging us to
play gin. We suggested his hotel room but his wife was hanging
around there. The poolside was out because our mooches were
everywhere and they might get suspicious. Besides, the guy was
allergic to the sun. Before we could settle on a location, he got
tired of waiting and walked away. If only we had somewhere to
take our marks, a prop of some kind. Where was Chucky Douglas
when we needed him? He always came up with the best props.
Chuck wouldn't think of making a drug run to Mexico without
a kid in tow and a camera around his neck.

Thanks to Jack Kearns, we found just the thing—a 42-foot
Owens. The boat needed a few repairs and a coat of paint, but
its wood hull and two Chevy truck motors checked out. Most
important, it had all the "bait" to lure our "fish." The price was
right, too—only eight grand—me and Bob split 50/50. The bow
held a big bed, the head actually worked and the boat even had
a fair-sized galley. Best of all, the galley was fitted out with a
fold-down table, tailor-made for card games. We wracked our
brains for a name. It finally came to us—the *Knot Guilty*.

Our timing was perfect. A reasonable berth in Haulover, a
popular dock north of Miami Beach in Sunny Isles, opened up,
and the activity in the area suited our needs to a T. Local sport

fishing outfits catered to large parties of wealthy businessmen. They all came for one purpose—to conquer the sea and flash photos of their prize catch back in Podunk. When these clowns weren't reeling in the "big one," drinking and whoring took top priority.

Me and Bob had the perfect setup to snag a few of our own. It so happened our slip was close to a restaurant and bar where all the groups hung out. Our prop was almost too good to be true, like a stage waiting for the actors to make it spring to life. We dusted off the old "peep joint" idea we used before under different circumstances. The scheme was simple. When I came across a sucker, I struck up a conversation and turned the subject to the *Knot Guilty*, parked out front.

It happened just the way we planned. I met Joe, a loud-mouthed New Yorker, at the neighborhood restaurant in Haulover. The routine bullshitting out of the way, I said, "Ya know, that's my boat out there and I'm expecting a couple of girls to come over. My friend can't make it, so why don't you join me?"

"Sure," Joe said, slightly drunk and drooling at the mention of girls.

Before I left the restaurant, I phoned Bob. "I'll stall him," I whispered. "Get there as soon as you can."

Once me and Joe were on the boat, I filled in with small talk and poured Joe a Scotch. Through the partly opened window curtain, I caught sight of Bob's car pulling up.

"How about a few hands of gin rummy while we wait?" I suggested casually.

The minute Joe agreed, me and Bob snapped into action like perfectly tuned machines. Joe sat facing me at the table. Bob was secretly stationed topside. From there, he could study Joe's hand through a slit in the curtain that didn't quite cover the open window over Joe's shoulder. Bob could overhear every word we said. If Joe accidentally discovered Bob, we even had a little story cooked up to explain Bob's presence. Everything was set.

Here's where our special code came into play. Each card and suit had a different word associated with it.

CARD	WORD
ace	play
deuce	do
three	terrible
four	fair
five	fine
six	cinch
seven	lucky
eight	easy
nine	nice
ten	time
jack	beat
queen	good
king	pair

SUIT	WORD
club	could
diamond	damn
heart	hell
spade	sure

For example, if I was getting ready to throw the queen of spades, I'd say something like, "I *sure* got a *good* card for you," sure being spades and good being queen. With this system there were a lot of ways we could work the cards.

The crowning touch, a small white towel attached to a fishing line, lay on the bed behind Joe. Since I faced Joe, I had a clear line of sight to the bed behind him. Bob had a firm grip on the other end of the line slinking its way along the deck. If Joe needed the card I was ready to throw, Bob tugged hard on the line and the white towel popped up behind Joe's head, like a ghost floating in midair. It took all I could do not to laugh.

Joe never got wise to us. Other suckers came and went, but no one discovered our secret. Still, the more we made, the more I squandered at the track. Money flowed through my hands like mercury.

One morning I lounged on the deck of the *Knot Guilty,* waiting patiently for Bob and Jack to show up. This was my piece of paradise—cream-colored yachts, cloudless sky, calm water. Our boat made a perfect prop to hook suckers and the Newport Beach Hotel was just minutes away. I tallied the number of women I brought over from the Newport. Gee, the money I saved on hotel bills alone could have paid for my share of the boat.

Bob eased into the parking lot, only a few yards from the dock.

"You want coffee, Slick? I'll get it." Bob wandered into the restaurant.

A few minutes later Jack came by with his friend, Greg, groceries spilling from their arms. I took an instant liking to this Greg, a well built, five-foot-seven-inch, dago-Spanish mixed breed with black curly hair and devilish black eyes. Greg was so laid-back, that if there was a dead body on the deck he'd step over it without saying a word. There was talk of Greg running drugs around Miami—serious stuff—but it was none of my business so I just kept my mouth shut. We busied ourselves storing the groceries below. Everything was set.

"Are you two landlubbers ready for your first voyage on the high seas?" Jack gave Greg the high sign to cast off. Me and Bob grinned like a couple of dopes. Big deal. A two-hour ride to Bimini. Nothing to it.

Jack set our course for 111° on the compass. He expertly maneuvered the *Knot Guilty* out of our slip, following the Intracoastal Waterway south toward Government Cut. But in my mind I was already in Bimini lying in a hammock strung between two shady palm trees, a gorgeous native girl catering to my every whim.

The ocean changed into a dark, cobalt blue. The wind turned brisk. I thought back to when I was a kid daydreaming about the tiny boats out on Lake Michigan, longing to be on one of them. Presto. Here I was. Two hours later, like Jack predicted, we were tying up at the dock in Bimini.

A friendly guy named Brown—the color of dark molasses— owned most of the island. He greeted Jack with a backslap and "Hey, mon! Good to see you." The sun glinting off Brown's teeth temporarily blinded me.

"Same here," said Jack pumping Brown's hand. "We're out for a couple of days."

Jack was in his element. All this gladhanding got us free dock- age and electricity. I couldn't find two palm trees close enough to string a hammock, but it didn't matter. On Bimini, I noticed glumly, you brought your own women or you went without.

That night while some fat native girl stumbled through a lame fire dance at the local bar, the couple at a nearby table carried on a full-blown shouting match. The woman's shrill voice ricocheted off the walls like bullets.

"If you don't shut up," she threatened her drunken husband, "I'm gonna give someone ten dollars to shut you up."

No sooner were the words out of her mouth than Greg sprang to their table, clipped the guy on the jaw so hard he went out cold, and snatched the $10 lying on their table. Greg slid back in his chair smiling that crooked smile of his. "Drinks are on me," he announced, slapping the ten-spot down on our table.

Now the guy's wife screamed at Greg, "What did you do that for?" He just grinned at her over his shoulder and shrugged. I knew there was something I liked about Greg.

"Hey Greg," Jack joked, "You don't start a beef in Bimini unless you want some cop in a white hat and shorts throwing you in a dungeon to 'cool off, mon!'"

A squadron of sand flies circling the dock forced us to anchor out by the reef that night. Early the next morning we dove fifteen feet into the warm, turquoise water. Visibility was so good, the bottom seemed an arms reach away.

During one lobster dive, I spotted a giant sea turtle with a hard-on. "Hey!" I shouted to Bob and Greg, "Get a load of this turtle!"

Greg stuck his head over the side and let out a low whistle. "You better get on the boat quick. It's mating season and you can't be too careful." I wasn't sure if Greg was joking so I followed his advice. No use inviting trouble.

Topside, Jack showed us how to pull the tails off the five or six lobsters we caught. A quick dip in a kettle of boiling water and they were ready for the melted butter. Jack went off to spear fish some 50 yards away. While Greg cleaned up below, me and Bob cast our lines over the side.

Immediately Bob's line went wild. Whatever he caught was jerking Bob all over the place. Bob slowly reeled in the line pulling with everything he had. His fishing rod bowed straight down toward the water. I was sure the line would snap any minute. Then we saw it. Bob had snagged a four-foot Blue-tip shark. By some miracle me and Bob managed to hook the thrashing giant into the boat. Holy mackerel! It looked as big as a whale flopping all over the place. I rushed below, pulled my Beretta out of my gear and charged up on the deck. "Stand back!" I announced. I fired two rounds at the sea monster, taking it permanently out of action with the second shot.

Greg ran up to see what all the noise was about. "Shit man. What are you doing?" he laughed, swinging open the double doors to the hatch where the motors were housed. We heard the bilge pump grind into action.

"We're taking on water," Greg shouted. "Bullets went right through the hull . . . good thing you didn't hit the motors." He looked up at me with that funny crooked grin.

I scratched my head in disbelief. "Boy they sure make these boats flimsy," I said.

Greg scrounged below for plugs. He found a pencil, broke it in two and jammed the ends into the two holes that lay just below the water line. We tossed the shark's carcass—evidence of my foolhardy deed—over the side.

Jack returned with enough reef dwellers to put us in the fish business. Most of them he presented to Brown. No wonder we were treated better than the governor of the Bahamas.

As we headed for Miami Jack said, "What you guys need is a ship-to-shore radio in case of an emergency." I looked at the water—smooth as a baby's ass—not a ripple. Who needs a radio?

The next day I filled Kitty in on my trip. She's the only person I know who can give me hell without shouting.

"Personally, I don't care if you rot in Bimini," she said. "But you have a little girl who's been asking for you. Next time would you please let me know where you are?"

I could see this conversation was heading down a path I didn't care to go, so I agreed with her and quickly changed the subject.

"By the way," Kitty said, "I met a multi-millionaire at the Bonfire named John Bell. He wants to show me his boat." She said it as an afterthought, but I knew Kitty was trying to get to me.

"Big deal," I countered. "I got a boat."

"Yeah, but Bell's custom yacht is 130 feet long with a seven-man crew plus he happens to own the Bell Fiber Company in Marion, Indiana. What's more, he has an estate on Collins near the Bath Club." She said all this like she was laying down a winning poker hand.

I could see it was no use trying to play her little game so I folded. "Okay, John Bell's got a bigger boat than mine, but I bet I went places Bell never heard of," I added lamely.

From then on, Kitty traveled everywhere with John Bell. The Ambassador East Hotel—one of Chicago's finest—became their headquarters on business trips up North. On one trip Kitty came back with a new nose; on another, big boobs.

"How amazing," I told her, admiring the latest upgrade. "Maybe they have a machine that stretches you to make you taller." She didn't see the humor.

Geez, I thought laughing to myself. Between
Mousie, Jackie Cerone and Tony Spilotro, these
guys could open their own cemetery.

I**T WASN'T LIKE** Bob to act moody. We swung by the Travelers
after a night at the track, but Bob seemed unusually quiet.
Finally he spilled what was eating him. "I think I'm losing my
grip on Rhonda."

"Why's that?" I asked.

"Aw," he mumbled. "Rhonda's been acting funny lately. She's
seeing some building contractor from Kentucky. They go off on
his yacht for two, maybe three weeks at a time." Bob looked like
a hound dog that had just lost his rabbit.

"Maybe you're imagining things," I said, trying to cheer
him up.

"I don't think so. She forgets to put her jewelry away . . . never
does that. I know the signs. She's nuts about this guy."

He didn't say anything for a few minutes. The silence made
me edgy.

Finally Bob spoke. "Ya know, me and Rhonda have a lot of
dough hanging out there, so I figure I better invest it before
everything goes away."

Bob continued, a little more upbeat. "I've been talking to my
brother-in-law, the one in Chicago. He can get me credit at the
Merchandise Mart where there's a warehouse full of goods from
closeouts and bankruptcies. Says I can resell the stuff down here

and turn a decent profit. I take off for Chicago tomorrow. You want in? We can split everything fifty/fifty."

Bob lost the hangdog look. He seemed excited at the thought of making an honest buck. My mind sifted through the possibilities. "Hey Bob, maybe you hit on something."

I was killing time playing Seven Card Stud at the Travelers Lounge one night waiting for Bob to return. Who should walk over with Bob Mann, one of the owners, but an Outfit guy named Mousy and Jackie Cerone, Tony Accardo's most trusted hitman.

At that time, Jackie "the Lackie" had worked his way up to the number two spot in the Chicago Outfit. I knew Mouse, this ugly pip-squeak with the thick lips, from the Crossroads. When Mousy, John D'Arco's strong-arm blinked, people jumped.

"Hey, what are you doing out here?" Mousy shook my hand while me and Jackie traded nods.

"Oh, I guess you two know one another?" Mousy may have been surprised that Jackie would acknowledge a nobody like me, but he didn't let on.

Yeah, I thought. I know Jackie Cerone. . . .

It was back when I managed Lee's Lounge. Leroy and Loreny had just gotten out of prison. All they could talk about was this Class A counterfeiter by the name of John something or other.

We went into business with John, rented a big store, printing equipment—everything he needed—with our phony IDs. Back in the fifties you could lay your hands on most anything. Drivers licenses, social security cards, even passports were as easy to get as ordering a cup of coffee. In the middle of the night we moved the whole lot to a new location so no one could track us.

We walked in a few days later to inspect the work. John hummed a little tune as he carefully hung one fresh counterfeit bill after another on a clothesline, like they came straight out of the Maytag. Clothespins kept the wet bills securely in place.

"This ain't good enough," said Loreny examining the dripping paper.

"Neither are these," I echoed. "You better keep trying."

Weeks passed and John still didn't have shit. I swear, my own kid could have done a better job with crayons. Loreny threatened to break John's neck if he didn't shape up.

Well, one morning we went to see John. Damned if the place wasn't cleaned out. John gave us the slip the same way we tricked the guys who leased us the printing equipment. Loreny was out for blood. No doubt about it. He would have killed John on sight. Word got around that we were gunning for this John.

Now Bob ran our book joint in Lee's basement. Me and Bob didn't want to wind up as "trunk music" so, naturally, we split everything with the Outfit 50/50. The Outfit's collector came in one night and introduced me to none other than Jackie Cerone.

Jackie was congenial enough. He even managed a smile.

"I hear you're looking for John?" he said, his cold fish-like eyes giving me the once over.

"Yeah, the fucking guy made off with some stuff of ours."

"Well," said Jackie, no longer smiling. "If you want to remain on friendly terms, you'll forget it. John's with me now."

Of course, I got the drift. No one in his right mind would cross Jackie Cerone. And that's how we met.

The present circumstances were a tea party compared to that time in Lee's, but I didn't take any chances. Jackie could turn violent without warning, depending on his mood. I conjured up the gruesome picture of Cerone torturing a juice collector, 300-pound William "Action" Jackson, with a cattle prod while Jackson hung from a meat hook in some guy's garage.

Mouse said, "Have you seen Tony Spilotro? We're supposed to meet him here."

I searched my mind. Tony Spilotro? Then I remembered that Sammy the Rock, "Hard Rock," was under Tony, an up-and-coming mob enforcer. I never actually met Tony but I noticed the respectful way guys spoke about him when I visited Tony's haunts like the Dream Bar on South Collins and A Place for Steaks, another Mafia hangout. Later I found out Tony was in Miami working with Lefty Rosenthal, the Outfit's sports betting authority.

Geez, I thought laughing to myself. Between Mousy, Jackie Cerone and Tony Spilotro, these guys could open their own cemetery.

"No," I answered thoughtfully. "I ain't seen him."

Bob came back from Chicago with the line of credit. Now all we had to do was find a storefront, display cases, buy us a sign and some start-up merchandise and we were set.

"Okay," said Bob. "I figure it'll cost us each five grand."

Boy, I wondered. What am I getting myself into?

Rhonda kicked in Bob's half, which meant he hadn't lost his grip on her yet. I talked Kitty into fronting my share.

"If you're not on the up and up with this, I'm taking back every penny and John Bell won't be too pleased," she warned.

"Don't worry," I assured her. "I swear this is legit. Bob got us a credit line through his brother-in-law in Chicago. It's a cinch."

Within a week me and Bob were the proud owners of a wholesale house on Flagler. "*Sunshine Sales—Open 9–5,*" the sign proclaimed.

I think the saying goes, "Don't ask a leopard to change his spots," or something like that. Me and Bob should have realized we weren't geared for this sort of thing. More and more often Bob had pressing business at the track—namely a horse that couldn't lose in the third. Guess who wound up minding the store? I got bored earlier every day, so I locked the place and went home to sleep. Sometimes I wouldn't open till noon if the previous night's poker game broke up late.

Living with Kitty and her crazy double standard, I should have known better than to flirt with a couple of stewardesses who lived in the same building. Flirting was no big deal, but it didn't stop there. The leggy blonde named Debbie really knocked me out. I invited her to Sunshine Sales, hell-bent on impressing her. My efforts paid off. She acted like a kid in a candy store.

"Ooooh, I want one of those!" she begged.

"Take it," I said.

"Can I look at these earrings?"

"They're yours, sweetheart," I said opening the case.

Talk about bad timing. In walked a couple of wholesale hustlers. While they were admiring the pearls we just got in—two gross to be exact—I was admiring Debbie's butt. I should have hung the closed sign on the door, but now it was too late.

One of the guys walked over. "I'll give you $864 for the two gross, take it or leave it."

That amounted to three dollars per string, which sounded like a lot of money at the time. I vaguely remembered Bob saying something like "never go below $4," but I wasn't in a haggling mood. There was pressing business I wanted to conduct in the office with Debbie, so I agreed.

Two unfortunate events happened as a result of my overactive sex drive. The warning shot, a rock zinging through our plate glass window, kicked off round one.

Kitty charged through the front door. From her "take-no-prisoners" look, I knew the rock was only the beginning.

"You lousy bastard! I know you're cheating on me. You left Kathy alone while you nailed that stewardess."

There was no reasoning with Kitty. She conveniently ignored the fact that she was going everywhere with John Bell and they sure as hell weren't playing Gin Rummy. What did she expect me to do, join the priesthood? Before this thing went too far, I phoned Bell. I explained quietly that Kitty was going nuts. Bell talked to Kitty, calmed her down and advised her to leave. Later she told me Bell was itching to have Miami's police chief, Rocky Pomerance, arrest me, but she nixed it. It so happened Pomerance doubled as John Bell's bodyguard.

"Isn't that a conflict of interest?" I asked Kitty. She answered with a look that would turn a stewardess's warm, inviting flesh into cold marble.

John Bell leased Kitty a luxury apartment at 5415 S. Collins, in the magnificent Hampshire Towers situated on the ocean between the Hilton and the Four Seasons. He wanted to protect Kitty from "that maniac" me, so he paid a whole year up front for the pad with the beachfront view. What a laugh. Who was going to protect the maniac from that wild Sicilian?

Round two, the second unfortunate event, hit when Bob stepped on our plate glass window scattered all over the floor. "Shit, I can't leave you alone for a minute. And I told you not to take less than we paid for the fucking pearls. Can't you see, we're losing money! Now I gotta go to Chicago and see if I can straighten things out." What could I say?

I could tell Bob was not a happy camper. He told his family he'd sell everything we had left at closeout prices to pay off our debt. If he did that, I knew I couldn't pay Kitty back so I thought fast. "Listen, I have a couple of ideas. We can say we were robbed and collect the insurance money. Or we can burn the place down and collect the insurance money. Whatta ya say?"

Bob didn't answer, which meant it was a no-go.

Not long after that, Bob and Al Massey from the Travelers went into the real estate business. Guess Bob thought he could do better on his own, so we went our separate ways.

Without Kitty to share the rent, I was forced to find a cheaper place further down on Flagler. With no more Sunshine Sales, I concentrated on improving my poker game at the Travelers.

It was there I kept bumping into Lucio, Mussolini's twin. I would have swum to Cuba to play this guy, he lost so often. Getting Lucio to cough up what he owed was another matter. "I'll take care of ya," he'd say, raising those bushy black eyebrows. When he lost more than $60, he'd go on the cuff for a couple of hundred. What could I do? Lucio was a mob guy. I knew all too well what could happen if I dared to make waves.

One night Lucio's debt hit the $1,000 mark. He said, "Look. If you'll forget the grand, I'll make you an equal partner in my restaurant."

"Okay," I said, "You've got yourself a deal."

Maybe Sunshine Sales was a lost cause, but Lucio's would more than make up for it, I reasoned. Turns out the restaurant was losing money on account of the fact that Lucio was a lousy businessman. Whatever caused it to lose money, in my gut, I knew I could turn the restaurant around.

The next day I inspected my new investment during the lunch hour. Lucio's was dead. It didn't take a genius to figure out why. An old scratchy Enrico Caruso record played over and over on the jukebox. Ten small tables broke up the otherwise bare room. Nothing decorated the walls. As if that wasn't enough, harsh ceiling lights killed any hint of an inviting atmosphere.

When Lucio brought the food, a delicious steaming mound of spaghetti marinara topped with homemade garlic bread, I knew how I was going to fix things. Lucio sent for the Sicilian cook who doubled as the waitress. She was a very nice lady with two major problems: First, she could barely squeeze through the kitchen door. Second, her black mustache was so thick, she needed a shave worse than I did. From that day on I called her Mama Mia.

What a stroke of luck. Lucio announced he was leaving for Sicily the next day, leaving me in charge. Now I came up with a plan to get Mama Mia away from the customers. Her looks would drive away a starving man, but I couldn't afford to offend her.

I took Mama Mia aside. "I've decided to give you a raise plus I'm gonna make your job much easier," I told her. "From now on, all you have to do is stay in the kitchen and cook."

"Datsa so good," she gushed. "You are a wonderful boy." She planted a kiss on top of my head, which was no trouble since Mama Mia towered over me by a good two or three inches.

Next I hired Mama Mia's pretty young niece, Annie, as our waitress. Then I plastered the walls with travel posters of Venice, Rome and Naples. I strung white Italian lights around the posters, added red and white checkered tablecloths to the bare tables, stuck candles in Chianti bottles for centerpieces, and hung plants from the ceiling. I replaced Lucio's scratchy, out-dated records with Dino and Al Martino. Only one thing left to do—fix the air conditioner.

Now we had an Italian restaurant with excellent food and plenty of atmosphere. *Buono appetito*! The place really started to go.

Imagine my shock when Lucio came back and instantly flew into a rage. "Five hundred dollars you spent on this? It was fine as it was," he shouted. "And what have you done with my priceless Carusos?"

Kitty, on the other hand, flaunted the power she had over John Bell. All she had to do was hint that she liked something, and it was hers. The guy was so rich, he owned the forest they used to make his paper. In fact, one of his biggest accounts was the Miller Beer cartons. So what if Bell was this ugly, fat, bald guy who drank too much. He was worth $68 million.

Bell pleaded with Kitty to move into his estate but she refused unless he married her. Once Kitty had a guy hooked, she worked the situation to her best advantage. There was only one small detail standing in the way of their marriage—Bell's alcoholic wife Livonia, who refused to divorce him. Bell had her stashed away in some sanitarium.

Now that Kitty and Kathy were set up at the Hampshire

Towers, I got rid of the apartment and moved in with Lucio to save money. The restaurant buzzed with activity once the nearby college kids discovered us, but our limited seating of only ten tables, kept us from turning a profit. I told Lucio we ought to go into carryout. For once we agreed. Lucio ran the carryout from the kitchen, which kept his ugly mug away from the customers. I hired another good-looking waitress to fill in up front.

One observant customer noticed the change. "Hey, Slick, you're a genius," he said. "You've got the ugly ones in the back and the good-looking ones up front, but no one's the wiser."

There was one other reason our books stayed in the red. Lucio's drew a lot of mob guys for dinner on account of Lucio's connections. Meyer Lansky came by one night with three other Mafia big shots. You'd think Jesus Christ strolled in with the apostles. Lucio insisted on picking up Lansky's tab. It wouldn't have been a big deal except Lucio insisted on picking up the check every time Mafia guys showed up, almost every night. I should have realized the joint was just a front for other mob interests, like racketeering. They didn't need to make money on the restaurant.

As if we didn't have enough of a worry, business began to fall off when two uniformed cops made it a habit of parking their squad car in our lot while they schmoozed with the waitresses. The customers got fidgety with the cops always hanging around, so I called this friend of mine. He was a young kid who came around occasionally peddling hot TVs.

"Do you think you can find me a big snake?" I asked him.

"No problem," the kid answered with a smirk. "I can get anything you want."

Pretty soon the kid came back with this enormous snake. I broke out in a sweat just looking at it.

The next day the cops visited Lucio's as usual, their patrol car parked in the lot. While the two yacked it up, me and my young accomplice placed the snake carefully in their car. Actually, the kid put the snake in their car while I supervised.

Half an hour went by. That snake is going to die of heat exhaustion if those guys don't hurry up and finish their "brave cop" story, I groaned.

Finally, the two paid their bill and left. I studied my watch. Hell-raising screams pierced the silence exactly 30 seconds later. Then rapid gunfire. Every conversation in the joint froze in mid-sentence as dozens of shots rang out. That poor snake was history when those courageous cops had finished with it. After that, the cops didn't come around much.

Another snake slithered into my life the very next week. It all started when I ran into Vince Giannani, a jockey's agent out of Chicago, in the clubhouse at the Tropical Racetrack. On the side, Vince managed to find time for some strong-arm collection for the Outfit. We exchanged warm greetings.

"How are you doing, Vince?"

"Doing okay," he answered. "I've got Vasquez, one of the best jockey's in the business."

"I'm hustling like always," I piped in. "Hanging out at the Travelers Lounge."

"Yeah, I know the place. Bill Hardtack lives out that way."

With the small talk over, I could ask Vince what was really on my mind. "Anything look good today?"

Vince shrugged. "Naw. I like one horse in the seventh; he's five to one. After that, I'm going home." Vince fared a hell of a lot better touting horses than booking his jockeys. God knows, he had the perfect setup—access to the business side of a track, car pass stickers, and a standing invitation to visit the paddock.

"I've got a piece of a restaurant out on Coral Way called Lucio's," I told him. "We close around midnight. Why don't you come around for some of Mama Mia's famous pasta?" I reached in my pocket and handed Vince my card thinking that if I hooked up with this guy, maybe he'd give me more racing tips.

A few weeks later, Vince looked me up at Lucio's. He asked if

I'd like to go duck hunting with him the next day. Having nothing better to do, I agreed. I'd barely closed my eyes that night when Vince's persistent honking horn jolted me awake.

In the Everglades, Vince hired an outfitter guy to run us to our destination in one of those airboats, perfect for skimming over the shallow, grassy water. The outfitter expertly maneuvered the boat into a quiet part of the Everglades. He deposited me and my gear in these weeds. Then he left off Vince on the other side of the weeds just out of sight.

I perched myself on this T-shaped stick—a funny contraption that lets you "sit" while you're standing up—blowing my little duck caller for maybe 10 minutes.

Uh oh. I spotted a snake the size of a freight train coming straight at me. I pointed my shotgun at the Loch Ness monster, pulled the trigger and watched it rain tiny snake parts. Meanwhile, I beat a rapid retreat. That was the end of Mr. Snake. The only problem was my shots came within inches of hitting Vince. That was the last time he invited me to go duck hunting, which was fine with me. A snake I could kill. No problem. But I couldn't kill a duck. Who could kill something that goes quack, quack?

19

I figured if we were going to sink, maybe
it would happen while I was sleeping
and I wouldn't know what hit me.

IT **WAS ONE** of those days that made you feel like a million bucks even if you didn't have a dime in your pocket. I picked up Kathy on my way to the *Knot Guilty*. Kathy, a miniature version of Kitty, was really a grownup disguised as a little girl. Instead of playing with other kids, Kathy helped me handicap football games. She was just one of the guys and that's how they treated her. Whenever an outsider remarked, "Isn't she cute," Kathy would roll her eyes skyward and wither them with one of her looks.

Bob stopped by and the three of us sat around not doing much of anything. While I was busy admiring the scenery on a nearby boat—a shapely blonde in a bikini made out of three band-aids—a wolf-whistle five inches from my ear made me jump. Greg had sneaked up behind me. He brought along his friend, Joe, who installed windows for Greg's dad. When their window business slacked off, I'd drum up new customers with my slingshot and a few strategically placed BBs. Joe had a lean, muscular build and acted tough, but I was about to find out that he talked the talk but didn't walk the walk.

Out of the blue, Greg said, "Hey, let's go to Bimini!"

I dropped Kathy off at her mother's before we left. The last thing I needed was Kitty on my case. "We'll only be gone for a day," I told Kitty, still smarting from the chewing out she gave me after my last trip to Bimini. She shrugged, turning away in her backless spike-heeled shoes and closed the door.

The Knot Guilty sped toward Bimini fixed solidly on Jack's 111° heading. The water turned that unreal color you see on the cover of those exotic travel magazines, and the seas were so calm the boat could have steered itself. Nothing could spoil this perfection, I thought, with the breeze gently whipping my cotton shirt. Even the Hammerhead sharks racing beside the boat seemed like puppy dogs out for a romp.

Twenty minutes later the engine began to sputter. Then it died. We had to shut down the other motor because Jack said the boat would go in circles with only one prop. What we didn't realize during the hour or so it took Greg and Joe to fix the engine, was that we were drifting more and more off course. Finally we had power, but it never dawned on us dummies to correct our heading for the change of position. Because of the curvature of the earth, if you're more than seven miles away from land, you won't see it. And that's exactly what happened. We cruised right by Bimini without realizing it.

Now Jack's words came back to haunt me like a piece of undigested liverwurst: "You guys ought to get yourselves a ship-to-shore radio in case of an emergency." But I didn't have much time to dwell on our screw-up. We were losing daylight rapidly and we had to figure a way to attract the attention of a passing boat.

We scoured the *Knot Guilty* looking for a flashlight. In a pile of junk under the bunk, I located two flares and a flashlight with weak batteries. Great! Now when we spotted a boat we could signal it—except there were no other boats.

Around 2:00 a.m. Greg spotted a plane flying at low altitude. I lit one of the flares. It fizzled out; must have been old. A while later we heard the engines of another plane. I carefully lit the other flare. That one fizzled, too.

Much later that night we heard a third plane. Desperate to attract their attention, I signaled with the only code I knew—Dot

dot dot, dash. Dot dot dot, dash. It was the "V" for Victory sign we all learned during WWII. Miraculously, the plane blinked its lights at us. We jumped up and down yelling and cheering, convinced we were about to be rescued, but many hours passed and nothing happened. Too bad I never learned the code for SOS.

The entire next day was a blur of failed attempts to make contact. What an adventure, we laughed, joking about who would be the lucky guy to dive for our next meal out in the middle of the ocean. We had plenty of beer aboard, enough to stock a bar, but the only food the four of us had left between us was a lousy sandwich. At least our water supply would last a while.

No sooner had the sun abruptly exited the horizon, than ominous black clouds appeared out of nowhere. A brisk breeze kicked up the waves into frothy white-tipped tents that grew steadily into hills. Within a half hour the hills had turned into steep-sided mountains, dropping away into bottomless valleys.

The storm couldn't make up its mind what to do with us. It carried us to the peak of a monster wave only to plunge us down the other side. The plunging did a number on my stomach, just like the Bobs Roller Coaster at Riverview Park. As if up and down wasn't bad enough, the *Knot Guilty* rocked wildly from side to side nearly swamped by the giant sheets of water crashing on its deck. If a guy lost his grip, he'd get swept overboard. Things looked pretty bleak. Without power, we couldn't head into the waves to avoid capsizing.

This is it, I thought. We're going to sink. Imaginary headlines formed in my overactive brain: Bermuda Triangle Claims New Victims!

Resigned to my fate, I went below to lie down. As I savored every bite of that last sandwich—probably my final meal—the old optimism kicked in. I figured if we were going to sink, maybe it would happen while I was sleeping and I wouldn't know what hit me.

The next thing I remembered was the sound of complete quiet. I was afraid to open my eyes for fear I was dead. I was even more afraid to find out where I'd ended up.

"Hey, you gonna sleep forever?" A human voice, Bob's irritating one to be exact, brought me crashing back to earth. I bounded up the stairs squinting at the sun glancing off the mirror-like water. I couldn't believe it. The sea was as calm as a fishpond on a summer day.

But hour after hour dragged by with nothing in sight, not even a lousy gull. What's more, I seemed to be the target for Bob's frustration. "I should have known you'd eat the last sandwich. You think you're the only one who's hungry. . . ."

Loud mumbling interrupted our one-sided conversation. Oh, geez. It was Joe on his knees praying again. When Joe had pulled the praying bit before, Greg told him to "Knock it off! You want to spook us?" Now we all stared silently at Joe hoping he was getting through to the Head Guy.

While I watched Joe praying, reality hit me like a hard punch in the solar plexus. This wasn't an adventure; it was a nightmare. I tried to see the funny side, but my sense of humor registered "empty," just like my stomach. It looked like I'd never see my family again.

Meanwhile, Kitty was getting worried—so worried, she put in a call to the U.S. Coast Guard. The Coast Guard was ready to write Kitty off as a nut. "This crackpot dame says her friend's lost at sea in a boat called the *Knot Guilty*. What a joke."

Later Kitty told me her persuasive manner changed their minds. "If you lazy sons-of-bitches got off your asses, you'd find out the *Knot Guilty* is way overdue at its dock in Haulover."

It was our fourth day of drifting. I was so bored that I caught myself counting the number of hairs in Bob's ear as he snored away in a deck chair. I noticed a speck on the top of Bob's left earlobe. But the speck moved around. Then it got a little bigger.

Now I thought I was seeing a mirage. Nope, it wasn't a mirage. The speck was really a boat on the horizon that was inching toward us. I almost cried out. But I was afraid if I told the others, the boat would disappear. So I just watched the little boat come closer and closer. No one else saw it but me. Maybe I'm going goofy out here in the blazing sun? The way my luck's going, I thought glumly, it'll turn out to be a ghost ship looking for lost souls. Ours.

We went crazy with relief when it hit us that we weren't going to die. For some time, our rescuers had tracked our suspicious boat that was making no wake. Whew! If they hadn't been so observant, there would have been a wake, all right—the kind before you bury someone. The boat's red-faced, good-natured skipper agreed to tow us to Bimini, which was out of their way, for a hundred bucks.

I could hardly believe my ears when I overheard good old Bob trying to bargain for a better price. "Please shut up!" I wailed. "What's a hundred bucks? We're saved!"

Several hours later we docked in Bimini. I didn't even mind the pesky sand flies carving a meal out of my arm. Pretty soon I'd be eating a nice juicy steak of my own. But first I headed for the nearest phone to call Kitty. I thought she'd be happy to hear I was okay. Boy, was I wrong.

Kitty's shrill voice crackled over the wire. "See, you asshole. You almost took Kathy."

We docked in Miami Beach dog-tired but relieved our ordeal was finally over. A guy from the local newspaper sniffed around eager for any bone we might throw in his direction by way of a scoop.

"Get lost," I told him, too exhausted to deal with the annoying press.

Later that night I checked to see how things were doing at the restaurant. As soon as I walked in, there was Lucio wringing his hands. "Don't ever leave me like that again. I had to run the restaurant all by myself."

"I'm glad everyone missed me so much," I said mock seriously. "I promise. That's the last time I'll ever get lost in the Bermuda Triangle."

20

"He was standing by the open window and must have fallen out, officer." . . ."Ten feet from the building?"

LUCIO'S MAFIA BOSS, Dominick Marino, a Lucchese captain, managed the mob-run Lum's Restaurant across from the Miami Dog Track. His mood changed faster than Miami's weather. Dominick actually skipped along next to you until maybe you didn't laugh at his joke. The next thing you knew, his hypnotic eyes bored a hole through your brain with this meltdown stare. And he had an ego the size of Bensonhurst.

"You know if it wasn't for me," he boasted, "certain New York bosses wouldn't be where they are."

I had to admit, all the young bucks from the Lucchese Family checked in with Dominick the minute they hit Miami. Aside from playing strongarm for the family business, Dominick ran a crap game in Miami Springs. That's where I entered the picture. The Lucchese Family believed that my partnership with Lucio gave them ownership rights to me. Of course, I saw it differently. I went along with their cockeyed notion for only one reason—to stay alive.

Right about now an interesting thing happened regarding my future. It all started with these nice poker chips of mine that Dominick loaned to his friend, Tony Esperti, an ex-boxer who belonged to another New York crime family, the Gambinos. Tony operated a gambling joint in Miami Springs that attracted all the high rollers. I guess poker chips were in short supply.

Now most of the wiseguys from New York, including Dominick, hung around a mob joint called A Place for Steaks on the 79th Street Causeway. It was a mile down from the Bonfire and Jilly's, a restaurant owned by Jilly Rizzo, Frank Sinatra's bodyguard.

One night Tommy, a classy mob guy who owned A Place for Steaks, gave Tony Esperti a hard time over something. Tony was so upset he decided to whack Tommy. When Tommy walked into the club, Tony casually came up behind Tommy and emptied a few rounds into his head. Bystanders saw the whole thing, but Tony wasn't too concerned about witnesses. He counted on his ace in the hole—mob protection.

Maybe five or six hours later, Tony heard the police were looking for him. What did he do? He marched right into the police station. When the police asked him whether he fired a gun within the last 24 hours, he vehemently denied it. The police weren't as stupid as Tony thought. A paraffin test on his hands proved that Tony handled the murder weapon. Mob protection or not, Tony Esperti went to prison for life and that's how I lost my poker chips.

This led to a disturbing situation for me. With Esperti, Dominick's competition, out of the way, Dominick got the bright idea that me, Lucio and him ought to open a nice, quiet gambling establishment.

"After all," Dominick said, "Lucio's is doing so good we won't have no trouble financing a club." Geez, I thought. I'm getting in awfully deep with these thugs. I might be a lot of things, but a killer isn't one of them.

I was fishing for an excuse to get out before it was too late. "All this time we're partners," I told Lucio, carefully watching his reaction, "I've never seen any money because of all the comp meals and stuff. I need to make some dough."

Lucio raised his Mussolini eyebrows. "You'll have 20 percent of the new gambling hall. So what's your beef?" I could see it was useless to argue.

We found a loft on Seventh Avenue in Miami that at one time belonged to Lefty Clark, a gambling legend. The place was made to order. It had a steel door complete with a peephole from the old prohibition days. There was even a slide in the back of the club, a quick exit from the second floor down to street level. We converted the pool table into a crap table, and used four empty rooms for private poker games. During the day, customers could play short cards like gin rummy—small fry stuff. But nights were reserved for no-limit poker games. At $500 a night poker room rental, plus the take from the crap table, we began to turn a profit.

One day Dominick found out a Jew named Hymie was operating his own game down on the beach. Worse yet, the little guy was moving in on our customers. Dominick ordered me to bring Hymie over to the club. From the look in Dominick's bloodless eyes, I had a pretty good idea what was in store for Hymie. Reluctantly, a few mornings later I paid Hymie a visit. When I broke the news to Hymie that Dominick wanted to see him, raw fear registered on Hymie's crinkly brown face. I tried to reassure him that everything would be okay, but neither one of us believed a word I was saying. We both knew there was no refusing to see Dominick.

We arrived at the club about 10:30 and I made the pre-arranged call to Dominick. At 11:00 sharp the Mauro Brothers arrived, the Lucchese Family's muscle. There was no "Hi, how are you." Robot-like, each brother grabbed one of Hymic's arms and legs, walked him over to the second story window and pitched him out like he was yesterday's trash. The Mauro Brothers took off without saying a word.

Now Hymie was in his sixties. I knew the possibility of him surviving was slim to none. As soon as the two thugs left, I ran over to the window. Hymie was still moving. Thanks to the fact that the Mauro Brothers threw him so far, he landed on the grass. I wasted no time dialing the fire department. "A guy just fell out the window," I yelled into the receiver. "Send an ambulance over here right away." I ran downstairs to see what kind of shape poor Hymie was in.

After they took Hymie to the hospital, the police questioned me about the accident. I scratched my head like I was puzzled. "He was standing by the open window and must have fallen out, officer."

Long pause. "Ten feet from the building?"

Hymie lived, but it took him years to recover from all his broken bones. The more I thought about Hymie's condition, the more I worried. Was I next? It was clear I had to get away from these mobbed-up killers. If I had any brains, I'd leave while my health was still good. But it wasn't in me to bail out before I made some money for my trouble. Things got a whole lot worse—one week later, to be exact. . . .

. . . *Which brings me back to the* Knot Guilty *and the visit from the Mauro brothers with their disposable bundle that started this whole history. But, as it turned out, I didn't become food for the fishes after all, as I had feared. After completing their little task, one of the brothers grunted,* . . .

"We're done. Let's get the fuck out of here."

I finally exhaled now that I knew the party wasn't for me. But I wouldn't let down my guard until I planted my feet on solid ground. I was thinking how quickly Marshall Caifano flew into a rage at Valentino's a few years back. You just couldn't tell what they were going to do, especially the New York guys.

The sun was just making an appearance when me and Lucio slid into a booth at the restaurant. I wolfed down a big breakfast and plenty of hot black coffee. I drank so fast, the coffee burned my throat, but I was too hungry to notice. Funny how famished I was now that the fear had gone. Thinking back over the last several hours, I figured I was lucky to be the one doing the eating.

A couple of days later this idea popped into my head. Miami was swarming with old people who were dying like flies. In fact, they were exiting so fast, the city was running low on cemeteries. Dominick knew this judge who could be bought so, the next time I was in Lum's, I laid out my plan to Dominick.

"You know," I said, avoiding Dominick's creepy eyes. "With all these old people dying and nowhere to go, we could have burials at sea. It'll all be legit and think of the money we'll make?"

Dominick went crazy. If looks could kill I'd be dead. "YOU MORON!" he yelled. "Don't we have enough heat on us? If I ever hear you mention it again . . ."

One of Dominick's goons came over and whispered something in his ear. Dominick almost laughed until he remembered I was still there. But the mood had shifted. I never mentioned burials at sea again, but I still thought it was a great idea.

I couldn't seem to shake my association with the Lucchese Family. Another incident followed soon after our early morning drop. Me and Dominick were headed to our club late one night. We turned onto Seventh Avenue and nearly collided with two young Cubans driving some beat-up jalopy. One of the punks gave Dominick the finger as we passed them. We pulled over. Dominick slapped the kid who insulted him, which quickly turned into a full-blown fight. The four of us were going at it when a Miami police car screeched to a stop.

After the cops cooled things down, the two of us wanted to forget the whole thing. But the Cubans insisted on filing assault charges. One of the cops told Dominick he could file a counter charge.

Dominick answered, "Just because they're assholes, officer, doesn't mean we have to be assholes."

The cops had no other choice; they arrested us. On the way

down to headquarters Dominick whispered, "Keep your mouth shut. Everything will be okay."

The Cubans failed to show up in court, all right. Dominick had predicted as much and I knew it wasn't on account of his ESP. In fact, all attempts by the police to contact the Cubans led to a dead end. They just disappeared. A chill ran through me when I remembered what happened to Hymie. If I don't get away from these monsters, I thought, I'll be next.

While suspicious trash disappeared over the side of the *Knot Guilty*, something very different exited John Bell's yacht. Kitty phoned me at Lucio's with an invitation.

"You realize it's Kathy's fourth birthday tomorrow. I'm taking her to dinner at the Villas, and I want you to be there."

"Sure," I said. "I wouldn't miss it."

The Villas was the sort of restaurant where the strolling violin players flashed smiles that screamed, "Tip me." And all the waiters looked like they had a terminal case of boredom. I guess fun was strictly for the lower classes. But when they serenaded Kathy with "Thank Heaven for Little Girls," and brought out a birthday cake as fancy as the dress she wore, I could see Kathy got a big kick out of all the fuss. That's all that mattered.

Kitty launched into a fascinating story. It seems John Bell got wind that Aristotle Onassis was planning to sail his 325-foot yacht, the *Christina*, to Nassau on a certain date. Bell decided the timing was perfect to meet the famous Greek shipping magnate. Shmoozing with celebrities gave Bell a big charge, but he was fussy. A couple of years earlier Richard Nixon asked Bell if he could borrow Bell's yacht, the *Livonia*, to impress some big shots during the Republican National Convention in Miami. Bell turned him down flat. I had to hand it to Bell; at least he had good taste.

"We were cruising around the Bahamas looking for Onassis's yacht," said Kitty. "But Onassis wasn't showing up. The constant rolling was making me seasick so John anchored and we waited."

I heard that irritation in her voice that meant this was only the tip of the iceberg.

"On the third night out we argued in the yacht's dining room while our lobster dinners sat on our plates getting cold. I was wearing my designer evening gown—you know—the one John bought me the last time we went to Chicago." I glanced at Kitty's new cleavage and nodded.

"Well, I had enough of all this sitting around so I told John I wanted to go home. John shook his head no. That did it. I was so mad I told him *he* could wait on his fucking boat, but I was leaving. I stood up and ran out on deck. Without thinking I jumped into the shark-infested water. Naturally, John's crew pulled me out right away. I glared at him through my sopping wet hair. The smart ass just stood there laughing at my nerve. But I got my way. John ordered the captain to head for Miami."

Kitty sure had some balls, I thought. With a guy like Bell on the hook, all she had to do was crook her little finger.

Aloud I said, "Why don't you ask Bell to buy you a fancy house or give you some money? That way if he dies you'll have something."

Kitty smiled smugly. She'd come a long way from the insecure, tough-talking kid of five years earlier. She dropped the insecure part.

"I'm gonna let you in on a little secret," she whispered. "I plan to have it all."

Just when I thought my run of bad luck had turned the corner, another life-threatening experience knocked that foolish idea right out of my head. Kitty stopped by Lucio's to see me. Whenever she paid me a visit I figured that either a) I was in deep shit over something I supposedly did, or b) Kitty needed a favor. This time I lucked out; it was the second reason. Kitty's car wasn't running right so I loaned her mine until I could have a mechanic who hung around Lucio's fix hers.

That same night me and Lucio were enjoying a few hands of Five Card Draw at the Travelers. As usual, I was raking in the chips on account of Lucio's lousy poker playing when Kitty phoned. Now my car wouldn't start and she was stranded near a restaurant called Pumpernickel's across from the Hotel De Ville. Me and Bob Mauro had patched up our differences over Sunshine Sales and he owned jumper cables, so we headed over in Bob's car.

We had no trouble locating my '63 Bonneville on a corner behind Pumpernickel's. Bob pulled his car next to mine and I was about to hook up the jumper cables when a squad car with its lights off drove up behind my car to see what was going on. I stood between the Bonneville and a Buick parked in front of me.

Without warning this uninsured Cuban busboy, driving a piece of junk, plowed into the rear end of the squad car. The squad slammed into my Bonneville pinning me between my car and the Buick. Both of my legs were twisted into my curved front bumper and now my right leg bone stuck through my pants at a weird angle. I collapsed on the pavement. Through the stabbing pain I heard the cop's calm voice telling me not to move; help was on its way. Then everything went black.

The next thing I knew, I was lying on a table in the hospital with Bob bending over me.

"Do I still have my legs?" I whispered. "I can't feel anything."

"Yes," he said. "They're going to operate."

I came to on a gurney outside my room to the sound of someone's loud TV. It took me about 15 seconds to realize the noise wasn't coming from any TV. A real live loony was jumping around and hollering a few inches from my legs. The hall was deserted and I couldn't move to save my life. "Oh, God," I prayed aloud. "Please let me get to my room in one piece."

For the next couple of weeks I lay flat on my back in the hospital, my right leg strung up in a cast. I never realized how bad daytime TV could be. I was about to go nuts when Bob paid me a visit. "You know, you're really lucky you didn't lose both legs," he said. "If it wasn't for the curve in your front bumper . . ." How crazy, I thought. Here I am with a broken leg and it wasn't even a mob hit.

Kitty stopped by the day before they released me. "John wants to marry me," she said, clearly excited by the thought of being filthy rich. "But we can't get married until his wife, Livonia, gives him a divorce. Remember I told you she's in this asylum for alcoholics? Well, he can't serve her with divorce papers until she's out." I nodded my head yes, even though I was having trouble following Kitty's ramblings.

"Listen," she continued. "We're going to Chicago for a while on business, so you can stay at my place and recuperate . . . maybe spend time with your daughter."

"That's a great idea," I said. "Kathy can help me handicap the up-coming games."

"Yeah, that's nice . . ." Kitty floated out the door before I could tell her to have a good time.

Bob picked me up at the hospital, helped me in on the passenger side and threw my crutches in the back seat of his car. I felt like somebody's helpless grandfather. On the way over to Kitty's apartment, Bob reminded me that Nicky Pasquale, a friend of ours from the track, had only one leg due to an accident. "Why don't you invite him over?" Bob said. "Two good legs out of four ain't bad."

Nicky with his funny stories and gimpy leg became a regular at Kitty's place. One afternoon Bob was showing Kathy how to "middle" a bet when in stomped Nicky carrying a covered birdcage. "Okay you guys. I've got a little surprise." Nicky whipped off the cover to reveal a large black myna bird he won in a bet. The way the bird strutted around kind of reminded me of my father so we named the newcomer Charlie. Not only was he a knockout with his shiny black feathers and bright orange bill and feet, but Charlie the myna bird caught on to sounds amazingly fast. In less than a week the clever bird could match any truck driver's wolf whistle. His favorite phrase was "My name's Charlie and I like to play the horses." And after Kitty came back from her trip, Charlie learned to swear like a sailor. If they needed a myna bird in a mob movie, Charlie would have fit right in.

The apartment's location on the beach helped speed my recovery. I remembered hearing that horse trainers walk lame horses in salt water to heal them more quickly, so I did the same thing. I threw my crutches on the beach, grabbed my little inner tube and sloshed through the waves up to my thighs. Every day I went a little farther down the beach. At first I could only manage a few blocks without tiring. Then it was a mile. The more I walked, the better my leg felt. In about a month I could follow the beach all the way to the Eden Roc Hotel and back, nearly six miles. So much for the doctor's prediction that I'd probably never walk again. I think doctors say that to make you so mad you'll walk just to get even.

When I was off crutches I strolled along Collins Avenue for a change of scenery. Every day I saw Meyer Lansky, who lived next door at the Four Seasons, walking his dog. And each time he passed me he nodded. Funny, he never invited me over for coffee. With Lansky, that was about as likely as the president asking me over to the White House.

Jack Kearns found me a lawyer who agreed to work on a contingency basis. While we waited for my case to go to court, my lawyer told me the cop was totally negligent driving without any lights. He assured me the jury would award me a bundle.

If it weren't for Bob driving me to the track every day, I would have gone bananas. The guys I bumped into knew I wasn't working due to my accident so they tried to cheer me up. "Hey, Slick! Don't worry. Pretty soon you'll be driving a brand new Caddy compliments of the Miami Police Department." It better happen soon, I thought, because they just repo'd my car.

21

"Just remember," Dominick said.
"Sicilians never forget."
"That may be true," I answered.
"But the Irish don't give a fuck."

ONE OF THE guys who hung around Lucio's was Artie, a junketeer. He herded groups of customers to places like Las Vegas on pre-paid gambling trips called junkets. The casinos sponsoring the junkets usually came out way ahead because the customers were required to put up $5,000-$10,000 in the casino bank. Out of that front money, the casino returned only 10–15 percent in the form of customer comps. Lured by the hope of big winnings, the customers figured they'd take most of their cash back with them. They didn't count on the house's extremely favorable odds that sent most of them home with nothing more than lint in their pockets. The junketeer received a fat commission on the casino profit. And that's how Artie made a bundle.

Well, Artie had a private plane that seated eight. Every Friday night he flew me, Bob Mauro, Lucio, Dominick and a few other guys to the Lucian Beach Hotel and Casino on Paradise Island in the Bahamas. The odd thing was that these "up-and-backs," or quick, one-day junkets, didn't cost us a dime. We ate all the gourmet food and drank all the premium whiskey we wanted without forking over one cent. Artie just happened to be a good friend of Meyer Lansky who just happened to own a piece of the Paradise action. I figured since the mob was behind the operation, they had to be laundering money or something.

The next time Artie stopped by Lucio's I asked him, "Are you sure you want us to go along this Friday?

"Yeah, of course," answered Artie. I should have known he wouldn't tell me anything, but I couldn't let the thing rest.

We were flying over to the Lucian Casino one Friday in time to make the 7:00 p.m. opening. I turned to Dominick. "Artie must be losing a ton of money. What's the deal with these junkets?" I asked, knowing Artie couldn't overhear us on account of the din from the engines.

"Enjoy the food and mind your own fuckin' business." Dominick threw me one of his famous dagger looks that made his words seem like honey.

Kitty had her own take on Paradise Island. We were alone in her apartment when I told her my suspicions about Artie's junkets. "Funny you should mention it," she said. "You know my friend, Ronnie, the guy who owns the wig shop on Flagler? Well, he asked me to carry this wig box through customs on a trip to Paradise Island. I looked all over but I couldn't find him until I left the building."

"Kitty," I said. "Something funny is going on at Paradise Island. I don't think you should go there anymore."

"Maybe you're right," she said, her voice trailing off. "By the way," she continued. "Ronnie wanted to know would John Bell pay the ransom if anything happened to Kathy?"

I went nuts. "The motherfucker asked *what*?" I demanded. Charlie the myna bird went crazy, too. I could hardly hear myself think over his high-pitched screams. "My name's Charlie and I like to play the horses. Squawk! Screech! My name's Charlie and I like—"

"Will you please shut that fucking bird up!"

Kitty turned pale. She didn't realize Ronnie's real intentions were to kidnap our little girl. We talked it over and I decided to keep a close eye on this Ronnie.

Soon after our conversation an awful thing happened. Kitty was half an hour late picking Kathy up from school one day. By the time Kitty arrived Kathy wasn't there. Kitty searched the school grounds but no Kathy. When Kitty called me in a panic, I knew right away Ronnie was behind Kathy's disappearance.

A single event saved Ronnie's life—Kathy showed up. She got tired of waiting and decided to walk home. The wig man never realized how lucky he was to be alive.

We still went to Paradise Island once in a while, but I kept my mouth shut like Dominick told me. I was just getting over one broken leg.

Nicky Pasquale played poker at the club almost every night. I was surprised when he told me Dominick's crew was bad-mouthing me on account of my long absence due to my accident. They said I wouldn't get my share until I worked my shift. I got the same treatment when I went by the restaurant. Lucio's story was, "Business is off right now so you don't get your cut." Something better happen fast. Not only was I broke and without wheels, my court case still hung in Limbo.

When I finally made it to the club, I saw my big chance to get out of the hole. The place had a no-limit poker game maybe once a month that rented to a bunch of high rollers. It was nothing to see a hundred grand sprawled on the table. Just to buy in took a whopping $10,000 bankroll. No one would be dumb enough to take off a game with Dominick and his watchdogs sniffing around—except a guy desperate to make a score. An idea was taking shape in my brain that was too good to pass up, but it took a lot of skill and expensive props, plus $10,000 for the buy-in.

Bob Mauro got cold feet around Dominick and the Lucchese Family. Can't say as I blamed old Bob this time. That left me looking for another partner. Nicky, that likeable, one-legged character who played around with the numbers racket, was my second choice. He seemed cool-headed most of the time, but could Nicky handle the pressure while we were taking off a game? The scales tipped in Nicky's favor when he agreed to finance his own trip to the KC Card Company in Chicago to buy the props we needed. The KC Card Company was a legitimate outfit that sold mostly to magicians. We were about to perform a little magic of our own.

Our shopping list included a pair of infra-red, plastic contact lenses that allowed someone to read specially marked cards—the same red plastic used for the discard holder on a blackjack layout but much thinner. The invisible green paint on the doctored cards is made visible through a red filter that washes out the red pattern of the card so the green ink clearly stands out. That meant we could only use cards with the red pattern on the back. We also needed eight marked decks for practice and two decks in their original wrappers for the game. You need money to make money even when you cheat. In this case, Nicky's investment set him back $1,000 for the plane fare, props, motel room, and expenses plus ten grand for the buy-in.

When no thugs were around I'd put the "luminous" or marked deck into the high-stakes game. Already in the game and wearing the contacts, Nicky just had to read the cards and rake in the cash. We figured if I wore red contacts on my light blue eyes, I would have looked like one of those "red eye" photos. But Nicky's brown eyes easily hid the red tint.

For two weeks me and Nick huddled around Kitty's kitchen table playing poker until Nicky could read the cards, bing, bing, bing. When Nicky made a mistake, he'd throw the cards down in frustration. That was Charlie's cue to show off his new vocabulary with a "Fuck you."

The instant I returned to work, Lucio's was robbed to the tune of $600. No doubt about it—this was an inside job. What's more, I had the uneasy feeling that the Luccheses were trying to frame me for the robbery. Dominick pointed a finger. "You have the key to the office and you also know where the bank is kept."

In my defense I said, "So does Lucio."

"Yeah, but Lucio's Italian," Dominick snapped back.

I could see what was coming. They were either getting ready to move me out or take me out. I think the Lucchese Family was a little wary of Kitty because of John Bell's association with Rocky Pomerance, Miami's Chief of Police. I hoped the Luccheses just wanted me out of the state. Me and Nick had to move fast.

The following week a major Five-Card-Stud game came up. I took the doctored cards from the cabinet where we kept all the decks, breaking the seal so everyone could see. Nobody else seemed to notice, but Nick looked nervous when he anted up. Before long the pot held over $50,000. Nicky kind of stared bug-eyed at the cards because the lighting in the room was much dimmer than Kitty's kitchen. He had a huge stake in this game and couldn't afford to blow it. Everything was going smoothly when in walked Dominick.

"Hey, how are things going out front?" I stammered, trying to draw his attention away from the game. Dominick dismissed my question with a shrug and a piercing stare. He scanned everything in the room like some space alien with X-ray vision. I flashed him a phony grin hoping it would pass for the genuine article.

Had Bob been in the game, he would have played legit or maybe got up and sat out a hand or two until Dominick was gone. But Nick continued the scam, blind to everything but the game. Dominick caught Nicky's eyes burning a hole in the backs of the cards. Jeez, I thought, sweat collecting under my white shirt. Now what?

Watching Nick the whole time, Dominick asked me, "Are those cards okay?"

"Sure they are," I answered a little too quickly.

"Put in a new deck and hand me that one," he ordered, eyes still riveted on the game.

Dominick studied the deck, holding some of the cards up to the light. Then he shrugged and threw the marked deck in the waste basket.

"Well," he yawned. "I'm goin' home. I'm beat."

I waited maybe three minutes, then I casually walked over and retrieved the deck from the waste basket. Dumb mistake. Dominick walked back in, nailing me with his you're-going-to-die look.

"I wasn't gone five minutes and you flew to that deck like a homing pigeon. So why did you take the cards out of the trash?"

I thought fast. "Hey, you know how I hate to waste anything. The deck's brand new. I can use it for gin rummy." I gave Dominick my most innocent, unblinking blue-eyed look, but I could see he didn't buy it.

Dominick snatched the deck out of my hands. "I better check these out," he said, walking toward the door. "And they better be okay."

None of the guys knew what to make of our conversation except for Nick, of course, who had turned the color of chalk. We had a clean up guy who went for coffee and stuff. I called him in to watch the game and gave Nick the signal to meet me in the office. Back at Nicky's place, we hashed out our next move over coffee and some day-old donuts. Nothing came to mind. But the next day Nick and his wife decided the timing was perfect to head for Newark to visit the family. I checked into a motel on Biscayne Boulevard and laid low. I needed a safe place to think over my next move.

A few days later me and Bob quietly paid a visit to the *Knot Guilty*. I planned to cruise over to another spot to buy some time. We walked over to our slip. A couple of gulls were playing tag on top of the wheelhouse. The rest of the boat was under water. So much for that idea.

I phoned Kitty with the news. She responded in typical fashion. "Fuck 'em. Why don't you go to my place till things blow over? Those lousy bastards wouldn't dare try anything with me dating John Bell and you staying at my place. Dominick knows

Pomerance is moonlighting as John Bell's bodyguard." I decided to take Kitty up on her offer. Besides, where else could I go?

Now Kitty began getting threatening phone calls from Dominick's crew. She told them she didn't know or care where I was. To top it off, one time Kitty was stopped at a light on Collins. The Mauro Brothers pulled along side her and asked if she'd seen me.

"Look," she said. "If you want to find Slick, go ask Rocky Pomerance, our upstanding police chief. Otherwise, leave me the fuck alone!" Good old Kitty. In spite of her faults, she was the most loyal person I ever met.

I had to get out of this lousy situation in one piece, so I started phoning around Chicago trying to contact my old cellmate, Sammy the Rock. Sammy had come through for me in the past. I sure hoped there was something he could do for me now.

In the meantime, I was going wacky sitting around Kitty's place. I let Charlie out of his cage to stretch his wings. Watching him swoop around the apartment made me feel good. At least one of us could enjoy some freedom. Kitty came in one time and Charlie made a beeline for her. Shielding her head with her hands, she screamed, "Who let that fucking bird out?" I guess she had a bird phobia or something. While I coaxed Charlie back into his cage I thought, I know how you feel, Charlie old boy. I'm a jailbird, too.

Holing up in the apartment was driving me nuts, so me and Bob worked up a plan. I sneaked down the back stairs of the Hampshire Towers to the beach, climbed over a wall to the Hilton next door, crossed the lobby and met Bob out front. We'd drive to the Pompano Race Track north of Miami where we weren't likely to bump into any of Dominick's thugs.

I waited for Bob to pick me up one day, but no Bob. Forty-five minutes later I phoned him from the Hilton lobby. The guy couldn't even talk he was so broken up. Just as he feared,

Rhonda left him for the building contractor in Kentucky. With Bob out of commission and only Kathy and Charlie the myna bird for company, I felt like my life was ticking away and I was helpless to stop it. If only Sammy the Rock would call, maybe I'd have a chance to escape from those cold-blooded killers, the Lucchese Family.

My day in civil court finally arrived. Everything looked like it was going my way. Even the jury seemed sympathetic, winking and nodding in my direction. After all, the cop had no business turning his lights off. He should have had his squad light flashing. I knew something was up when the judge asked the two attorneys and me to talk in his private chambers. The judge threw out the negative testimony about the police officer. It seems my past felony conviction combined with the fact that I could produce no visible means of support were unfairly held against me. In spite of the new orders, the jury awarded me $5,000 in damages from the busboy. What a laugh. It cost me more to get my suit pressed for my trial than I ever saw from the lousy busboy.

A week later, which seemed more like a month, in waltzed a dazed Kitty. She couldn't stop gushing over her new present. John Bell had just given her a brand new 1968 Lincoln Continental, one of the first out on the market.

"That's great," I told her, still smarting from my trial. "You finally have something to show for all your hard work."

Even my sarcasm couldn't upset Kitty's good mood. Gee, it looked like she was on the verge of actually marrying Mr. Moneybags. Bell wanted to pay me a lot of money to divorce Kitty and make him Kathy's legal guardian. I told Bell to keep his money. I'd consent to a divorce because I didn't want to stand in the way of Kitty's happiness. But no amount of cash—not even a million dollars—would buy anyone the right to be Kathy's legal father. I was her dad for life.

Now only one thing stood in the way of their marriage—his alcoholic wife, Livonia. The soon-to-be ex-Mrs. John Bell had the nerve to threaten Kitty over the phone. "You won't live long enough to marry John. I'll make sure of that." I remembered how coolly Kitty handled the Lucchese threats. So it was no surprise when Kitty laughed off Livonia's menacing words.

John Bell exploded over his wife's phone call. He retaliated with a threat of his own. "That's it," he warned Livonia. "I'm cutting you and John Bell, Jr., out of my will and nobody can stop me." Bell was livid. He vowed to make Kitty and his other son, George, the sole inheritors of his multi-million dollar estate. John Bell and his namesake were on the outs. There were plenty of reasons why.

John Bell drank more heavily than ever. In a fit of temper, Kitty marched over to his estate one night, and broke all his whiskey bottles screaming, "You're drinking yourself to death!"

"That's okay," he said. "If I die you won't have anything to worry about. You'll inherit a fortune. I'm seeing my lawyer tomorrow to draw up a new will."

Kitty was a lot of things, but I know she really had feelings for Bell. When she said, "I hope he lives forever." She meant every word.

After a while I retrieved Kitty's Lincoln myself from the lower level garage. My car had been repo'd after my accident since I had no cash to make the monthly payments. First I cleared it with Pedro, the Cuban doorman at the Hampshire Towers. Only valets were allowed to bring up the residents' cars, but Pedro liked me. I'd spend a few minutes with him, ask him about his family. And I always made sure to tip him big. He never questioned why I wanted to get my own car. In Pedro's line of work it paid to mind your own business.

The jangling phone woke me. It was Sam's calm voice on the other end asking me how I was doing. I couldn't be happier if Ed McMahon had called. Sammy told me his hands were tied as long as I was in Miami. The Lucchese's wielded too much power. But he might be going to Las Vegas with Tony Spilotro, the new front man for the Chicago outfit. No one would touch me in Las Vegas, Sam assured me. The Mafia considered the town off limits for mob hits. I vowed to go even if Sam wasn't there. Now that I had hope, life was good again.

In less time than it took to read the obituary column, everything came to a head. Four days after their argument over Bell's heavy drinking, Kitty called Bell's private number. His housekeeper answered. "I'm so sorry but Mr. Bell died yesterday from a heart attack."

Thinking it was some kind of a hoax, Kitty immediately drove to Bell's estate. The guard ordered her to leave the premises. Kitty was too stunned by the news to think straight, but the situation seemed perfectly clear to me. Bell died right after he warned his wife he was cutting her and John Bell, Jr. out of his will. My suspicions didn't amount to a hill of beans. We couldn't prove foul play caused John Bell's death.

My old buddy, Jack Kearns, found Kitty a lawyer. She hired him on contingency to locate Bell's new will and report back to her. According to this lawyer, there wasn't any new will. Here I was the target of a vicious Mafia grudge, nearly broke, and Kitty's world had come crashing down around her. For once I knew better than to ask, "What more could go wrong?"

The next time Pedro the doorman saw me, he looked like he was having a heart attack. "Hey, Pedro, what's wrong?" I asked. "You look terrible." Pedro started to cry and shake all over. At first Pedro refused to talk, but I told him I wouldn't leave until he spilled what was bothering him.

"You know," he said in a hoarse whisper. "This tough-talking man came by earlier today and told me my family is in real danger. He knew my address and the names of all my kids. The man threatened to kill my family, one by one, unless I do exactly as he says."

Pedro looked like he still hadn't made up his mind to tell me everything. After a long pause he blurted, "I'm supposed to wipe my forehead with this white handkerchief when you drop off your car. The guy waited for over four hours in the room over there where we keep the keys, but you never showed up. He said he'd be back later. You're lucky . . . he just left." Pedro covered his face with his hands moaning.

It didn't take a genius to figure out that Dominick had read about John Bell's death in the *Miami Herald*. With Bell dead, Rocky Pomerance posed no threat. I studied Pedro, this religious little Cuban guy, who just wasn't cut out to be a stool pigeon.

I tried to convince Pedro he did the right thing. "Look Pedro," I reasoned. "Whether they shoot me or not, they'll have to kill you because you know too much." I repeated my favorite phrase, "Don't worry, Pedro. I have a plan." Pedro didn't look too reassured.

Next I checked into a motel. I dialed Kitty, told her where I was staying and repeated Pedro's story. "Listen, Kitty. Las Vegas is the only safe place for me to go. It's kind of a no-man's-land from mob hits. There's nothing for you here right now. Besides, you can hire a lawyer in Las Vegas and sue the shit out of the John Bell estate. So why don't you go with me?" I detected a faint sigh.

Even though Kathy didn't want to be left behind, me and Kitty thought it best to let her finish third grade in Miami. She could stay with the family of two kids from her school then spend the summer in Montreal with Kitty's folks. As soon as we were settled, we'd send for Kathy. But where would we come up with dough for Kathy's room and board, and her plane fare to Canada? My pockets were empty. Except for some jewelry Bell gave Kitty that she was saving for an emergency, the only stuff worth anything was Kitty's Thomasville living room furniture and bedroom suite that John Bell had bought for her. Through a newspaper ad, she sold it all for a fraction of what it was worth. There was no time to haggle for a better price. We needed the cash in a hurry.

I had a pressing matter to settle before we left Miami. The Lincoln was so loaded down with Kitty's clothes we needed heavy-duty shocks to carry the extra weight. Charlie the myna bird rode quietly in his covered cage in the back seat as we inched our way through traffic on South Collins. "Drive over to Lum's Restaurant," I told Kitty, patting the .25-calibre Beretta in my coat pocket. "I need to talk to Dominick one last time."

"You're crazy," she answered. "You're going to kill him. Don't go."

"No," I said. "I've got to tell Dominick I'm leaving town for good, try to convince him to call off his bloodhounds. It's our only chance to make it to Las Vegas. . . ."

Kitty's temper started to flare but this time I stood my ground. "You can't change my mind. It's made up."

The street corner in front of Lum's was packed with the early lunch crowd, but a guy was just pulling out. I turned to Kitty. "If anything happens to me, don't wait around. Drive straight to Las Vegas." I checked my pocket one last time and walked over to the restaurant.

I spotted Dominick talking with a couple of customers. My sudden appearance threw him off guard. For a second his jaw dropped like he saw a ghost. Then his face turned an ugly shade of purple when he realized I wasn't dead.

"Join me for a cup of coffee?" I tried to act casual, but my knotted stomach was telling me something else. We slid into a back booth facing one another. I counted on the fact that Dominick wouldn't want any trouble in his place. It would be too messy.

I met Dominick's famous stare like a steel plate facing a blow torch, talking fast so he wouldn't interrupt me. "Okay, Dominick. I'm leaving Miami for good. Why not let bygones be bygones? And don't forget the things I did for you. Hey, remember the time I fenced that diamond and then split the take with you? And I couldn't exactly tell you ahead of time that me and Nick were taking off the game. Naturally, we were planning to cut you in all the time."

This was all bullshit, of course. But I knew we wouldn't make it out of Miami unless I cooled things down with Dominick. Dominick hadn't moved one muscle while I was talking. If it wasn't for the scorching heat from his eyes burning a hole through my forehead, I'd have thought I was looking at a department store mannequin. Dominick's thin lips began to move. Here it came . . . the final decision.

"Just remember," Dominick said. "Sicilians never forget."

"That may be true," I answered. "But the Irish don't give a fuck."

My job was finished. I got up and walked out.

We sped along the highway south of Miami wrapped up in our own thoughts. That was the second time I'd heard the line about Sicilians. The first was when an old prohibition gangster named Roger Toughy was gunned down by the Mafia after he did 20 years in the joint. He lived near me and Betty on Polk Street in Chicago. Toughy had made a lot of enemies with the Mafia because he refused to knuckle under. It was Sammy the Rock who told me, "Some of those old Sicilians never forget." This was one time I prayed the Sicilians had a short memory.

PART THREE

Las Vegas
1970–1993

22

Everyone you ran into in Las Vegas had their
monogram on their cuff . . . except for Vic Damone.
He didn't think VD would look so good.

WE FINALLY HIT Las Vegas just in time to catch a postcard-perfect sunset. I had that old tingling feeling like when I first stepped off the train as a skinny kid in an Air Force uniform. I could almost hear the ding, ding of the slot machines paying out. Boy, the city had grown. This new, glitzier Las Vegas was a beautiful sight, especially to an ambitious guy with a yen for excitement and a fatter bankroll. Already I felt better with the heat off, and I'm not talking about the temperature. Even Kitty's mood improved.

Our westerly route took us along Tropicana Avenue to the Strip. Only in Las Vegas would you see a drugstore sign that read, *We offer sympathy and aspirins.* We cruised down Las Vegas Boulevard checking out all the hotels and billboards to see who was appearing. Thousands of flashing lights spelled out big names like Sinatra and his Rat Pack at the Sands and the hot new act, Siegfried and Roy, in the Stardust's Lido show. By the time we reached Sahara Avenue, traffic had thinned out and the wattage had dimmed. Cheap motels and wedding chapels, both touting "great deals," popped up about half a block further north. I spotted a motel across from the International House of Pancakes, got us a weekly rate, and we crashed for the night.

In the morning after breakfast, I walked down to the Sahara Hotel and Casino to see what the action was like. I noticed one of the poker dealers was Lou Goldman who I'd known from the Devonshire. His daughter, Brandy, married Buddy Greco, the singer. I met Lou on his break and we arranged to get together after his shift. Connections are everything, especially in a big "juice" town like Las Vegas.

With several hours to kill, I decided to check out the Stardust Casino about a block down the street. I remembered the last time I was there with Kitty on our way to California, just passing through. This time I was scouting for permanent action. I ran into Wheels, a Chicago getaway driver Bob Mauro introduced me to on that last trip. Wheels was a "line-loader" just like Bob. And there was Harry Tinderella, a Chicago maitre d', working as floorman. Geez. The place was crawling with Chicago Outfit guys, more than the last time. Almost every direction I turned, there was some mob guy I recognized from the Devonshire dealing blackjack, roulette, craps, poker or working in the pit.

I made sure everyone knew I was job hunting. As Bob Mauro had found out, there's no way a guy can make a living hustling cards in Las Vegas. The mob would chop you into little pieces if they caught you. On the outside chance maybe things were different, I asked a few guys about short card games like pinochle or gin rummy. No dice. The casinos shut out all competition. I'd been a thief most of my life so I really didn't want a legit job. I'd tried that and it didn't work. But at the moment, I didn't see any other option. Dealing sounded as good as anything until I could find another angle.

My informants told me my best bet to break into Las Vegas as a new dealer was downtown Las Vegas, or Glitter Gulch, as the locals call it. But how would I do that, I wondered? Mind you, there were no dealers' schools. The casinos did hire shills—salaried players—to start up games. Eventually, you learned the ropes and could wind up as a dealer. Maybe it was worth a try?

I walked back to the Sahara and played blackjack until Lou's shift was up. He took me to a little place on the Strip across from the Tropicana called The Leaning Tower of Pizza, a big mob hangout. In the parking lot I noticed a bunch of guys in black pants and white shirts. That was the official Las Vegas dealer's uniform. You could guess how much a guy made by the name printed on his green felt dealer's apron. If it said "Sands" on it, you could bet the guy was taking home at least $200 in tips a night. He'd make sure the name showed clearly for everyone to read.

All dealers on the Strip were still men, by the way. It would be some time before Stardust manager Al Sach's girlfriend became the first woman dealer on the Strip. But in 1970, women were only allowed to deal downtown.

Lou introduced me to Jasper Speciale, the owner of the Leaning Tower. Jasper preferred to hang out in the restaurant away from the swinging bar that attracted the big names and a hoard of wannabes. Jasper was a made Mafia guy and probably the biggest loan shark in town. With no legalized sports books in the hotels, business was brisk for Jasper. He'd only book your bet if someone okayed you. Then you settled up with him on Tuesday after the Monday night football game. Me and Jasper became friendly, but I watched my step around him because he was with the New York mob. The bad taste in my mouth from the Luccheses still lingered like spoiled Italian meatballs.

If you didn't do business with Jasper, there were two other sports books—Lefty Rosenthal's Rosebowl, and the Churchill Downs. Frank "Lefty" Rosenthal, or "Mr. Rosenthal" as he insisted people call him, brought sports book betting to Las Vegas. Lefty really knew his stuff, starting out as a bookie for the Chicago mob when he was still a teenager. Too bad Lefty's ego needed constant feeding. Later, that attitude would hurt his career. Most of the time I hung around Bob Martin's Churchill Downs where I met even more guys I knew from the Devonshire. I felt right at home.

A couple of days after we moved in, our motel manager told us the guests were going crazy on account of Charlie the Myna bird's wolf whistle. The manager liked Charlie so he agreed to let us keep the bird in the office until we moved into an apartment. People came in off the street just to hear the talking myna bird say, "My name's Charlie and I like to play the horses."

We started at the bottom—Kitty as a keno runner at the Frontier and me as a shill at the Castaways, the worst casino on the Strip. It happened to be directly across from the Sands, the best casino on the Strip. The longer I stuck around, the more I realized the Strip was where it was at.

Before I could work, I had to take the referral slip I got from Marty Kutsin, the casino manager at the Castaways, over to the Las Vegas Police Station so I could get a gaming card required by state law. I felt uneasy going into a police station voluntarily, but I knew I'd be barred from working in this town without the proper ID. The form I filled out asked about a felony conviction. If I lied, they would have traced my police record from my fingerprints and discovered my felony anyway, so I checked the box marked "convicted of a felony."

When I took my completed form up to the clerk, she asked to see my "pink card." She explained that in Las Vegas, a felon has 48 hours to register with the police in order to receive a sheriff's card, or "pink card." Convicted felons could work legally in Las Vegas as long as they registered with the police. Now I really felt weird talking to a police lieutenant, but he didn't give me any trouble. He saw that my felony was over 15 years old, so he signed the paper saying it was okay to work. When I brought the original clerk my paperwork, she told me how lucky I was they let me work. Lucky to work? What a town!

In no time the blackjack dealers at the Castaways were teaching me how to deal, even though I was a lowly shill. I already knew how to handle a deck of cards and "cut" chips. That's when a dealer takes a stack of chips out of his rack and breaks it down so everyone, especially the pit boss and the eye-in-the-sky, can see exactly how much he's paying out. Dealing cards in a casino has a special procedure. For example, the cards are shuffled exactly the same way every time, two shuffles, a riffle and a shuffle. And a dealer learns how to "pitch" cards using the index finger so they land precisely where they should without being exposed. About

80 percent of these procedures are the same no matter where you work. The other 20 percent vary from casino to casino.

When a dealer altered his moves from the accepted system, either by accident or on purpose, he immediately called attention to himself. If the pit boss missed it, the eye in the sky—a guy pacing a catwalk above the dealer—usually spotted the error.

Once in a while the shift manager let us shills deal for a couple of hours. I gained valuable dealing experience and made good tips, but my real income came from cheating. I couldn't resist the temptation of all those chips sitting right in front of me, like a kid in a candy store. So, after my first time dealing, I asked Al Sorentino to be my agent. He was a Kansas City mob guy—a fellow crossroader—who owned a wig shop in the Commercial Deli Center, a retail strip where all the Las Vegas insiders hung out. It was nothing to see entertainers, casino workers and mobsters kibitzing with one another. Me and Al worked out a set of complicated signals to cheat the house, like leaning on the table a certain way. It took exact timing to outfox the pit boss and the eye-in-the-sky, but we managed.

Now that we both had jobs, me and Kitty found a furnished one-bedroom apartment off Flamingo, a few blocks from the Strip. It was time to collect Charlie the Myna Bird and send for Kathy so she could start fourth grade. Kitty kept her jewelry, worth maybe fifty grand, stashed in a box in the dresser. She didn't trust banks.

Kitty took out a ring she'd pawn for Kathy's plane fare and held it up to the light. "I don't know," Kitty sighed. "It seems like we're going down instead of up."

"Don't be silly," I answered. "You'll have a ton of jewelry. As long as we can both work, money ain't gonna be a problem."

"Maybe you're right," she said, but didn't sound too convinced.

Life was very different from what Las Vegas became later. It was a side that visitors rarely saw—a small, friendly town where everyone knew one another. If a guy asked for a ride home, you always said yes because you knew he couldn't live more than ten minutes away. The entertainers and casino employees mingled like one big family.

For instance, I usually hung out across the street in the Sands lounge killing time before my shift. Louie Prima, who was appearing there, spotted me sitting alone and said, "Hi Slick. Have you eaten yet?"

"No. Not yet," I answered.

"Well, come over and eat with Keely and me."

Everything went swell until Louie and Keely got into this big argument at the dinner table.

"Hey, you two," I piped in. "Me and Kitty argue exactly the same way except we don't have to keep smiling while we sign autographs."

We all laughed and went our separate ways.

People liked to dress sharp in Las Vegas, especially at night. In fact, almost everyone you ran into in Las Vegas had their monogram on their cuff . . . except for Vic Damone. He didn't think VD would look so good. The town wasn't the best place for Vic. He liked to gamble too much. But Vic was great—just one of the guys.

Then there was Lefty Rosenthal with his narrow-toed shoes when everyone else was wearing round-toed shoes. Now, Lefty was a very smart dresser—one of the best, but those shoes had to go. When I pointed to mine and told him his were out of style, he just walked away. The next day I happened to see Lefty again. Without cracking a smile or saying a word, he pointed to his shoes. They had round toes.

By a stroke of luck, me and Kitty had the same day off so we decided to take Kathy to a movie. There was only one movie house in town, the Red Rock Theater on Charleston, usually packed with locals. The tourists were too busy gambling. Besides, they could always catch a movie back home.

We arrived at our apartment to find the door wide open. I stopped Kitty from running inside, fearing someone might still be in the place. Borrowing her little Cobra 38 snub-nose, I cautiously made a sweep of the apartment, decided the coast was clear and waved to Kitty and Kathy. Kitty made a bee-line to the dresser. By some miracle, all her jewelry was lying in a heap on top but nothing was missing. We couldn't figure it. Why bust in and leave the jewelry? Then it dawned on me. Charlie must have gone into his act in the other room. The guy dropped everything and took off thinking someone was home.

"You know, Kitty," I laughed. "We've got ourselves a $50,000 burglar alarm named Charlie. Ain't that something?"

The next day Kitty went straight to the bank and put her jewelry in a safe deposit box.

Later, I told Jasper and some of the guys at the Leaning Tower what happened. One guy said, "You're lucky they didn't steal the bird."

"He's right, Slick," said Jasper. "You know maybe you should keep him here for a while? It'd be a lot safer and the customers will get a kick out of him."

Within 24 hours, Charlie was holding court at the Leaning Tower of Pizza.

A few days later, opportunity appeared in the unlikely form of a little Silver Nugget dealer by the name of Bitsy Ross. I bumped into Bitsy, an old-time Chicago bookie and friend of Lefty Rosenthal's, at the Rosebowl. It was hard not to like Bitsy, this short, bald, friendly little Jewish guy with the gift of gab. It seemed like everything he did was on the up and up, but Bitsy liked to talk a lot, so I watched what I said around him.

Bitsy may have been a friend of Lefty's, but he didn't think twice about describing Lefty's misfortunes in vivid detail. It seems there was some "evidence" that Lefty was cheating on his income tax. The FBI indicted him and threatened to close down the Rosebowl. Bitsy got Lefty a young upstart attorney nobody had heard of by the name of Oscar Goodman.

Just then Shecky Green, the wacky comedian, made an appearance. Fearless Shecky wasn't afraid of anything and started singing, "The FBI is breaking up that old gang of mine." Everyone in the joint cracked up except Lefty, of course. Lefty had a very strange sense of humor, like the time he put a tear gas bomb in one of his own bathrooms that cleared the place out. No one could figure out why he did it. But this time, Lefty wasn't laughing.

On Bitsy's advice, I drove over to the Silver Nugget in North Las Vegas to ask the owner, Major Riddle, for a job. Riddle also owned a piece of the Dunes. If anyone had a lot of juice, this guy sure did.

I passed by the old Moulin Rouge, a black and white club, closed long ago. Back in 1947, when I was in the Air Force, you saw more prejudice in Las Vegas than in Mississippi. Colored people had to stay in their own neighborhood on the West Side and all the hotels and casinos were strictly off limits to them except when they were on stage entertaining. It was years later during the Rat Pack era when Sammy Davis, Jr., became the first colored guy allowed to stay in a "white" hotel on account of Frank Sinatra's pull. Sinatra threatened to take the Rat Pack elsewhere unless Sammy could stay at the Sands. Sands big shot Carl Cohen reconsidered when he thought about the revenue he'd lose.

Bitsy also told me that Joe Louis, the ex-boxing champ, was host at Caesars Palace, one of the ritziest places in Las Vegas. Boy! Things really were changing.

I was to look up a guy named Obie Orlander, a one-time bookkeeper for a lot of Rush Street nightclubs in Chicago. Obie used to bet big time with Riddle and that's how he wound up as general manager at the Nugget. Obie gave me a warm reception on account of Bitsy sending me. In no time I was introduced to

Obie's casino manager, Jimmy Payne. I could tell Jimmy was the kind of guy who knew everyone worth knowing in Las Vegas. He told me to keep in touch. Judging by his friendly attitude and strong eye contact, I figured I had a good shot at working there.

One day that same week I was playing poker at the Stardust. Sitting at my table was a gum-chewing, hyper guy named Southbend Johnnie, a high-stakes poker player from—you guessed it—Chicago. Johnnie looked as dago as they come, but he talked like a used car salesman. A suitcase brimming with jewelry, which I figured had to be hot, lay on the floor next to him. We made small talk between hands.

"Hey, Slick," Johnnie asked. "You want to make some money?"

"What do you have in mind?" I said, never one to pass up an opportunity.

Johnnie immediately began ticking off the prices of the rings, gold watches, chains and other stuff in the suitcase. Then he made me an offer.

"Take the whole lot and get what you can for it. Then come back and we'll settle up."

I couldn't believe my ears. For all Johnnie knew, I could hop a plane out of there before he left the table. But I acted like it was no big deal, picked up the suitcase and walked out.

About two hours later I came back with $1,200 plus the jewelry I didn't sell. Johnnie peeled off three $100 bills for my efforts. Not bad for a few hours of easy work. Chomping his gum, Johnnie suggested I meet him at the Riviera the next day and maybe he'd have a little more business for me. His brother was partners with E. Walker, who owned a piece of the Riviera, so Johnnie's room was comped.

The next day I met Johnnie at the Riviera and we went to the Leaning Tower of Pizza for a bite to eat. I noticed that the air conditioner was set higher than usual. I warned Jasper how Charlie was a tropical bird and couldn't stand too much cold. "No problem," he said. "I'll take care of it."

At my suggestion, we headed for the Silver Nugget where I quickly spotted Jimmy Payne talking to one of the pit bosses. Even though I was with Johnnie, I really wanted Jimmy Payne to offer me a job. Within a few hours, Southbend Johnnie had dropped nearly $5,000 at the crap table and it didn't look like he was about to quit. Now Jimmy, who was watching the action, must have been mighty pleased by what he saw because he took me on the side and told me I could start dealing there tomorrow. Only a few months in Las Vegas, and I was already juiced into my second job.

The only problem was that the Silver Nugget, located in North Las Vegas, had different gaming cards than Las Vegas. And if you worked downtown, you needed a third gaming card. The routine was familiar. Before my shift, I marched over to the police station and got myself a second gaming card. If it was any other town and someone saw me hanging around the police station that often, they might have wondered. But this was 1970s Las Vegas. There was a whole new set of rules and the mob called the shots.

I'd been working at the Nugget a few weeks so now me and Kitty could afford a nicer apartment. It was time to take Charlie home from the Leaning Tower. Jasper collared me the minute we walked in. I sure didn't like the look on his face.

"Remember you told me to keep Charlie out of the cold air, Slick?" Jasper was as nervous as an ex-con in a lineup. "Well, I put him outside and he had a sun stroke and died."

Kitty went ballistic. She called me every name in the book. I shouted back that it wasn't my fault and then all hell broke loose. By the time the cops arrived, Jasper barred us from ever stepping foot in the joint again. Great. This was just what I needed. Now I had another New York mobster breathing down my neck.

Kitty kicked me out of our new apartment. I didn't want to stir up more trouble with Kathy around, so I moved in with a guy named Marty, a dealer at the Frontier. He had an apartment way south on Las Vegas Boulevard, out in the desert, called the Paradise Spa. The complex had a fantastic gym with punching bags, a whirlpool, and two swimming pools—my kind of place.

I liked to work out on the heavy bag and so did Jimmy Flood and Al Sicliano, two ex-boxers. Years later, Al ended up as a highly respected judge for the boxing matches held in Las Vegas. Jimmy Flood was a real crowd pleaser, but he liked to bug people. Maybe that's why a couple of mob guys shot him in the stomach. He was also a bodyguard for Al Sachs, the GM at the Stardust, until Jimmy made fun of Al's son's long hair and Al fired Jimmy.

Once in a while world heavyweight champ Sonny Liston came around to work out. This guy had superhuman strength. Mike DeJohn, a heavyweight fighter from Buffalo, New York, told me that when he fought Liston on February 18, 1959, Liston hit him so hard that Mike had to lie down. And Mike's no slouch. One time I asked Liston about his fight with Mohammad Ali. Liston just laughed and winked. Later Liston would die from a drug overdose. Funny how no one ever heard about Liston using dope until after his death? I remembered all too well how it did a number on my boyhood chum, Jack Bailey. Taking dope's a crapshoot and it always wins . . . which leads to a tragic story about a guy named Brady, a craps dealer I met when we both worked at the Castaways.

Late one night while I was dealing, a huge ruckus broke out at the craps table. The cause of the problem was none other than Frank Sinatra, taking a break from the Sands. Sinatra screamed at this poor craps dealer Brady that he'd placed a bet on number six, but Brady held his ground and politely insisted that Sinatra was wrong. You could hear a pin drop. Every eye in the joint was riveted on the craps table. This would have been a perfect opportunity to snatch some chips, but I was more interested to see what happened. Just when it looked like Sinatra was about to punch the kid out, Dean Martin stepped in.

"He's not worth it, Frank." Dean's familiar voice soothed Sinatra's ruffled feathers and the whole thing died down.

I walked over to Brady in the dealer's break room. It was the first time we'd really talked.

"You know, Sinatra could have had you fired," I told the tall, lanky guy whose shirttail never stayed tucked in.

Brady shrugged and laughed. "Yeah," he said. "But he was wrong and I just couldn't let him get away with it."

From that minute on, I decided Brady was my kind of guy and we started to hang around together. In spite of his surprisingly bold move, Brady was laid-back and easy going—just like me—so we hit it off right from the start.

Brady would say, "Let's go gamble."

"I'm broke," I told him.

"That's all right," he said. "You're my partner. We'll split my tips."

When we blew his tips, we went home.

Brady may have been the most generous guy I ever met—generous to a fault, in fact. But it was his trusting nature that set him up for trouble.

I'd been working at the Nugget for a couple of weeks when a frantic Brady called me one night while I was on my break. We met in the coffee shop after my shift. Poor Brady was so shook up he could hardly talk. Then everything came flooding out like someone pulled the plug on a drain.

"You see, Slick. This Texas jerk started to come around every night and shoot craps at my table. Well, the guy was a real loser but he had this beautiful girlfriend named Gloria who started coming on to me. At first I didn't believe a girl like her would give a guy like me the time of day. Maybe she was just playing around to make her boyfriend jealous. Anyway, me and Gloria began to see each other on the sly. I couldn't bring her to my place with my mom living there and everything. So I set Gloria up in an apartment." Brady threw me a hesitant look.

"Go on," I said, realizing Brady was really hooked on this Gloria. "Then what happened?"

"To make a long story short, this bad ass boyfriend—who Gloria said deals dope—asked around and found out about Gloria's apartment. He even knows where it is. Tonight he came by on my shift and made a big scene, saying he'd kill me if I didn't leave Gloria alone. I could tell he meant it."

Brady took a deep breath and tried to pull himself together. I was getting hotter by the minute, but I wanted to hear the rest of Brady's story so I kept my mouth shut.

"Slick, you gotta come over to Gloria's with me right now. I'm afraid this creep is gonna be there and I don't want to go alone."

I didn't need any coaxing. Brady was in way over his head and I sure wasn't going to stand by and watch my friend go down the tubes over some crazy broad and her dope-dealing boyfriend.

"What are we waiting for? Let's go."

We pulled up just as Gloria and badass were leaving her apartment. The pair looked way too chummy. Brady and him got into a shouting match. I tried to break things up when in waltzed the cops. They took everyone's name and escorted us three guys to our cars. I told Brady to forget about Gloria, tried to convince him that she was just using him. Of course he didn't listen. Suckers like Brady never do.

Maybe two weeks later I decided to go over to Brady's. His mother told me she hadn't seen him in a few days—not since these two men came by looking for him, flashing some Texas Ranger cards. They told her they wanted to talk to Brady. She said he'd be back in a little while, but he never showed up and the so-called Rangers never returned. If his mother looked worried, I was downright sick at what I was dead certain had happened to Brady. I forced a smile, thanked her and told her I'd check things out.

I gambled that maybe the police could do something. I was wrong. Without any hard evidence to back up my story, homicide didn't seem overly concerned about my suspicions. Brady's disappearance nagged me for a month. The longer he was missing, the more convinced I was that Brady met some awful fate.

Then an item appeared in the *Las Vegas Review-Journal*. It read something like, "Hand discovered sticking out of the desert attached to dead man's body." Cause of death was a single bullet hole in the back of the head. Gut instinct told me it had to be Brady. It was. A police detective took a full statement from me. Naturally, I cooperated. But it was a little late to save Brady, I thought with disgust.

The Nevada state's attorney asked me to appear as state's witness after the FBI pinched the dope dealer and Gloria in Texas. I figured I had to do anything I could to avenge my friend. During my testimony I was asked to point the dope dealer out in court. He threw me one of those you-mess-with-me-and-you're-history stares, but I looked him squarely in the eye.

"That's him . . . that's the guy who murdered my friend."

The dope dealer got a life sentence and I had the satisfaction of putting him there. I knew I did the right thing even though it meant working on the same side as the law. In a way, I did it for Jack Bailey, too.

23

His wife answered the door wearing nothing but a
flimsy nightgown, a ton of makeup and a smile.

WHO SHOULD I bump into at the Churchill Downs, but Sammy
the Rock. He was the same as always—quiet and deep.

"Boy. If it wasn't for you, Sam," I said pumping his hand. "I'd
probably be lying at the bottom of Biscayne Bay chained to a
cement block."

Sammy just smiled knowingly and nodded. He took me
down to the Bacchanal Room in Caesars Palace, one of those
ritzy restaurants which means they can serve you cold soup on
purpose. Our meal was comped by Mokey the casino manager,
a good friend of Fifi Buchieri, Sam Giancana's top strong-arm
enforcer. The Feds nicknamed Fifi the "lord high executioner"
after Buchieri, Jackie Cerone and others brutally tortured then
killed William "Action" Jackson. Lefty Rosenthal had learned
a thing or two from Fifi back in Chicago. Even though Lefty
wasn't a made guy on account of being a Jew, he still carried a
lot of weight in the Outfit. And Sammy the Rock was friends
with Fifi's brother, Frank. With Mafia guys, you didn't use the
word "friend" loosely. If you said he's a friend of "mine," it meant
the guy was an outsider. But if you said he's a friend of "ours," it
meant the guy was at least a mob associate.

A few days later, Sammy introduced me to Tony Spilotro. Sam
was part of Tony's crew. Of course, I'd heard all kinds of stuff
about how Tony, a feared enforcer (some say at least 22 hits) ran
Las Vegas for the Chicago Outfit now that Marshall Caifano was
out. Tony also operated a jewelry-theft ring on the side. When
the Outfit found out about Tony's moonlighting—especially

since they weren't getting their cut—it was the last straw following a string of problems that eventually cost Tony the biggest price of all.

Tony seemed to take a liking to me, not that I tried to get on his good side. It wasn't my thing. Plus Tony would have spotted anyone sucking up to him in a minute. Through the years, I came to know a different Tony from the stone killer who could whack a guy as easily as ask him the time of day. I had no complaints. Only eight months after hitting town, Tony juiced me—an average dealer at best—into the Chicago Outfit's premiere casino, the Stardust. I still couldn't get used to the fact that when you have juice, nothing's impossible in Las Vegas.

Kitty was doing pretty well for herself, too. I stayed in touch on account of Kathy, plus communication got a lot easier now that Kitty was mellowing out over the "Charlie incident."

I wasn't the only one to work out a juice deal. Kitty landed a job as cocktail waitress at the Aladdin because she knew Stevie Blue, head of the powerful Culinary Union. Funny, even though she couldn't tell a seven-seven from a seven of spades, she still made a damn good waitress. In fact, it wasn't long before she was serving cocktails in the Starlight Lounge at the Stardust, and hauling in tips by the truckload. No doubt about it. Kitty had balls—the kind that attract guys like John Bell. Even Tony Spilotro became a fan of Kitty's when she shared an apartment with Tony's girlfriend. He told her he made buttons when he was really a "button man," or Mafia soldier for the Outfit. I laughed till my sides ached.

One time me and Tony were having a cup of coffee at his brother John's restaurant, the Food Factory. Tony remarked how tough it was to find dependable help.

"You know Slick," Tony said, appraising me with those unreadable, dark eyes. "That Kitty's a real standup broad. I'd pick her before a lot of guys if I needed something important done."

It didn't take a genius to realize Tony wasn't talking about waiting on tables. I just nodded agreement.

Dealing at the Stardust might be okay for a guy who wanted a legit job, but I was getting burned out real fast. The same grind would have killed me after a while. Back in Chicago, when I had a bunch of mouths to feed, I would have done almost anything to bring home a steady paycheck. But going to work now was like doing time in Cook County Jail. I figured I had to steal enough money so I could retire. Besides, I was never one to hang around a joint too long. I got bored after a while.

Another Stardust dealer who wasn't geared for work was Jimmy Kodolinsky. I called him Twiggy because he was skinny, just like the British model. Our boss, shift manager Frank Cursoli, me and Twiggy would sometimes bullshit over coffee during a shift break. One time Frank asked me and Twig to go with him on a business trip for some Outfit guys.

"You know," Frank said. "Some of the guys in Chicago want me to check out a casino down on the Nevada-Arizona state line. If it looks like a good deal, maybe I'll get a piece of the action and there'd be something in it for you guys, too."

The following week, the three of us flew down on a private plane. We landed on a small dirt strip next to the highway in Bullhead City, Arizona. Problem was, to get to the casino we had to take a cab north to Davis Dam—the nearest bridge that crossed the Colorado River—then drive south once we were in Nevada. One hour and a car-load of dust later, we pulled up to crumby little Riverside Casino and the sorriest-looking ghost-town sort of a motel. There was Bullhead City across the river where we'd just been—so near yet so far. The casino owner, a guy named Don Laughlin, took us on a tour.

"Right now the dealers live above the casino, but that's going to change," Don informed us, flashing a smile that would have put any Las Vegas marquee to shame. "I bought this bankrupt bar for only $35,000 down back in 1966. Eventually, I plan to build a bridge across the river just north of the casino." Frank rolled his eyes at me and Twiggy when Don's back was turned. We all knew the place was hopeless, but we went through the song-and-dance routine anyway. No sense wasting a plane trip.

Frank told his Chicago connections to forget it. "The place will never go," he laughed. Little did Frank know that, a few years later, Don coughed up $4.5 million out of his own pocket to build that bridge between Bullhead City and Laughlin, as it was now called. Now that Laughlin was easily accessible to both states, it became one of the hottest areas in the entire country and it's still going strong. With my rotten judgment, no wonder I ain't rich.

But Las Vegas was filthy with deals. I met a crazy guy at the Stardust—crazier than most, that is—called Gil Fracassi. Gil brought up-and-back junkets to the Stardust from L.A. or San Diego. Gil, who owned a fancy house in L.A., would fly in free as many people as could fill a plane. They'd stay ten hours, eat, drink, gamble then fly home. The Stardust picked up their tab and Gil charged each person a $20 service fee. Management recouped their costs when the gamblers became victims of the thing every savvy casino boss banked on: the big house advantage. Gil started to have trouble when his customers took their fat wallets elsewhere to gamble. Naturally, the Stardust lost money.

"Gil," I said, trying to cheer him up. "You ought to see Bitsy Ross at the Trop. He might be interested in doing a junket deal over there."

Gil went to see Bitsy on my advice and the two wound up as partners. The way Bitsy got into the Tropicana—the best tipping casino on the Strip—is very interesting. He started hanging around with Spinning Wheel Sam, a world champion "middle bettor." It was hard to tell who Sam was actually betting since he got a lot of numbers on a single game from around the country—places where he had good credit. Then Sam placed bets on both sides of a game in order to "middle it" for the best return. (It would take too long to explain how middle betting works, but there are plenty of books that describe this type of hedge betting to the uninformed. If you don't know how to middle a bet, you ain't a pro and you're missing out on big money.) Everyone wanted Sam's picks, even Lefty Rosenthal.

Most of the time Spinning Wheel Sam was a loner, his residence a well-kept secret. Or maybe nobody wanted to hang around Sam's 20 cats. But Bitsy would invite me and Sam over to feast on his wife's great dinners. I stopped going when I realized I couldn't get any insider tips with these two betting both sides. You needed a larger bankroll than I had to do that sort of thing. Sam was in tight with the owner of the Tropicana, a guy named Deil Gustafson who had just bought the Trop in 1971. And that's how Bitsy got in as a blackjack dealer, another juice deal.

Something told me it was my turn to make a little dough when this big, flabby guy wearing a navy blue running suit with red and white stripes on the pants sat down at my blackjack table. He had to be the worst player I ever saw, but he was full of himself. Las Vegas chews up guys like this and spits them out every few minutes and I loved watching it happen. Funny thing was that this goofball didn't seem to care whether he won or lost.

Every time I asked Mr. Macho, "Sir, do you want a hit or are you gonna stay?" he'd just shoot me this shit-eating grin like he was laughing at some private joke.

When the three other players left in disgust, the guy asked me if I knew Nick Pasquale from Miami. Uh oh. It sounded like some kind of a setup so I shrugged. Now that it was just the two of us, I had a chance to check out the leather pouch the guy carried over his shoulder, like a giant purse. Boy, I hope this jerk isn't coming on to me, I thought. When he suggested I meet him in the coffee shop after my shift, I had to admit, curiosity got the best of me. Did Nick really send me this character?

We took a booth in the back of the restaurant. Right away I didn't like the guy's pushy manner, but I was itching to find out his angle.

"Hi, my name's Dr. Siegel," he said, reaching out a damp hand. "I've lost a ton of money in these Las Vegas casinos through the years. But I met a fellow in Miami recently—a friend of yours, he says—by the name of Nick Pasquale. He guaranteed that if I could find you, not only would you get me my money back, you'd show me how to make a few extra bucks. So I tracked you down to the Stardust."

Dr. Siegel couldn't be more pleased with himself if he'd discovered a foolproof way to mint money. Nick must have realized I could make a killing off this greedy sucker. That cagey Nick sent him to me, like a big present just waiting to be unwrapped. I went right into my act.

I leaned close, looked Siegel in the eye and said, "So you want to cheat with me, right?" Siegel barely nodded, but his cocky grin said volumes.

"When you cheat a casino you have to be good," I continued. "And I mean very good. Your timing has to be absolutely perfect. You know, it could take years to teach you all this. It's very dangerous and, if we get caught . . ." I let my voice trail off on purpose to see whether he took the bait. By the dollar signs glittering in Siegel's eyes, I could see he was hooked.

"Let's go up to your room," I suggested, mentally rubbing my hands in glee. "I might be able to help you out."

I noticed Siegel left a measly 50-cent tip. When we were walking out, I told him I left my keys in the restaurant, went back and gave the waitress an extra two dollar tip. Now I knew another important bit of information: this guy was unbelievably cheap.

Siegel didn't have his room key so he knocked. After a few minutes, his wife answered the door wearing nothing but a flimsy nightgown, a ton of makeup and a smile. She gave me "the look." It was probably the same look she gave every guy she met, meaning she didn't object to using her "charms" if she really wanted something. I wondered what she could possibly have in mind, especially with her husband in the room. Then I remembered a certain judge and his perky, blond wife who put the make on me years ago in Miami. Hell, you never could tell what screwy things people had on their minds.

The suite was loaded with extras—wet bar, two TVs, sitting room, two baths . . . the works. Knowing how cheap Siegel was, I figured it was probably comped. It was. We sat down and I picked up the deck of cards lying on the table. I gave the cards my expert Las Vegas shuffle. Then I silently flipped up every card in the entire deck, stopping just before the last card.

"Okay, the next card's gonna be the eight of clubs," I announced. Naturally, I called it right. It was a very old trick that looked like I had a fantastic memory but was actually simple card-counting. A ten-year-old could do it on his first try. In fact, Siegel was so impressed by my little show he promptly pulled out a stack of $100 bills from that big leather pouch of his, counted out five crisp bills and handed them to me.

"Let's go down right now and you can play for me, Slick." I didn't mind spending his money so I agreed. Before you knew it, I was up $1,500. Of course, Siegel was happy about that. Then, as luck (and the house odds) would have it, I lost it all. I thought Siegel was mad, but he just shrugged. That gave me another clue: Siegel had deep pockets.

At my suggestion, we went back up to his room. Siegel and his wife were leaving in the morning, but my con was just beginning. First, I had to win back their confidence.

"You know, even if you have a fantastic memory for cards, you can still lose because there's a lot of luck involved. The football season is about to start and I happen to know a fantastic handicapper by the name of Jimmy K, who everyone calls Twiggy. He knows all the big bookies in town so he gets strictly inside tips. If I can talk him into booking some football bets for us this season, it's guaranteed we'll make a lot of money."

The Siegels looked like a pair of billboards with the words

"greedy sucker" plastered all over their faces. "Okay," Siegel said. "How much is this little venture going to cost?"

"Well," I scratched my head like I was trying to figure the whole thing out. "First you have to rent an apartment, put in some phones, take care of the local cops and the rest is bankroll. I don't know exactly how much we'll need until I talk with Twig. He's the expert."

I gave Siegel my phone number, so they could talk it over, and left. If they didn't turn me down right then, it was a cinch they'd go for my pitch. I swung into action. I called Twiggy and filled him in on the details.

"I gotta hand it to you, Slick. You sure come up with some real winners. How much do you think the guy's worth?"

"If his big pouch loaded with money is any indication, I'd say we could quit our jobs after we've milked this guy."

Siegel called the next morning, just like I knew he would. He wanted to meet Twiggy as soon as possible. I waited maybe three hours, like I had a hard time tracking Twiggy down, then I called Siegel back. I told him Twiggy was tied up until the following day so it would look like Twig was a very busy guy.

I swear Twiggy should have been an actor. The next day in the Siegel's room, he went through this spiel like he'd done it all his life. He even looked the part with his unshaven beard and fat cigar clenched between his teeth.

"Listen, you two, I don't have time to do favors for just anyone, but seeing as you're friends of Slick . . . With the right amount of cash, plus my years of experience, we can make a fortune."

Now Twig just sat back, took a few puffs on his cigar and waited for everything to sink in.

Siegel popped the question me and Twig had been expecting, "How much will we need?"

"Around twenty thousand," Twig fired back.

"I've only got ten?" offered Siegel.

Twiggy looked at me and said, "Let's go. They're wasting my

time." All the way to the door my heart was in my throat. Just as I was about to grab the door knob, Mrs. Siegel stopped us.

"Wait a minute. Do you know who I am?" She saw our blank looks.

"I'm Bob Hope's cousin . . ." She revealed this bit of info as if I gave a shit. Personally, I didn't care if she was married to the Pope, but I knew we had to let her ride out her little power play.

" . . . and our credit is excellent so you can get your twenty grand tonight." Well, Siegel may have been carrying the purse, but Mrs. Siegel pulled the strings.

Ignoring Mrs. Siegel's talent for name-dropping, I turned my attention to her husband. "Here's what we're going to do . . ."

According to my plan, Siegel started playing blackjack. After a while, he asked to take out a marker for a large amount of money. The pit boss gave it to him right away since his credit was so good. I waited a little while and then I had him paged. "Dr. Siegel, Dr. Siegel," came the impersonal voice over the paging system. Siegel followed my directions and left the casino. Then we went to another casino and pulled the same stunt, then another. At the end of the evening, Siegel handed over $20,000.

The next morning, me and Twiggy dropped the Siegels off at the airport. I was all smiles and reassuring pats on the back. "When you two return, we'll have everything ready," I told them. "And don't worry about the markers. You have two months to pay them off."

The Siegel's plane hadn't even left the ground when me and Twig were chopping up the twenty grand. That same day we both quit our jobs at the Stardust and Twiggy and his wife went on a vacation. As for me, I wasted no time doing my favorite thing—playing poker every day. The MGM (now Bally's) had a good poker game going. The dealers no longer stole from the pot like the old days when a dealer was hired by how many chips he could snatch during his shift. I haven't missed too many days at the table. I guess you could say I'm serving a life sentence playing poker.

We weren't done with the Siegels yet, by any means. Twig returned in a few weeks, rested and raring to go. We rented a cheap apartment and put in a couple of phones. Then I called Siegel with the new phone numbers. I'd show him the setup when they came out the following week. Just to give the operation a hint of secrecy, I whispered the code name Siegel was to use whenever he called. It was the word "sucker" in Japanese—a little phrase I picked up while dealing. Had Siegel done his research, he might have realized we were out to cheat him, but I gambled that greed gave him tunnel vision. I figured right again.

The Siegels flew in two days after pre-season started. I held the door open to the white Cadillac Seville for a beaming Mrs. Siegel, the car I rented for $200 a month with her money. I checked them into the Frontier on another comp of Mrs. Siegel's and we went up to their room.

Once we were behind closed doors I spoke in a confidential whisper. "Everything's in place, but you'd better wear dark glasses just in case the Feds are watching. It's just a precaution."

Mrs. Siegel turned pale and her makeup cracked ever so slightly. "I think I'll wait here, if you don't mind."

Twiggy was "taking bets" over the phone when me and Siegel walked into the apartment. Actually, Twig was talking with Jolly Joe, a bookie who turned up dead years later at the bottom of Lake Mead. Siegel was so antsy he barely glanced at the place, nodded to Twig and headed for the door. Good thing me and Twig didn't make eye contact or one of us might have blown our cover. Siegel was like a nervous kid with his hand in the cookie jar, praying he wouldn't get caught.

During dinner with the Siegels that evening, I continued the con. "Twig is going like gangbusters," I explained in my sincerest voice. Someone told me that if I didn't blink, my large, blue eyes took on a kind of innocent look. "But the winning/losing patterns haven't been established—it's too early in the season—which means we're not bringing in the big money yet."

I went into a long, technical explanation that the Siegels

couldn't possibly understand. It was strictly bullshit. They bought the story and came up with another ten grand.

Two days after the Siegels left, I drove over to see Kathy. It had been a while since I'd seen my little girl. Kitty's anger toward me had disappeared, which always seemed to happen just when she needed something from me. She told me how she got in a big fight with her roommate, who called the cops, and now Kitty was being thrown out. Okay, I had some extra cash from the recent score. Maybe it was time to bring Kathy and Kitty to live with me? Realizing I was setting myself up for another Sicilian eruption, I decided to do it anyway. That's because I either forget easily, I'm stupid, or both.

Me and Kitty made a down payment on a new two-bedroom condo at Maryland Parkway and Tropicana for $18,000. It even had an attached garage, plus the mortgage payment was only $75 a month. Then I bought new furniture and fixed the place up. Gee. It was the first time I owned my own place.

We continued to bleed the Siegels to the tune of about $80,000. Our last story was that we were robbed, but Siegel finally had enough. He went so far as to come out to Las Vegas and threatened to have me and Twig killed if we didn't return his money. Here was another golden opportunity. I got on the horn right away and called good old Bob Mauro in Miami.

I explained the situation. "Listen, Bob. You can offer to do the hit, which you got from an anonymous tip. You negotiate for half up front, then me and you split the front money 50/50?"

Bob called me a week later. "Just like you said, Slick, the guy wanted to hire me in the worst way, but he was broke. Nice try, though."

24

At his wake, I looked at Chucky and all I could
see was that little red-haired Irish kid whose
parents moved out and didn't tell him.

I WAS WINNING AT poker, but since I never worried about tomorrow, money went out about as fast as it came in, just like the
ocean's ebb and flow. It never occurred to me that one day that
would all change. . . .

Now my ex called urging me to talk to our daughter, Betty,
about moving to Las Vegas. She was depressed and things weren't
going too well for her. I still had some dough from the Siegel
business. With no job to tie me down, I figured this was as good
a time as any to visit Chicago.

I discovered Betty, around twenty-three, had turned into a
fine young woman with a sweet personality. She reminded me
of my mother. But I noticed a kind of tired, strained look on
her pretty face. She lived in an apartment around Western and
Belmont and tended bar in a blue-collar tavern within walking
distance. The area had fallen on hard times, a seedy version of
the old neighborhood where I'd met Betty's mother at Riverview
Skating Rink many years ago. Betty seemed happy enough to see
me but I could tell something was missing in her life.

"Hey, sweetheart, why don't you come to Las Vegas and check
the place out? There's a ton of good jobs out there. You know I
have a lot of connections."

Betty smiled and mumbled something vague, but didn't answer.
I let her think over my offer and flew back to Las Vegas.

In about a week, Betty and her girlfriend, Kathy, stepped off the plane at McCarran Airport. The airport was so small and had so little traffic that I could park by the side of Tropicana Road and watch their plane land. When Betty introduced me to her friend, I recognized her last name. Me and her dad, Bob, who died quite a few years ago, grew up together. I remembered the time we had two hot TVs in the back of Bob's car when the cops pulled us over.

"Who owns the TVs?" one of the cops growled.

"You do," I answered. They took the TVs and left.

I smiled at Kathy, thinking how lucky she was to get out of that lousy environment. Maybe here she could make something of herself. I escorted the girls down to the Culinary Union hall, since they needed union status to work as waitresses in Las Vegas. We went to the Aladdin and I got Betty a temporary waitress job on account of knowing Stevie Blue, head of the union. After two days, they were going to transfer Betty to cocktails, but she didn't like the place and was going to quit and go back to Chicago. As luck would have it, while they were packing to leave, both Betty and Kathy got a call that the Union Plaza downtown badly needed cocktail waitresses. They both landed the jobs and that was that.

Speaking of jobs . . . Lucky for me, Tony Spilotro got me back into the Stardust. My old boss, Phil Diaguardi, was none too pleased but what could he do? The main guy had spoken and I don't mean Lefty Rosenthal, the Outfit's Stardust frontman. Phil would have loved to bust me because he had nothing to do with hiring me. I was juiced in by Tony.

Money wasn't the only thing coming and going in my life. The first of a string of old friends drifted into the Stardust. It was none other than Chucky Douglas from the granny scam. On my break Chucky filled me in on the latest. It seems Jerry Patten died some time ago and Chucky married a girl he met on vacation in Australia. Friends my age were dying like flies . . . from unnatural causes.

"Yeah, Bill. I'm still doing the granny bit but it's about burned out. Too many people are wise to it. I got busted a few years ago and did some time."

Now Chuck launched into what he was doing in Las Vegas. "My wife met this international burglar in Chicago—first rate—while I was in the joint. He happens to be in tight with Tony Spilotro and that's how we came to Las Vegas, on account of Tony."

I could see that his wife was basically supporting him now and it didn't sit too well with Chucky. He needed to make money on his own. This time around I asked Chucky to be *my* agent. Before long I was flashing the hole card to him on first base—the seat to the dealer's left—when nobody was looking. Or I'd make change for a black chip ($100) when he'd only given me a green chip ($25.) Our cons worked especially well when Orientals sat at my table. They turned a blind eye no matter what went on. Me and Chuck had an unspoken rule: Never force the con. If everything wasn't absolutely perfect, we waited.

The Stardust used the Griffin Detective Agency for their security, the guys who came up with a black list of all the undesirables in town. But the agents never spotted a thing. I always checked out Phil Diaguardi to see if any detectives were lurking around. Funny, how Phil would fidget with his collar and act sort of jumpy when the private dicks were near the pit. I could read him like a "tell" in a poker game. Or Phil would disappear for a while thinking he'd come back and catch me in the act or something. I gave him a pleasant smile and a wave. Secretly, I laughed my ass off.

Soon the old restlessness took over and I was itching to get away. But I needed a plan to take off work since I'd only been back for a couple of months, but what? I was standing at my dead table waiting for live action when a guy passed by whose arm was in a cast. That's it!

The very next day I had this Outfit doctor friend put a cast on my arm and give me a note saying I'd broken it. He made it so I could easily slip in and out of the cast. Phil Diaguardi looked at me like an executioner whose victim was snatched away at the last minute. He knew I was up to something, but there was this cast and the doctor's note. He had to let me off. The employment rules were in my favor in another way. If a guy couldn't work due to sickness, he was entitled to half his share of the dealer's combined tips. Hey, I could use that money to pay for my plane ticket! When I asked Phil to autograph my cast, he turned his back in disgust.

That night I told Chucky I was going to Chicago for a while —did he want to come along?

As soon as he said, "No thanks, Bill. I think I'll give the granny game one more go," I had a bad feeling in my gut that maybe he should have accepted my offer.

Instead I said, "Good luck, Chucky. I'll see you when I get back."

This time I looked up my son, Tom, now in his early twenties. He was scratching out a living as an auto mechanic and home was a lousy basement apartment. Tom was polite enough, but you could cut his resentment with a knife. I sure didn't blame him for feeling that way. When had I ever been around? Here was my son, my own flesh and blood, and I realized I hardly knew anything about him. If I hadn't been conning my way around the country, I would have been there for Tom.

I tried to find a bridge that might connect us if only for a minute. "Tom, why don't you just come out to Las Vegas for a vacation? You know Betty's doing great and she wants you to stay with her if you decide to look for a job."

"Yeah, maybe . . . I'll have to think about it." Tommy forced a smile, not wanting to open up years of unspoken feelings.

I left Tom with a lump in my throat. Maybe if I checked out the action at a few of my old haunts, I'd cheer up. The familiar scene hit me the minute I stepped inside the Hawthorne Racetrack. Air filled with stale smoke and shady-looking guys scrambling to place their bets changed my mood. I looked down on the track where the jockeys paraded their horses before the second race. Now I was in my element. I breathed a sigh of relief.

There was Mousy who I hadn't seen since I bumped into him at the Travelers Lounge in Miami. To complicate matters, Mouse was a good friend of Phil Diaguardi, my boss. Uh-oh. He was walking my way and I didn't have my fake cast on. If it got back to Phil, I was history.

"Hey, how ya doin'?" I said, silently checking out the guy he was with. It was Mugsy Tortorella. Even other mob guys feared Mugsy because he'd do absolutely anything for a buck. Mugsy was tight with an old friend of mine who introduced us when I lived in Chicago. We exchanged greetings, then Mugsy wandered off to place a bet.

"So you two know one another, eh?" Mousie was clearly impressed that I knew Mugsy.

"Yeah, he worked with a couple of friends of mine," I answered.

"Did those friends know that Mugsy thought Marilyn Monroe's ass was the best he's ever seen?"

Now, any ordinary outsider would have said to himself, "Where did that remark come from?" But I knew how mob guys talked. Mousie was testing me, but he had to do it in a roundabout way. He couldn't come right out and ask, "Do you know Mugsy was the guy who killed Marilyn Monroe and put dope up her ass to make it look like she died of an overdose?" No. Mousie and I both would have been hit—him for talking and me for knowing too much. So, Mousie used this indirect way of finding out how much I knew. I'd heard about Marilyn being taken out by the mob through extremely reliable sources, but I never let on to anyone. Okay, there was only one way to play this if I wanted to live a few more years.

"Gee, I never heard that one." I managed to sound like maybe Mousie was making a joke and I didn't get the punch line.

He glanced at me with these watery eyes that seemed to take in my every thought. Apparently he was satisfied I didn't know anything because he let the subject drop. I was itching to ask a ton of questions like, was the FBI in on it? . . . and were they afraid she was getting too close to JFK? . . . but I just nodded. The less you said to these Outfit guys the better. And the fact that I didn't pump them, made them trust me and want to open up about stuff. I first noticed this with Sammy the Rock. The more I kept my mouth shut, the more he talked. I guess it's a natural instinct with people who know a lot of stuff they can't talk about in public. They get the urge to show what a big guy they are. My one real slipup had been when I asked Dominic's goons what was in the bag they were wrestling aboard the *Knot Guilty*. I had to be more careful.

Just then I spotted Big Joe Smith from the Crossroads, the first strip joint I'd worked in when I was a green kid who knew nothing about conning marks with fake champagne. I told Mousie I'd catch him later and walked over to Joe. He was the same big, ugly guy—a Frankenstein monster knock-off. He took down my phone number since him and his wife were planning to move to Las Vegas. Was anyone I knew staying in Chicago?

I was back in Las Vegas and pretty soon my son Tom came out, which kind of surprised me considering our last meeting wasn't exactly a festive occasion. Tom's best bet was to become a valet parker, which meant he had to join the Teamsters union or no job. Tony Spilotro got the head of the Teamsters union to let Tom join even though it had been closed to new members for some time. In a few weeks, Tom started parking cars at the Union Plaza where his sister Betty worked. He pulled in about $150 a day in tips. Not bad for the new kid on the block.

As for Billita, she was raising a family in a Chicago suburb and writing for a local newspaper and Mary trained race horses in New Orleans. It made me happy to see my kids had their lives squared away. That's more than I could say for myself.

My instincts were right. While I was in Chicago, they busted Chucky for the granny scam again. His case came up and he went to prison in Tehachapi, California. Just before Chucky's release, I visited him out there. He told me his wife sold their house in Las Vegas and moved back to Australia with the burglar friend of Tony's. She said she didn't want anything to do with Chuck, that she was divorcing him.

Chucky swore revenge. "I'll kill that cocksucker when I get my hands on him and spill the whole setup to the Feds."

Now I could see what was coming. Word gets around fast. As soon as Chucky got out, Tony Spilotro would be laying for him. So, one day soon after the incident with Chucky, I walked into the Food Factory looking for Tony. Good. He was in a back booth by himself. I slid across from him.

"Hey, Tone, how's it goin'?" I heard the words come out of my mouth, but it sounded like someone else talking. You never tried to bullshit Tony. Anything other than straighttalk and he'd crucify you.

"Okay. And you?" Tony probably knew why I was there, but he let me take the lead.

"You probably heard that Chucky's been shooting off his mouth about what he's gonna' do when he gets out, but I know for a fact he won't do anything. No way would he beef. I grew up with this guy and I'll vouch for him. Please lay off Chuck for my sake. I promise nothing will happen, Tone."

Tony just nodded. I knew better than to ask him what he planned to do. I said what I had to say, thanked him for his time and left.

From the moment Chuck got in my car, I started to sweat. It was broad daylight, but that never stopped any Outfit guys from teaching someone a lesson. I kept a lookout for boards with nails sticking out of them and other debris the Outfit would wedge under your tire so you'd get a flat, check it out and end up with your head blown off. Our long trip back to Las Vegas went without a hitch, so I guess Tony decided to trust me. Maybe he admired my loyalty or maybe he figured it took a lot of balls for me to pick Chuck up. Of course, I never heard a word about it.

Chuck wasn't the same the few times I saw him after that. He just fell apart. Eventually, Chucky hooked up with some chip hustler whose father was a retired cop. Chucky got in a fight with him, the old man pulled a gun and killed Chuck. At his wake, I looked at Chucky and all I could see was this little red-haired Irish kid whose parents moved out and didn't tell him.

Phil Diaguardi couldn't catch me stealing on the blackjack table so he put me on the Big Six, a game based on the "Wheel of Fortune" TV show. Besides using my old standby of palming chips, I put in play an old trick that can work at any gaming table. First, I brought in about three inches of two-sided transparent tape stuck to the top of my watchband. I had to make sure the eye-in-the-sky, a guy pacing the catwalk above my table, wasn't watching. The absence of dust filtering down on my head meant he was somewhere else. I took the tape and attached it to the paddle that pushes the paper money into the drop box under the table.

Now if a customer gave me a small bill, it wasn't worth taking, so I turned the paddle a certain way and let the bill fall straight into the drop box. But if someone gave me a $100, I made the bill stick to the paddle. Then I announced that I was "dropping a hundred." The pit boss would look over and see the bill go down. When I was sure the coast was clear and my customers had moved on, I pulled the paddle up, retrieved the $100 and put it in my pocket.

I snatched a lot of bills and chips—several hundred dollars worth—and needed a place to stash the loot until I could take it home. An idea came to me. I put the money in a small, Crown Royal cloth bag and hid it in one of the men's room stalls behind a metal door that covered all these pipes. I hung the bag on the pipes and shut the metal door. I did this for months. After my shift one day, I went to the men's room and found it "closed for remodeling." Shit. The workmen were sure to discover my stash.

Lefty Rosenthal was the Outfit's front for the casino, but the Nevada Gaming Commission refused to give him a key-employee license. So, Lefty took a variety of hotel positions that didn't require a privileged gaming license, including entertainment director. He arranged all sorts of "busy-work" to hide the fact he was skimming for his Outfit bosses. Remodeling the joint was one of Lefty's current coverups. It was a riot watching Lefty's gofer, Bobby the Midget (aka Bobby Kaye), scurry behind Lefty trying to keep pace with his long-legged friend.

Some days later in the casino, I bumped into Tony. He took me aside, "Look, Slick. If they catch you stealing, I can't bail you out." Geez, was there anything this guy didn't know? He must have been psychic.

For the record, misinformed people still think Lefty fronted Las Vegas for the Outfit. I watched Tony order Lefty around many times. Sure, Lefty was the Outfit's watchdog at the Stardust to make certain the big guys got their share of the skim. Tony wasn't supposed to do everything. Some people also thought that Bobby Stella, the casino manager, consulted Lefty about Stardust goings-on. Anyone in the know realized Bobby Stella, as well as Frank Cursoli and Phil Diaguardi, were some of the sharpest casino men in the business. Bobby Stella sure didn't need to consult with Lefty, who knew almost nothing about casino operations.

For a long time Tony kept a low profile while Lefty strutted his stuff on his live TV show that made the guys in Chicago cringe. The last thing they wanted was for Lefty to call attention to himself. But Tony gave them even worse headaches. His Hole-in-the-Wall Gang—the theft ring he kept secret even from his top bosses—got out of hand and the Feds finally exposed it. Then there was the small matter of Tony's indictments for murder, among other crimes. You can't bring in that kind of heat *and* fail to cut the Chicago Outfit in on their share of the pie.

My old buddy, Bob Mauro, was the next guy to hit town. Ever since Rhonda hooked up permanently with that Kentucky building contractor, Bob's bankroll had dwindled. There was nothing to keep him in Miami so I sent him money to come to Las Vegas and worked out a poker-dealing job for Bob at the MGM. Soon after that, Bob got into the Desert Inn as a shift manager. Me and Sam Gambino, Tony Spilotro's cousin, paid Bob a visit.

"Hey, Bob. We want to go eat in the restaurant. How about a comp?"

"I don't know, Slick. You guys haven't been playing yet."

I couldn't believe what I was hearing. Did I need to remind Bob that I paid his way to Las Vegas and got him into the MGM? I was steamed.

"Bob, are you gonna give us a comp or be an asshole all your life?"

Tony Spilotro laughed his ass off when Sam told him what I said. It was great having old Bob around, but the couple of times I tried to use him as my agent on the Big Six, I found out he'd lost his nerve. It seemed like Bob had no spark after Rhonda left.

I bumped into Gil Fracassi. He moaned how him and Bitsy Ross had a major disagreement at the Trop and split up. I already heard that Bitsy was disgusted with Gil's lack of business sense and took their junket operation downtown to the Four Queens. I could see now that Gil wasn't too bright. I'd helped him with his junket business and he blew it again. Here was my chance to take advantage of a goofy guy who thought life was as simple as all those movies he watched.

"Listen, Gil," I said. "Don't worry about Bitsy. I just found out an important Outfit friend of mine is coming to Las Vegas by the name of Big Joe Smith. He's just the guy you need."

I collared Big Joe the minute he showed up. "Hey Joe, I know how we can make a good score and take over this guy's business. Are you game?"

Joe puffed out his chest. "So, you're finally wising up to my talents. It's about time."

Big Joe was like that—all bluff and ego, but I didn't care as long as my scheme paid off. I had it all planned out. Joe was going to pretend to be an Outfit big shot and I'd be Joe's gofer. He looked and talked like a typical wiseguy, and packing those two .38 calibre revolvers he nicknamed "The Twins" didn't hurt. Everything went like clockwork . . . at first.

Now I got on the horn with Gil. "That guy I told you about is here in Las Vegas, Gil. Me and him have some business in L.A. Maybe we can meet you out there?"

I could tell Gil was excited by the way he stumbled over his words. Now me and Joe drove to L.A. to look up my old pal, Vince Eli, who was going to play a key role in my plan. I only prayed Vince would stick to the script and not ham it up. We pulled up to Gil's sprawling ranch house. I carried Joe's suitcases to make him look important. When I introduced him to Gil, Joe played his part like a pro. Little did Gil know that the big burly guy with the gruff voice stood on the bottom rung of the Outfit ladder.

I laid out the deal to Gil, but Joe kept interrupting. "Slick, go get me a cup of coffee, no cream," or "Slick, I need a pack of Camels." Of course I did what he wanted. Inside I boiled. Later in private I pointed out that Joe was taking this gofer thing a little too far.

Joe grinned and shrugged. "Whatta ya expect a guy in my position to do, get my own coffee and cigarettes?"

That night me and Joe took Gil to a fancy restaurant on La Cienega Boulevard. Gil acted like every sucker I'd ever met. He heard just what he wanted to hear, never thinking he was being set up. According to our pre-arranged plan, the three of us met Vince afterward in a strip joint. Vince did his bit perfectly. He made sure Gil, seated between Vince and Joe, overheard every word.

"I'm glad to see you, Joe. My friend who owns this joint needs a big favor that only someone with your considerable juice can pull off." Vince talked like that—using those big words.

Vince had bribed the guys who worked there to act like Joe was somebody important. So, the whole time Vince was talking, the employees fell all over Joe. One of the good-looking strippers slid up against Joe and cooed, "Can I get you anything Joe, honey?"

Gil leered at the stripper's cleavage. "That Big Joe sure has a following."

Yeah, I thought laughing to myself, if you only knew the truth. Geez, I thought. Ain't they laying it on a little thick? I gotta work with Big Joe.

Vince and Joe disappeared into the office for a private talk with the owner while me and Gil cooled our heels in the bar. Of course, there was no private talk with the owner. It was just part of the con. When they came out, Joe told Gil he was going to Palm Springs to see Frank Buccieri. Frank was Fifi's brother, at one time Al Capone's top gun.

"Here's the deal," Joe said. "If you want a casino to work out of, Gil, we have to give Frank Buccieri ten grand. In about two weeks, we'll have our casino. It's important I cut myself in for half of that as a partner so things will go without a hitch. Whatta ya say?"

Anyone else would have been suspicious as hell, but Gil bought it. He coughed up the $10,000, pumping Joe's hand and smiling the whole time like an idiot. I never saw a fool so happy to part with his money.

Me and Joe headed for Palm Springs to look up Buccieri. I was curious why we were actually going to see Buccieri and I asked as much. Joe answered a little too fast like maybe he was expecting my question. "You know Frank runs the West Coast for the mob. So, if we cut Frank in, he won't have no beef."

I agreed. Frank Buccieri was big enough that he could make it rough for all of us. Joe had five grand and I had five. Joe told me he was giving Frank two grand and he wanted me to kick in two. I didn't actually believe Joe was giving Frank two grand, but I figured I'd be in the clear if Tony Spilotro had any questions about all this, especially since Buccieri was involved. Any guy who's done business with the mob knows that everybody gets his cut in a certain order. If you skip someone important, you could get whacked.

Then there was Tony. Only a complete fool would think they could hide anything from Tony. And you never, never lied to Tony. Death would be merciful if he found out you lied to him. Many guys thought Tony got a piece of all the action in Las Vegas, but that wasn't the case. If you went to him for protection, he figured he deserved something for his trouble. But if you didn't ask for his help, he wouldn't get involved. He had enough on his hands. Or if the score was big, he felt he was the one taking the heat from Chicago, so he was due something whether he was in the deal or not. After all, it was his territory and his neck on the line. In my case, he wouldn't want anything, but he'd certainly know about it.

We had just two weeks to come up with a casino. If we found a joint, I owned half a junket business. If we didn't, I still made three grand. On a hunch, I stopped by the Landmark Casino on the Strip and looked up Frank Modica, the new owner. Modica had left his casino manager job at the Showboat to lease the Landmark because he could tell the place was really gonna go. I'd heard about Modica taking over the Landmark through the grapevine and I thought maybe he'd want some new business.

After introducing myself, I gave Modica a rundown of our

junket business—the up-and-up version. I could tell he was a straight shooter with no mob bosses telling him what to do. One other thing I learned, Modica didn't rush into anything. He gave me his decision a few days later. The outcome was better than I hoped for. Modica agreed to let us work out of the Landmark, plus, he covered all expenses. We were in business.

My job was to meet the plane at McCarran, and bus the customers to the Landmark. About 12 hours later, I'd load them up again and drive them back. I had a lot of time to kill so I started hanging around with Mr. Modica. I'd give him updates on how the junkets were doing while we waited for the customers to blow their dough. I even negotiated a fantastic price for Modica on an expensive demo TV at an electronics convention across the street. After that, he seemed to trust me. Naturally, Joe and Gil were never around.

Meanwhile, I ran into Bitsy and told him Gil was Big Joe's partner. He nearly laughed himself off his bar stool. He couldn't believe Gil was dumb enough to go into business with Big Joe who had no pull whatsoever.

"You mean Gil thinks you're Big Joe's flunky? What a riot!"

"Yeah, ain't it something?" I said. "Of course Gil can't find out I was the guy who set up the whole junket idea. That would mess everything up."

"I don't think you have any worries there, Slick. Gil's too stupid."

Now I was supposed to get half of Joe's action. Somehow every week Joe came up with an excuse to keep my share of the take. I knew it was absolute bullshit but I went along with Joe for a while, just waiting.

Everything came to a head one night when Joe called me to meet him at his place. He got straight to the point. "From now on, Frank Buccieri gets your end of the business."

I couldn't believe my ears. Where would this asshole be without me? I guess he expected I'd just roll over. "Who do you think you're bullshitting," I snapped back. "If I'm out, you're out."

Joe grabbed me by the throat. I countered by kicking him in his bad knee and down he went. I glared at Joe lying at my feet. "I created a Frankenstein monster. We had a good thing going and you had to fuck it up."

A few days later I told Tony Spilotro the whole story. Like always, he listened without saying a word. When I finished, a tiny smirk crossed Tony's face. "That's what you get for doing business with a guy like Big Joe Smith."

In the morning I informed Frank Modica that I quit the junket business. "I found out Big Joe was mixed up with the Outfit and I don't want any part of that," I lied.

Modica slapped me on the back. "You did the right thing, Slick." That same day he kicked Gil and Joe out of the Landmark. And that was the end of me and the junket business.

25

I stared straight down the barrel of that 38 snub nose she carried. With the gun only inches from my face, I could see the bullet wobble in the chamber.

A T 3:00 P.M. the Commercial Deli swarmed with patrons. I spotted Judge Potter, a powerful local figure, shoveling down lox and bagels. And there was fearless Shecky Green working the crowd like a politician—a real live tabloid in action. I scanned the room. Bruno, one of my agents, sipped coffee in the far corner, unfazed by the commotion. Bruno always had a good story under his belt so I headed in his direction.

I let Bruno in on my latest junket deal. "By the way, Bruno, that Tony Spilotro doesn't miss a trick," I said. "And you better not cross him. If he was going to kill you, he wouldn't call you an asshole. He'd warn you not to do it again, and if you didn't take the hint, he'd blow your head off without warning. Don't ask how I know."

"Yeah, Tony's . . ." Bruno didn't finish the sentence. Then in a lowered voice he said, "You know my son, Joey? He went to Tony with a crazy plan to take off some casino. Tony said, 'Listen, you desperado punk. That's not robbery. It's suicide.'

"My son got kinda loud so Tony slapped him a few times and said, 'You've watched too many movies, kid. Behave yourself.'"

Bruno looked around to see if anyone was listening. "A few days later, the Churchill Downs Race Book was robbed, in broad daylight, no less. A masked robber entered the back door, grabbed the dough while the owner was counting it, and walked out. He threw the mask and money in his trunk. Then he did a brazen thing. The guy walked in the Churchill Downs front door this time, right on the Strip, and played the horses. The robbery was in all the papers. Of course, Tony took a lot of heat because of it. No one knew who did it . . . except for Tony. It didn't take him two seconds to figure out who was wild enough to pull this stunt."

Bruno checked the crowd again. "Tony called my son in for a little talk. Good thing Joey cut Tony in for half the take, because he's still alive."

A lot of rumors floated around about who robbed the race book, but I didn't know for sure until now. I'd have another Tony story of my own to tell in a few short weeks.

It all started when this Outfit messenger, Guido, tracked me down to the Aladdin poker room about 4:00 a.m. I sat out the next few hands since I was losing anyway. In the coffee shop, Guido opened up.

"Slick, I gotta see Tony. It's very important."

"Okay, Guido. You wait for me here and I'll see what I can do."

I didn't have Tony's phone number on me but I knew he lived at 4675 Balfour, a regular middle-class neighborhood. In fact, Tony's house looked exactly like all the other ones on his block, just the opposite of Lefty's sprawling ranch house on the Desert Inn Golf Course. I'd driven Tony home a couple of times because he didn't like to drive. He figured you made an easier target in the driver's seat. Here's my chance to help Tony out, I thought listening to the doorbell's constant chime.

A long five minutes later, Tony answered the door dressed in his pajamas. "Oh, it's you," he said, a little surprised to find me on his doorstep at such an early hour. "What are you doing here?"

"This Guido from Chicago collared me at the Aladdin just now. He says he has something very important to tell you . . . it couldn't wait. So I came right over."

Very calmly, Tony asked, "Was it important for him, or important for me?"

I stood there with my mouth open like a fish caught in a net. My mind raced for an answer, but none came. Quietly Tony closed the door.

Tony nailed it. Who was it important for? Every time I was around that guy, I learned something new, like the fact that whenever Tony invited a guy to his house, he would say, "Let's relax in the Jacuzzi. What size bathing suit do you wear?" He'd glance at the guy's waist and shout, "Nancy, get him a 38." If the guy refused, Tony figured he had a wire on and the guy was in deep shit. Only a few people knew this about Tony. I decided to skip the Aladdin.

Things stayed surprisingly calm living with Kitty in the condo I bought with Siegel's money. I think this was a "cease fire" record for Kitty. She still hauled in the tips as a cocktail waitress at the Starlight Lounge, while I did my usual—playing poker at the Landmark. I was enjoying my freedom when, out of the blue, Frank Modica asked if I had a minute.

"What are you up to these days, Slick?"

"Just playing poker," I answered, wondering what was on his mind.

Modica paused and looked me squarely in the eye. "What do you think of my poker room?"

I wasn't expecting his question, but I decided to tell him the truth. "It's a joke."

"What do you mean, Slick?"

"It's really none of my business . . ." I said, testing the waters.

"It might be," added Modica. "I'm losing $30,000 a month, so I'm either going to close it or let you run it. What do you think?"

Right away I liked the idea, so I agreed. Seeing as this was Friday, I had the whole weekend to check the room out before the switch took place. Modica wouldn't make the announcement until Monday, per my request. I was lucky to get Sam Raguso, who just happened to look like Cary Grant's twin, to cover swing. He suggested Fred Curry, a guy working at the MGM, for the day shift. Later, I could add a graveyard shift when the room took off.

All weekend I played like usual, or so it seemed. I'd known for some time that the dealers were peddling coke in there. Even a blind man could spot it. Then there was the clique of foul-mouthed poker dealers, running off most of the older players.

On Monday morning, Modica walked me in and introduced me as the new card room manager. So many faces fell, you'd think it was a wake. They probably guessed what was coming. In my first official move, I gave all 15 poker employees their walking papers. Then I hired Fred Curry and Sam Raguso as my shift managers. Next move was to bring aboard polite dealers to lure back the seniors. I also started a few promotions, like free poker lessons for beginners. In another popular promotion, we gave players $22 worth of chips for $20. Since the only game we spread back then was Seven Card Stud, and dealers routinely got out between 35 and 40 hands per hour, I figured we'd more than make up the difference by taking in a bigger rake. It worked. Players practically stumbled over one another vying for a seat. And when things got a little slow, I'd use dealers as prop players which meant we could spread a game much faster. Prop, or proprietary, players were casino employees hired to play using their own money. The dealers loved it.

After the first month, the poker room went from losing $30,000 to breaking even. And by the end of the quarter, we were taking in $30,000 a month. Modica beamed like a new father.

I'd heard from Bob Mauro that our old friend Vince Eli wasn't doing too well in Hollywood. I figured, since the poker room was going so strong, it was time to open up the graveyard shift. The next day I phoned Vince. "I need someone I can trust, Vince. Why don't you come in as my graveyard manager?"

"Gee, Slick. Your offer's pretty tempting, but I don't know shit about poker."

"Don't worry, Vince. I promise I'll stick with you until you learn the ropes."

In a week I had my graveyard manager but at a price: I had to sleep in the joint—catching a few winks here and there—until Vince got the hang of things. You gotta understand that what Vince lacked in poker knowledge, he more than made up in people skills. For instance, whenever I asked him, "Who's that guy to the dealer's right on table four?"

Without hesitating, Vince would say, "Oh, that's so-and-so."

Now I had my team in place: Sam Raguso, "The Lover"; Fred Curry, "The Rule Maker"; and Vince Eli, "The Photographic Memory." Boy, everything was going great, especially after I moved the poker room near the showroom and table games to catch the walk-by traffic. Thanks to Modica, I had carte blanche with all poker room decisions. Sometimes when the poker room was packed, I noticed with satisfaction that the blackjack tables were nearly empty.

Our customers ran the gamut, from entertainers like comedian David Brenner to little Jewish ladies like Mae and Pearl who brought a different brand of entertainment to the room. They reminded me of Mortimer's nutty aunts in the movie *Arsenic and Old Lace*. Mae and Pearl made an entrance every night at 6:00 sharp. The pair exchanged a series of complicated hand signals no one could decipher. But even a kid could spot their game. When Bob Mauro paid me a visit one night and saw the volume of stuff flying between those two, he rolled on the floor laughing. I could have thrown the old girls out, except that no amount of cheating could make up for their lousy poker playing. Eventually, they'd go bust. Besides, the other players loved them. Mae and Pearl were to the poker room what the ding-ding-ding is to slot machines.

I pocketed $250 a day—not great, but better than I'd done in a while. Plus, I could count on a regular paycheck. Kitty popped in the poker room more and more often now that I had an important job. I guess she thought she could throw her weight around since I ran the room. Every other word out of Kitty's mouth was "Fuck this" and "Fuck that," so I finally had to bar her from the poker room. You can imagine how well she took that.

Good things had a knack of turning sour, and the poker room was no exception. First, I should give you some background on the Landmark. The casino manager was a guy named Steve Shunaman. As far as I could tell, Steve's only qualification for the job was that his wife was GM Gary Baldwin's sister. Gary was a real sharp guy, but even sharp guys have their blind spots. Steve had it in for me ever since I replaced his good buddy as card room manager. I knew I had to watch out for Steve, especially after Modica moved back to the Showboat. Now that I didn't have anyone touting me, I had to fight my own battles.

There's a saying that goes, "You are the company you keep." Well Vince Spilotro, Tony's brother, began bringing his friends around the poker room to help business. He didn't realize an FBI informant by the name of Bartolo was tailing him everywhere, including my poker room. Things really went bad when I hired Vince Spilotro's poker-dealing girlfriend, Sherry. Besides her upbeat personality, Sherry made few mistakes and could get out a lot of hands.

Steve Shunaman was watching my every move. A week after I hired Sherry, Steve said, "You gotta fire her. She's in with the mob. It's bad enough that her boyfriend, Spilotro, brings all his Outfit friends around." I told Steve I couldn't do that so he ran straight to his brother-in-law, Gary Baldwin. Naturally, I was called on the carpet to explain my actions.

"Look Mr. Baldwin," I said. "Sherry's a great dealer. On average, she gets out 42 hands an hour and the customers like her."

I took a gamble with my next line. "If I fire her on account of her association with Vince Spilotro, I should fire myself." I glanced at Shunaman to see his reaction. He stood with his arms folded looking smug. If Shunaman expected his brother-in-law to fire me, he miscalculated. Baldwin was a smart businessman. He knew the bottom line was raking in the bucks, so he told me to forget the whole thing. Baldwin and Shunaman were still arguing when I closed Baldwin's door behind me. From then on, Steve sent dagger looks my way, but I let them glance off my invisible shield.

A much bigger storm was brewing with Kitty. It began late one night when this tourist broad came on to me at the poker room. Nah, it wasn't my drop-dead looks and charm that attracted her. It was my powerful position. The fact that I always wanted to be Don Juan but resembled a balding, slightly overweight Don Knotts never stopped me from taking advantage of a situation dripping with promise.

Her long, dark hair and Oriental features hit all my weak spots, and the way she moved in her clingy red dress said more than a million words.

"Maybe we can have a few drinks when you get off work?" she purred, brushing against me.

I switched to my bedroom voice, the one I reserved for just such occasions. "I'm the boss so I can get off any time I want, sweetheart, but I don't drink. What I would like is to get you in a nice warm Jacuzzi, that's what. There's a place called Spring Fever that has little private rooms with hot tubs. What do you say?"

Three hours later, the hot tub had cooled down and so had I. Geez, it's a wonder this broad didn't give me a heart attack. I never knew you could do stuff like that under water? I paid the bill, stuffed the receipt in my pants pocket, and drove my Shanghai doll to her hotel on my way home. I was snoring before my head hit the pillow.

A few days later, I got all sorts of messages at work that Kitty was looking for me. She wanted me to call her the minute I got her message. I tried a couple of times, but no Kitty. When I made it home after my shift, Kitty wasn't there so I went to sleep. A horrible noise woke me out of an X-rated dream. I realized it was Kitty screaming at the top of her lungs.

"What's this?" She threw the Spring Fever receipt in my face.

How funny that Kitty could have all these guys but when I was with someone, it was different. I didn't think too long about this, though, because I was staring straight down the barrel of that 38 snub nose she carried. With the gun only inches from my face, I could see the bullet wobble in the chamber. Now my eyes focused on Kitty holding the gun with both hands, shaking as if she had a chill. Her dark eyes turned a shade I'd never seen before—the color of charcoal briquettes after you throw a match on them. I prayed that if she shot me, I'd die right away and not turn into a vegetable. At that very moment, Kathy walked in.

"What are you doing, Mom?

I used Kitty's distraction to grab her gun. Then I got dressed. That was it. I couldn't live with this crazy broad for another second. What made me think I could? That was the real question.

The drama wasn't over yet. Kitty lunged toward me screaming every obscenity. I shoved her out of my way. She tripped, reached out for the railing, missed and tumbled down the stairs. I looked at Kitty lying in a heap at the bottom. For once, I didn't care what happened to her. I threw her 38 snub nose as hard as I could, shattering the solid mirror that covered one of the living room walls. Glass flew everywhere. Then I walked out.

Looking back, I'm sad Kathy had to go through the pain and horror of watching her parents attack one another. I vowed it would never happen again. I'd finally had my fill of living with Kitty and this time I meant it.

I'd been at the Landmark for almost two years when who should walk in but Kitty.

"See my engagement ring?" She flashed a rock the size of Gibraltar in my face.

"Yeah, it's very nice, Kitty," I answered, hoping she wasn't going to start any trouble. But she seemed too upbeat to run off any customers.

"I'm marrying Dominick, one of Sam Manarite's sons," Kitty announced as if she were marrying the King of England.

This is going to be interesting, I thought. Sam Manarite, a Genovese Family capo from the East Coast, earned the nickname "Springfield Sam" by threatening to beat guys to death with a golf club. Another time Sam poured Draino down a guy's throat for being late on a juice payment. Even the mob's most ruthless enforcers feared Springfield Sam. With Kitty and that psychopath father-in-law of hers under one roof, anyone could wind up dead. At least we agreed that Kathy would stay with me until her mother adjusted to married life.

The happy event—a Las Vegas-style society wedding—took place at the Dunes, Manarite's hangout. With plenty of East Coast wiseguys in attendance, the guest list looked like the FBI's most wanted.

Only a few short weeks after the wedding, trouble erupted. Soon Kitty and Dominick's apartment featured fights every week, just like Madison Square Garden in its heyday. During one major shouting match, Kitty moved out. The next day she returned to pick up her clothes and discovered Dominick had changed the locks. Now their Maryland Avenue apartment was on the first floor near a beauty parlor and some other shops. Kitty pounded on the door, screaming at Dominick to open it. He told her to get lost. She stood back, pulled out her 38 snub nose, and fired at the lock. While Dominick was making a hasty retreat out the back door, the neighbors called the cops.

By coincidence, Sam Manarite was driving by and noticed all the squad cars parked in front of Dominick's apartment, so he investigated. Sam turned white with rage, promising Kitty she was "already dead." Kitty tried to kick him in the balls, but the police held her back. It's a good thing they took her gun or she would have tried to shoot Manarite on the spot, never mind the witnesses. The police forced Sam to leave, shaking their heads in disbelief at Kitty's nerve. They didn't even charge her with disorderly conduct, figuring her days were numbered with Manarite swearing to kill her.

A few days later, my friend Hy Powell, former head of the Las Vegas Police Department, handed over Kitty's gun. With Sam Manarite gunning for her, Hy figured she needed all the protection she could get. That night me and Vince Spilotro were walking through the Stardust when Sam Manarite came out of nowhere screaming at me.

Sam was in my face. "About that ex-wife of yours—I'm gonna kill that bitch after what she did to Dominick."

"Well," I told him, unfazed by his threats. "If I was you, I'd straighten out that son of yours."

Sam lunged for me but 250-pound Vince stepped neatly in front of him, like a linebacker protecting his quarterback in the pocket. Sam backed off for now.

Then I found out that Tony Spilotro called Sam in for a talk. If Tony had thought of Kitty as a "standup broad" before the Manarite incident, now Tony backed his words with strong actions.

"Go ahead, Sam," Tony said. "Do whatever you want to Kitty. I won't stop you. But, remember that whatever happens to her, will happen to you."

Even though Sam was a New York mobster, he knew the value of getting on Tony's good side, the guy who ran Las Vegas. Kitty divorced Dominick and she never heard a peep out of Sam Manarite again. Only Kitty could survive a death threat from Springfield Sam.

The year was 1980. It was a typical Christmas, meaning the card room was so slow I could have sold the poker tables and no one would have noticed. So when Steve Shunaman told me I'd have to close down the graveyard shift until business picked up, I could see his point. I made him promise that when we got busier, I could hire Vince Eli back. Naturally, Steve agreed. And, naturally, I didn't trust him.

Fred Curry, my dayshift manager, and Steve Shunaman played golf together. Everyone knows guys form alliances on golf courses. That's not the only game Fred played. Kitty's girlfriend, Barbara, who used to go with another Manarite son, was now seeing Fred ever since she began serving cocktails at the Landmark. Too often, I'd come in and find Fred schmoozing with Barbara in the coffee shop instead of running the poker room. But that wasn't the worst part. I'd known for some time that Fred stashed a gun in the locked cash drawer at the podium.

The day I discovered the gun, Sam Raguso was on duty. I made sure no one was listening. "Do you know who's gun that is in the cash drawer?"

"Yeah, Slick. It's Fred's. When we counted down the cash before his shift last week, Fred told me he was worried that Sam Manarite's son might try to get even, since Fred's seeing Barbara. The gun's for Fred's protection, just in case the Manarite kid gets any goofy ideas."

I kept all this to myself, waiting for the right opportunity. Well, everything came to a head when the cage manager, a very reliable friend of mine, told me Fred was after my job. The next day, sure enough, there was Fred yacking with Barbara in the coffee shop. The minute Fred came back, I motioned him over to the podium, handed him a pink slip and fired him on the spot. Fred's face turned the color of the crimson wallpaper.

"You can't do that!" he shouted.

"I just did," I answered.

As soon as Fred left, I tracked the time on my watch. Steve Shunaman stormed into the card room exactly five minutes later with Fred tagging behind him. The two looked about as friendly as a pair of gorilla's who caught an outsider messing with their females. I greeted Steve with a handshake and a smile.

"Gee, Steve. You must have run all the way from your office."

Pushing my hand away, Steve scowled. "You can't fire Fred Curry. I'm casino manager and I say he stays."

"Well, I'm the poker room manager and I say he goes." By now, all eyes in the poker room watched our little drama unfold.

"We'll see about that, Hanner."

The next day I got the phone call I'd been expecting from Gary Baldwin's secretary. Big surprise. I walked in to Baldwin's office just as Steve and Gary were discussing my fate.

Gary broke the ice. "You may have acted a little harshly, Slick. Maybe you should have given Fred a warning first?" I was weary of all this political bullshit so I played my ace right away.

"What about the gun?" Of all the things Gary Baldwin thought I might say, this clearly was not one of them.

"What gun?"

"Sam saw Fred hide it in the cash drawer," I explained. "I didn't want to mention it in my report because it would make the Landmark look bad."

Steve was too stunned to speak. That was it. Case closed . . . for now, anyway. But I knew things were just warming up.

By February, the room rocked again after the seasonal slump. I kept asking Steve if I could open grave but he always nixed it, just like I knew he would. I finally hired Vince back anyway, with solid proof I could justify the move to Gary Baldwin. Sure enough, Steve blocked Vince's rehiring. I'd finally had enough, went to Gary and turned in my badge. Thinking back, I should have accepted Frank Modica's offer to move to the Showboat. But I had the Landmark card room running like a well-oiled machine and I wasn't about to jump ship.

The more responsibilities, the more headaches. I never seemed to get it into my thick skull that I wasn't cut out for regular work. It was time to hang up the three-piece suits and haul out my poker shorts and flip-flops. Vince Eli worked brush at the Holiday Casino poker room, thanks to my connections. I couldn't stomach the Landmark, so I made the Holiday my regular hangout.

One night after Vince's shift, we went over to see an old friend of ours from Chicago named Tony Montana who tended bar at the famous Villa D'Est. The restaurant, also known as Joe Pignatello's place, catered to entertainers and mob guys like Sinatra, Sam Giancana and Sam's main squeeze, Phyllis Maguire. She could have had any guy in the world, but she settled on that ugly thug. There's no accounting for taste. The three of us guys were rehashing old times when in walked Tony Spilotro. Few people knew that Tony Spilotro was Joe Pig's silent partner.

Tony greeted everyone, turned to me and said, "So, Slick. Are you working?"

"No. Not yet."

"Here's what you do," Tony said. "Go to Vegas World. They just leased the poker room to a friend of mine by the name of Pete Keller. Tell him I sent you."

I recognized Keller's name. He was a high limit poker player who always carried a gun in his cowboy boot. I heard you didn't want to mess with him. At that time, it was legal for anyone with enough money to lease a poker room.

The next day I introduced myself to Pete Keller. When he found out Tony sent me, Keller got right down to business, as if he'd been waiting for me to show up. He hired me as his swing shift boss at $125 a day, no interview, no nothing.

"Your real job is to put our card mechanic dealer in any game where there's a high-rolling sucker and bring in the cold deck with the setup. For every cold deck you bring in, I'll give you $500 on top of your salary." That sounded better.

Now Keller took me over to meet Bob Stupak who owned Vegas World. Geez, here was this chain-smoking, creepy-looking guy who needed a bath in the worst way. Without looking up, Stupak told me to find the casino manager and get myself processed so I could start work right away. First, there had been

Bob Stupak's World Famous Million Dollar Historic Gambling Museum and Casino. I guess someone had a thing against long names, because the place burned down. Stupak took the insurance money and built Vegas World.

Huckster Stupak attracted folks with any gimmick he could muster, including a No Limit Texas Hold'em game meant to draw in high rollers. The exciting new game, featuring universal cards dealt face-up, descended on Las Vegas like a desert storm. Within days, the high stakes grabbed the attention of Keller and his crew, well-known World Series of Poker winners. But Keller and his boys didn't stop at honest gambling. They unleashed an arsenal of cheating tactics tailor-made to bust the heavy hitters. Everyone including me and the dealer had their role to play—everyone, that is, except for Stupak and the mooch-of-the-moment. Tony Spilotro got a piece of Keller's action and that's how I entered the picture.

Not long after I started working there, who should sit down but Bob Stupak himself. Keller figured just because Stupak owned the joint didn't entitle him to immunity. Nothing would go wrong because all the other players at the table were in on the con. I brought in the cold or doctored deck with the two-deck setup, just like always. The dealer spread the normal deck, shuffled and began dealing.

After a while, a player said he detected a crimped card and asked for the other deck. The cold deck was pre-set to give one of our guys the nuts and Stupak the second best hand.

Now here's where the dealer's world-class card mechanic skills plus the crew's timing came into play. The dealer picked up the cold deck and acted like he was going to spread it face up. That would have been a dead giveaway, so it was up to one of the players to distract Stupak. Ironically, Stupak's Greek bodyguard bumped Stupak's glass. The Greek was hired to alert Stupak of any funny business, but was actually part of Keller's crew. Stupak grabbed the glass so it wouldn't tip. By the time Stupak looked up, he thought the dealer had already spread the deck. After all, his Greek friend acted like everything was on the up-and-up. Then the dealer false shuffled and went right into dealing. The pot topped thirty grand. On the turn, it became a showdown between Stupak and the guy with the nuts. When the river came up, of course, Stupak lost.

Bob Stupak never wised up. In fact, after Keller's gang hustled a very sharp female player out of considerable money, she sued Stupak for cheating her. The court ruled in Stupak's favor for lack of evidence. To this day, I don't think Stupak guessed who was behind the swindle.

26

I looked into Dennis Farina's eyes. Then it
came to me where I'd seen them before. "You
cost me a lot of money," I told him.

DURING THE LATE 1980s, shooting began on a new TV show
called *Crime Story* based on Tony Spilotro's life. The show had
Las Vegans glued to the TV. Every guy who fantasized himself as
an actor tried to juice his way into a bit part on the popular show.
They were ready to start filming the second season, after scoring
a big hit with the first season set in Chicago. The second season
opened with *Crime Story's* main character Tony Luca's arrival in
Las Vegas—headquarters for the Chicago Mob's money-skim-
ming operations. Gee, that sounded familiar.

The show's popularity put a lot of heat on Tony Spilotro. He
hated the show because everything that happened to Tony in real
life worked its way into the *Crime Story* plot. Who could blame
Tony? He had enough heat on him already without calling more
attention to his Las Vegas activities.

I was hanging around with Sam Gambino, an ex-Stardust
dealer now working floor at the Aladdin. Sam was a retired
Chicago cop who happened to be Tony's Spilotro's cousin.
When I first met Sam at the Stardust, I couldn't get over how he
resembled an Italian John Wayne. Unlike his cousin, Sam led a
law-abiding life. We never discussed my con artist ways. As long
as I treated Sam fairly, he figured what I did was my business.
But Sam was in tight with Tony, whose genius and cool head
never ceased to amaze me.

One day I dropped by to see Sam at the Aladdin. "Hey, Sam, what do you think about all this *Crime Story* business?"

"Funny you should ask, Slick. The show's creator, Chuck Adamson, is a good friend of mine. In fact, I'm meeting him for breakfast tomorrow. Why don't you come along?"

The next morning I found Sam sitting with two other guys in the Hilton coffee shop. Sam introduced me to Chuck Adamson. Then I found myself shaking the giant hand of Dennis Farina, a broad-shouldered, dark-haired guy who looked every inch the Mafioso. Dennis caused quite a stir during the show's first season playing the wisecracking Chicago detective, Lt. Mike Torello. The four of us exchanged small talk for about five minutes, but I couldn't concentrate. I'd met this guy before, but where? I looked into Dennis Farina's eyes. Then it dawned on me where I'd seen them before.

My mind flashed back to the Devonshire Hotel, mob headquarters, where I lived thanks to Bob Mauro's mob connections. I remember these two cops pulled me over while me and Jimmy LaRue cased a jeweler's apartment on Marine Drive. I could still see the menacing look in that one cop's eyes, those meaty hands of his firmly planted on my car door, as if his brute strength alone would hold the car in place if I tried to take off.

"You cost me a lot of money," I told him, gulping a mouthful of hot coffee.

"How?" Dennis asked.

"Never mind," I said, knowing I couldn't mention the robbery. "It's a long story."

Dennis just laughed.

About 20 cop jokes later, I realized I'd been wrong about Dennis Farina. Now I could see this warm, funny guy with the quick smile was nothing like the mean killer I imagined. Every other phrase out of Dennis's mouth was "Gee, I love this . . ." or "I love that . . ." Not too many killers I knew used the "L" word that often.

Chuck told us how the show began. "You know, Dennis

served in my police unit as a detective for almost 20 years. We nicknamed him "the Great Wounder." Sam here used to hang around with us.

"Little by little, acting jobs came Dennis's way." Chuck winked. "I guess he thought he was too good for us because, eventually, Dennis exchanged his police-issued revolver for those props he wields in his movie roles. This terrific idea for *Crime Story* came to me during one of our bull sessions. Then I thought, hey! Who would be better at playing a tough Chicago cop than my good friend, Dennis Farina? As they say, the rest is history."

A hilarious true story came out during our conversation. Knowing Tony Spilotro, it really cracked me up.

Chuck explained, "I needed some jewelry for one of the show's main characters, a mob guy who flashed gold chains, rings and stuff. Well, Sam here told me Tony's brother, John, ran the Gold Factory jewelry store for his brother Tony so I dropped in to see what they had in stock. I was concentrating on some rings in one of the cases. When I looked up, there was Tony himself glaring at me with murder in his eyes. I nearly passed out. I dropped everything and beat it out of there, not wanting to press my luck."

Thanks to Chuck, I got a bit part during a chase sequence. In the scene, I played a gambler who's walking out the door of a casino with a bucket of coins. A policeman chasing a robber runs into me sending the coins flying everywhere. If those coins had been real, I would have said to hell with the show and made a dive for all that dough. Then, a small speaking role for a shift boss came up during filming at the Mint Hotel and Casino on Fremont Street. I begged Chuck to let me play it but he said, "No one will believe you're a manager, Slick." Gee, I thought shaking my head in disbelief. All those guys I fired at the Landmark sure believed it.

Playing poker all the time appealed to a goof-off like me—no responsibilities. I came and went when I felt like it and made enough to keep me in food and flip-flops. I learned a valuable lesson at the Landmark—at least for a while—stay away from jobs that give you a headache. Not that I made a fortune, but my poker earnings improved steadily due to tight playing, meaning I threw away all but the best hands. Just playing tight is only the beginning, though. Over the years, I got good at reading people, whether it was during an elaborate con or a poker game. A guy can't win without knowing how to spot a "tell." But the most important thing I've learned was how to act fast. Thinking on my feet probably saved my neck during the robbery with Gym Shoes and the nitro.

It all started in a Bally's poker game one day. I noticed a greasy-haired character sitting across from me who looked very familiar. While I was debating where I'd seen him before, the guy came over to me. "Aren't you George Romi's friend? I met you at Sherry's Bar in Hollywood years ago."

"Yeah, and you're Gym Shoes, right?" I remember George telling me the guy was a master safe cracker. He wore gym shoes to help him climb up drainpipes on those second-story jobs.

We continued our talk in the coffee shop. It didn't take Gym Shoes long before he was telling me about a job he planned to pull in Long Beach.

"There's a safe in this office building where they keep a lot of cash. The building's closed Sundays so I figure that's the best day to take the place off. I need someone to watch my back. Whatta ya say, Slick?"

"Who couldn't use a bigger bankroll?" I answered.

Saturday morning I drove out to Gym Shoes's house in L.A. Me and the wheelman, a guy named Phil, listened to Gym Shoes lay out the plan. This should be a piece of cake, I thought to myself. I tried to recall the last time I used that phrase, but it escaped me.

Early Sunday morning, the three of us were getting into Gym Shoes's car. I noticed he carried a small black bag, but I didn't give it a second thought. About ten minutes later, I was checking out my gun when Phil hit a bump in the road.

"Take it easy, Phil. You know I've got the nitroglycerin in the bag and it's extremely sensitive," Gym Shoes warned.

Nitro . . . Jeez, I sure wasn't in the mood to get blown up. We passed by the *Queen Mary* anchored safe and sound at Long Beach. For a fleeting instant, I wished I was aboard instead of bumping along in a car that might explode any minute.

The office building looked deserted. Gym Shoes grabbed the black bag and his walkie-talkie, to keep in contact with Phil. I picked the door lock in no time. We were walking up to the safe on the third floor, when a rent-a-cop patrolling the second floor stopped us in our tracks. Me and Gym Shoes looked at one another then at the security guard.

In my most authoritative voice I said, "What the hell are you doing here?"

"Checking all the office doors like I'm supposed to," he answered.

Thinking fast I said, "Nobody told us you were going to be here."

"Yes, sir. That's right, sir. This is a new account and I'm on duty every Sunday from now on," he said like he was talking to a VIP.

Playing off the guard's mistaken identity, I turned to Gym Shoes and said, "Remind me to put out a memo on this." Then I waved the rent-a-cop away. "Okay, go on and do your job."

Whew! Good thing we left the ski masks in the car. We beat it.

Back at the car, Gym Shoes unloaded a string of four-letter words that ended with, "Why didn't you shoot the fuckin' cop?"

"If I did that," I said calmly eyeing the bag of nitro still in Gym Shoes's hand, "I'd have to shoot you and Phil because I sure as hell couldn't leave any witnesses. Besides, we don't even know how much money is in the safe." I could see Gym Shoes was thinking about what I said, then he shrugged. The crisis had passed.

By the time we rolled into Gym Shoes's driveway, I figured I'd better hit him up for business expenses before it was too late. "Lend me $500 so the trip won't be a total loss. You can take it off our next score," I fibbed. No way in hell would I hook up with Gym Shoes again.

Now that I was driving back to Las Vegas, I started to breathe a lot easier. It finally came to me the last time I said, "It's gonna be a piece of cake." I was a running target for two bootleg whiskey smugglers in some snake-infested Louisiana swamp. "That's it. No more burglaries," I told the steering wheel. "I'm getting too old for this stuff."

I could have done nothing but play poker for the rest of my life, but fate had other plans for me. Out of the blue, I was offered the swing shift manager's job at the Orbit Inn, a funny little casino on the sleazy side of downtown. I got the job kind of by default. A man and woman tried to rob the place at gunpoint. While the man held a gun on the security guard, the shift manager jumped over a BJ table and wrestled the robber for the gun. Well, during the scuffle, the robber shot the shift manager and killed him, which is how the job happened to be vacant. By now, you can tell I have a rotten memory. Otherwise, I'd remember all the lousy, stress-filled jobs I left.

About a year after I started working at the Orbit Inn, a very beautiful Oriental woman by the name of Leslie Chow walked in. She wore one of those form-hugging satin dresses with the stand-up collar that looked like liquid green jade. Sparks of light reflected off her black shiny hair. Her every move spoke a universal language that any guy with a pulse could understand.

I watched her playing blackjack thinking she had way too much class to be in a joint like this.

Each time Leslie came in after that, I learned a little more about her. She was Taiwanese and lived in San Francisco with relatives. She came to Las Vegas job hunting and found herself a cheap room off Freemont Street across from the Orbit Inn. Things began to get interesting when Leslie asked to cash a check for $20. The check bounced and she didn't come in for a while, but I knew she'd be back. If Leslie was going to beat someone, it wouldn't be for a measly $20.

Sure enough. Maybe a week later Leslie walked in and handed me three ten-dollar bills. "I had a problem with my bank," she said. "The extra $10 is for your trouble." All the time she looked at me in that straightforward way of hers.

"That's okay," I told her refusing the ten. "Twenty dollars ain't no big deal."

Leslie seemed to relax now that she'd taken care of her debt. "I got a job dealing blackjack at the Lady Luck," she told me. It was a small grind joint a few doors down from the Orbit Inn.

"They have a dealer's school and, if you sign a one-year contract, they put you to work in their casino. I decided to accept their offer because I need to make a lot of money for my family."

Boy was she something! Leslie's ambition attracted me even more than her looks. We started seeing one another and that's when Leslie really opened up. "I was born in Taiwan where I lived with my husband, a U-2 pilot, until he was shot down and killed flying over China. In Taipei they even put up a statue in his honor. I brought our two sons to the U.S. to avoid the mandatory draft in Taiwan. It was bad enough losing my husband.

"My goal is to save enough money to bring my family to Las Vegas. Right now, I'm sending most of the money I earn to my sister in San Francisco. She's watching her son and my two boys. I still own a lot of valuable real estate in Taiwan, but it will be there when I return some day."

Leslie got very quiet for a minute. I could see she was deciding whether she should tell me something. She looked up and said, "You know, I married a man in San Francisco to get my green card but it was strictly business." I just nodded, thinking I didn't give a shit who she married or for what reason. Jealousy wasn't my thing. I didn't know it, but the "green-eyed monster" lay coiled in the background, ready to strike.

The next day we found a two-bedroom apartment at the Country Club Towers on Desert Inn Road and set up housekeeping. In two weeks our quiet paradise turned into a circus. Leslie's sister and the three boys moved in with us. As if that crowd wasn't enough to kill any romance, within a month, Leslie's mother arrived from Taiwan. Imagine four adults and three kids fighting over one lousy bathroom!

Did I learn how Orientals operate! Every trip to the grocery store meant buying another 10-pound bag of the Rose's brand rice we ate at every meal—breakfast, lunch and dinner. I knew if I swallowed one more mouthful of rice, my eyes would start slanting just like theirs. The boys behaved exactly the opposite from me when I was their age. Polite is one thing, but why did they call me "uncle" I wondered?

Leslie saw my blank look and smiled. "In our country, calling a man 'uncle' shows respect." The funniest part was when the three women switched from Chinese to English and back to Chinese. I felt like I was listening to a radio station that wasn't tuned in right.

Then my boss, Ron Zuber, accepted a job at the Nevada Palace out on Boulder Highway. There was a shakeup at the Palace and Bill Wortman, the GM at Ceasars, took over the Palace operation. Bill made Ron Zuber casino manager and Ron pulled me in to run his day shift. In a small casino like the Nevada Palace, it meant I was supreme commander from 10:00 a.m. to 6:00 p.m. Of course, there was all that responsibility again, but I figured I could stomach it for two reasons: the money was terrific and I got a kick out of the day-to-day challenge of running the place, at least for a while.

Power changes people. Now that I had pull again, women came on to me like I was Cary Grant. I didn't kid myself. Many guys in powerful positions never understand this fact and let all the attention go to their heads, but not me.

Then there was another angle. Taking off the casino big time would be as easy as writing a check. But that would mean I'd have to betray my friend Ron Zuber's trust. Many guys betray a friend's trust, but it wasn't my thing. Dealing's different because there's no loyalty in it. The idea of cheating as a dealer is more about knowing you can get away with it when everyone expects you to cheat. Tony Spilotro knew I was stealing and didn't give a shit. He just didn't want me to get caught.

I really liked Ron Zuber, but he was a screamer. When the house was losing, you could hear Ron's voice all over the casino. Bill Wortman tried to calm him down, but it didn't work. Ron didn't need to worry because there's something called the "twenty percent rule," based on the house advantage and law of averages. The rule works like this: The percentage that table games take in for the house varies from day to day. By the law of averages, at the end of every quarter, the house's profits or hold comes to about 20 percent. So why yell? I guess Ron didn't know about the rule for some reason, so he screamed. More than likely, an employee was ripping off the casino, which would change the hold percentage. Frank Modica found a way to increase the house's hold to 40 percent. He refused to do it because it would bust everyone out. Frank said, "Twenty percent is plenty." I like a guy who ain't greedy.

27

"Many times a girl washes a guy with
warm water to get him aroused. That way
she can negotiate a higher price."

ME AND VINCE Eli stopped by the Food Factory hoping to bump into Tony. Instead, we found his brother John taking orders. He slid into our booth after the lunch crowd had scattered.

"You guys just missed Tony. He flew out to see a Dr. Michael DeBakey in Texas for his heart. Tony says DeBakey is one of the best heart surgeons in the world. I hope to God he can help my brother." It wasn't like John to look so worried, but he had good reason.

It's a wonder Tony was still alive when you ticked off all the things he was dealing with. It seemed like every day there was another sensational item about him in the newspaper. Then there was Frank Cullotta, Tony's boyhood friend and, until a few years ago, a trusted member of Tony's crew. In 1982, Cullotta entered the federal witness protection program. He turned state's evidence against Chicago Outfit heavyweight Joey Lombardo and Tony. Some say Tony was going to whack Frank, but that was no reason for him to turn. In my book, there's nothing worse than a snitch. The guys I grew up with would crush any guy who ratted on a gang member. Guys who snitched in jail could look forward to an early exit—in a casket.

The Feds ended up indicting Tony for, among other things, murder. The Chicago bosses were plenty hot over the indictment. It didn't help matters that Tony was screwing around with Lefty's wife, Geri. Naturally, word got back to Chicago. Yeah, I'd have heart problems, too.

Las Vegas has two things stacked against it—July and August. I swore I'd punch out the next guy who said, "But it's a dry heat." Here it was only June but what a scorcher! The weather was nothing compared to the heat Tony was taking. I'd heard he returned from Houston, so I drove over to the Food Factory. Sure enough, there sat Tony hunched over in the corner booth scribbling on a slip of paper, the phone cradled between his ear and shoulder. He looked okay to me, so I decided not to mention his health. He probably hated talking about it.

He spotted me and walked over. "You want anything, Slick?"

"Just coffee, Tone."

"Glad you popped in, Slick, because I want to run something by you. This guy has a carnival on Paradise Road and needs to find a new location for it. Do you know any place he can put it?"

I thought for a minute. "Yeah. There's an empty lot that belongs to the Nevada Palace out on Boulder Highway. You know how much traffic that road gets. I could talk to the owner, Bill Wortman, see what he says and get back to you."

"Okay. If you can get it on, we'll wind up with a piece of the carnival. I have to go to Chicago, but you can let me know in a week or two when I get back."

The deal sounded great since I wouldn't have much to do and I was sure Bill Wortman would go for it. Besides, the extra dough would really help Leslie out.

In a couple of weeks, the story of Tony's disappearance hit the media. Rumors flew that it was a hoax on account of Tony's upcoming trial. Everyone thought Tony was in hiding, even his brother John.

Now three long weeks had passed since Tony disappeared. I knew in my gut that it was too long for Tony not to check in with his crew. I dropped by the Food Factory hoping I'd find Tony sitting in the corner booth as usual on the phone sipping his coffee.

John Spilotro didn't say a word. The tombstones reflected in his eyes said it all. In that instant, I knew for sure I'd never see Tony again. A few days later, Tony and his brother Michael turned up dead, buried in an Indiana cornfield after they were tortured. It didn't register at the time, but Tony's death hit me very hard. It marked the end of an exciting era. Still, life goes on. . . .

Kitty's current boyfriend, a little Jewish guy named Darryl Cronfeld, left her and took off for New Jersey. After Kitty hit rock bottom, I helped her get a cocktail waitress job at the Nevada Palace. Kitty hustled her way to a major comeback. Pretty soon, she was reeling in between $150 and $200 a day in tips. No sooner was Kitty flush again, than Darryl got wind of her good fortune, and hooked up with her in Las Vegas. He landed a job as a salesman for some security outfit. As luck would have it, someone in Darryl's family died and left him $60,000.

Right after Darrell inherited the money, the two of them made a decision that would radically change their lives. Darryl told Kitty, "You know, my boss must be doing pretty good because he just bought a Jaguar."

That comment started Kitty's wheels turning. "Why don't we open our own security business? If your boss can do it, so can we."

I had no doubts that the four-foot-eleven-inch Sicilian dynamo wore the pants in that relationship. Within a few months Official Security was born. By the end of its second year, Kitty and Darryl racked up enough business to flaunt "his" and "hers" Jags in their driveway. I had to hand it to Kitty. Two years earlier, she didn't have two nickels to rub together.

My nerves couldn't take it. One more screaming scene from Ron at the Nevada Palace and I quit. But playing poker for a living wasn't in the cards for me just yet. My good friend the comedian Jackie Vernon talked to the GM at the Marina Hotel and Casino where the MGM now stands and boom—I became the Marina's poker room swing shift manager.

A rough redneck named Big Al Rogers lugged a huge cellular phone everywhere he went including my poker room. (In the early days, cellular phones were so big they resembled narrow black bricks.) He was always on that cell phone with this guy and that guy and sometimes, when Al got a call, he took off. The more that cell phone rang, the more curious I got. But who could be calling so often? Drug dealers?

Turned out Big Al drove a limo for the Chicken Ranch, where more than eggs get laid. It's a famous whorehouse in Pahrump, Nevada, 60 miles west of Las Vegas. Maybe you wonder why a guy had to travel so far to buy sex when it seemed like everything was legal in "Sin City"? In a bold move to knock out all casino competition, the 1971 state legislature outlawed prostitution in every county with a population of 250,000 or more. That meant only Clark County—home to Las Vegas—became off limits to whorehouses. Now anyone with a yen for a prostitute had to travel to another county. The Chicken Ranch wasn't the only brothel servicing Las Vegas visitors, but it was one of the most popular. Some comedian observed, "Viewed from above, the limo traffic between Las Vegas and the Chicken Ranch looks like a trail of ants heading for the queen's chamber."

Big Al explained his setup. "It's like this, Slick. My boss has four Lincoln Town Cars. He has a deal with the Chicken Ranch owner, Ken Green, where my boss gets 18 percent of each customer's total bill, including the Chicken Ranch fee. Now I get 10 percent of my boss's take for every customer I drive to and from the ranch."

The picture Al painted whetted my appetite. Before he even finished, I was licking my chops for the same deal.

"A roundtrip to the Chicken Ranch" Big Al continued, "takes anywhere from three to four hours, depending on how long a guy stays. With one to four johns per trip, my boss averages $400 per customer and I wind up with around $80 plus tip. I figure I make at least $200 a day doing two trips. We're busy enough for another driver."

I wasted no time quitting my job at the Marina. It worked exactly like Big Al said it would and I even had my own cell phone. Now I played poker while I waited for a call, just like Big Al. All those years hanging around hookers made me think I knew everything there was to know about the world's "oldest profession." Boy was I wrong. My whorehouse education was just taking off.

On our first run, Al introduced me to the madam, a well-dressed smallish woman around forty with sharp eyes and a hard smile. She quickly turned her attention to the two new customers, fawning over them like a nervous schoolgirl. Her manicured finger hit a small button. In less than five minutes, 12 sexy girls decked out in brief costumes strutted into the main parlor for the line up. The johns asked the girls a few basic questions, but nothing too personal. Sasha, a dark-haired beauty in a black negligee and four-inch black stilettos, escorted her eager partner into her private room to arrange a price. The other guy picked a redhead named Honey with the palest ivory skin and wearing a plunging deep green satin gown. If it plunged any lower, we could have checked out Honey's toenail polish. Her john didn't seem to mind one bit when she led him to her room. I decided right then I was gonna like this job, but it might be a little difficult to keep from sampling the merchandise.

Out of earshot, Al whispered, "Now the girls wash the guys and check them for disease. A girl can refuse anyone who doesn't pass inspection. Many times a girl washes a guy with warm water to get him aroused. That way she can negotiate a higher price. Once the fee's set, the girls go to the madam with cash, check or a credit card. Except for tips, all services are paid for up-front."

We cooled our heels in the limo until the johns came out, in this case two hours after we dropped them off. The guys wore broad grins, hair still damp from their recent showers. They must have had a good time because me and Al split his take, which came to over $220 plus tip. I figured, with the extra cash I'd make, I could afford to sit in on those higher stakes poker games.

I learned plenty from the girls when I drove them to Las Vegas and back for their weekly medical checkup. According to state law, prostitutes were required to carry a current health card. If a girl missed her physical, she could lose her job, the state could fine the brothel or they might even lose their license. During one medical trip, Bunny, a smart brunette, dished out plenty of interesting tidbits.

"You know, Slick. Most of us girls have a boyfriend or husband—I guess around 85 percent. Another 10 percent are lesbians and not more than 5 percent are independents. Most of the last bunch needs someone to keep tabs on them because they're too stoned or drunk during their time off to keep track of their money. They need supervision so they don't blow all their dough." Bunny paused for a minute, taking a long drag on her cigarette. "I used to be that way until I met my old man . . ."

"What about the other independent girls . . . are they all into drugs or booze?"

"No, we get a few girls looking to make extra cash—like school teachers during their summer break—who hit and run. When they reach their goal, they go back to their regular jobs."

"It's all very interesting," I said, hesitantly. "But what about that time of the month?"

"Oh, the girls are forced to take one week off every month," Bunny said, smiling. "But most of the girls won't let that stop them. They go to Las Vegas, hook up with a john and use a surgical sponge so they can still make money."

I didn't have to ask Bunny any more questions. Once she got started, it was like a running faucet.

"By the way, the average age of a girl is 25. You might be surprised to hear the girls make around $2,500 a week." In answer to my low whistle Bunny said, "Yeah, we ain't in it for the kicks. The money's terrific. But we all pay income tax, just like everyone else."

Driving a limo for a whorehouse had certain benefits. I waited for Bunny to come out of the doctor's office then we headed back to Pahrump. Sometimes when I drove a girl into town I'd take out my $50 fee in "trade." This was one of those times.

I'd been driving a limo for three months now, bringing in roughly $200 a day like Al predicted. But why settle for $200 a day when I could do a lot better? There was another brothel a quarter mile up the road from the Chicken Ranch called Sheri's Ranch. Sometimes I'd talk a guy into trying Sheri's when I picked him up from the Chicken Ranch. "If you really want a good time, I'll take you to Sheri's, just up the road. Over there, the girls will do . . ." and I'd say whatever popped into my head figuring the grass always looks greener somewhere else. Any business I brought to Sheri's yielded a whopping 18 percent commission, the same as Big Al's boss.

But every silver lining has its cloud. Leslie hated my new work. She couldn't handle my "dishonorable" job, especially since her husband had been a war hero in Taiwan. It didn't make any difference to me, but to Leslie, driving a limo for a whorehouse was a huge step down from supervising a poker room. Then that green-eyed monster reared its head. Leslie turned insanely jealous at the thought of me hanging around all those hookers. To make matters worse, her girlfriend convinced her I was a pimp, which I wasn't. I should have realized how important that stuff was to Leslie, but it didn't register until Russell Reade, the fruity-looking manager at the Chicken Ranch, called me in one day.

"You're fired," he lisped, skipping the small talk. "A little bird told me you're taking customers over to our competition next door. I should break your legs." Russell tried to play the heavy, but the little wimp just wasn't cut out for it.

I knew right away Leslie tipped Russell off, and I didn't blame her. She'd pleaded with me to quit my embarrassing job. When that didn't work, what else could a strong woman like Leslie do but take matters into her own hands? I wasn't about to let Larry, have the last word.

"No," I said. "You're lucky I'm *letting* you fire me."

In September 1988, me and Leslie flew across the Pacific en route to Taiwan. Only a week earlier, we came up with a plan to manufacture casino chip knock-offs. "Look," Leslie said. "My boys are going to need college money. I have many important friends in Taiwan who can back us. All we need to do is show them what real chips look like and let them take it from there."

I agreed, trusting that Leslie's friends could pull this off. We collected casino chips in $25 and $100 denominations from five of the biggest casinos. That way, it would be harder to trace the chips with so many passing through those joints.

Our China Airlines flight lasted an ass-numbing 16 hours. Taiwan is so far from L.A., that once you get there, you're halfway around the world. I watched the sun, a bright orange ball, glowing on the horizon. It felt like we were chasing it because the sun never set. Time seemed to stop. All that water below stretching as far as the eye could see reminded me of another time when there was nothing but water around us. We were lost at sea on the *Knot Guilty* because none of us fuck-ups knew how to navigate.

I turned to Leslie. "It's a good thing you have contacts in Taiwan. Things can get tricky when you don't know what you're doing."

"What are you talking about?" Leslie acted surprised by my sudden caution. I usually went through life like a speeding freight train about to derail at any minute.

"Forget it. I don't know what made me say that." Then it dawned on me. Except for the time I spent in Cook County

Jail waiting for my trial, I hadn't sat still this long in my entire life. Inactivity forces a guy to think about things—the past, for instance. I remembered how Tony Spilotro considered all the angles before he made a move. No doubt, Tony knew what the Outfit had in store for him in Chicago, but he decided to go anyway. Nothing scared Tony.

I laughed to myself when I thought about the time Tony owed some high-ranking New York mob guy $100,000 from a gambling debt. The guy even tracked Tony down in Las Vegas demanding his money, but Tony hated New York guys so he told the guy to get lost. That started a big beef between Chicago and New York. Momo (Giancana) paid off Tony's debt to stop a war. Tony never paid Giancana back. Hundreds of guys ended up as "trunk music" for doing a lot less than Tony.

Our pilot turned out to be a friend of Leslie's dead husband. He left the cockpit and walked back to greet her. Even though they talked in Chinese, an idiot could see the respect he showed Leslie. Good. That meant she still had clout in Taiwan on account of her husband.

A limo whisked us from the airport to Leslie's mansion in Panchiao a suburb of Taipei. Her house looked like an Oriental palace in some old movie with its gardens and statues. I half expected Charlie Chan and his number one son to pop out of a bush.

The next day Leslie got busy on the phone. She sure knew all the heavyweights. When Leslie called, it didn't take long for six Tai gangsters to show up. After the formal bowing and drink pouring, Leslie took charge of everything. The guys only spoke Chinese, but Leslie translated that the gangsters wanted money up front. That wasn't in our game plan. I wanted to talk to these guys, man-to-man. They saw me sitting on my hands like Mickey the Mope while a woman called the shots. I would have tried to pull the same thing if I was in their shoes. The minute the giant red door closed behind the last oily-haired gangster, I couldn't keep the lid on my anger any longer.

"Your problem," I told Leslie, "is you always have to be in control, even if it means losing out on a score."

Leslie ripped into me with all her pent up frustration like a machine gun blasting anything that moved. "I didn't lose the deal. You did. What do you know about dealing with Taiwanese gangsters? We're not in the United States, you know."

"Of course I know that. But guys are the same no matter where you are. They want to deal with another guy, not some woman."

From this point on, I don't remember what we said, just that I'd had enough of Leslie's stubborn refusal to see the facts and stormed out of the house. I didn't have any idea where I was going until a few blocks away I spotted a bus that read "Taipei." I handed the driver a U.S. dollar bill and took a seat.

About an hour later, I exited the bus in what looked like downtown Taipei. The place was so crowded, I felt like a Salmon swimming upstream. Nothing made sense in this strange country where people talked in singsong sentences and the writing looked like chicken scratches. I walked down streets that smelled of raw fish and seaweed until I found a sign scribbled in English that said "Snake Alley." Some guys at a nearby stand were cutting snakes open and drinking their blood. Seeing as how I love snakes, I decided to pass on this.

I'll bet Taipei is the only city in the world where you find guys drinking snake blood while right around the corner people are wolfing down McDonald's hamburgers. I made a beeline for the familiar golden arches. Geez, was I starving. A Big Mac never tasted so good. The whole time I was demolishing my burger and fries, I could feel someone watching me. I turned around and there were three little Tai kids giggling. They made their fingers into circles and held them up to imitate my round eyes. When I was a kid, we pulled the corner of our eyes into a slant pretending we were Japanese. I got such a kick out of the new twist that I bought each kid a burger and fries.

A few streets from McDonald's I noticed a row of men standing in line at a ticket window. I thought what the heck and got behind them. The ticket taker held up five fingers. He seemed happy with the U.S. five dollars I offered him. I followed the men to an elevator that let us off on the fifth floor. The room held a big stage and theater that sat maybe a hundred people. It was so dark I could hardly see anything. Being a curious guy, I waited for the show to begin.

Out marched ten gorgeous girls all dressed in traditional Oriental gowns. One by one, the girls sang a song and left the stage. Great, I thought. It's gonna be some kind of a musical review. Then each girl came back wearing nothing but her high heals. Can you beat that? I'd wandered into a Chinese strip joint!

After the show, I spotted a hotel on the next corner, got myself a room and crashed. It's exhausting trying to find your way around in a strange country. In the middle of the night, a noise woke me out of a deep sleep. It was someone knocking on my door and they wouldn't go away. Who could it be? Nobody knew I was here. For a second the thought crossed my mind that those gangsters followed me from Leslie's. Cautiously, I unlocked the door. Standing in the doorway with only the back lighting from the bright hall were two young Oriental girls. This time I didn't need an interpreter. I knew exactly what they wanted.

For three days we partied. On the fourth day I looked over at the two sleeping girls on my bed, a kind of glazed smile spreading over my face. I opened my wallet and reality set in. When I walked out of Leslie's, I had $300. It was all gone except for a wrinkled twenty-dollar bill and Leslie's phone number. If I was the type who panicked, now would have been the perfect time, but I never get too excited. I figure things always work out.

Okay. It was time to quit fooling around and get hold of Leslie. I found a public phone down the street from my hotel, called Leslie and told her I was in Taipei. Leslie tried to sound matter-of-fact, but she couldn't hide the relief in her voice.

"Taipei is huge," she said. "Where are you?"

"I have no idea."

"Well, find a local and put them on the phone."

That wasn't hard. Everyone looked like a local so I collared the first guy who walked by and pointed to the phone. He got the picture. The guy said a few things into the receiver and handed it back to me. He smiled, bowed and melted into the human stream.

"Stay where you are," Leslie told me. "I'll be there in an hour."

Leslie pulled up driving her brother's car. Turned out she sold her house so she'd have money for her family. Things were cool between us. Resentment hung in the air like a cloud of stale smoke.

This time it got dark on our flight almost immediately. Now we were going against the turn of the world. I guess I had a lot in common with our plane. I always seemed to be going against the turn of the world. Leslie's sister met us in L.A. and drove us back to Las Vegas. In a few days, I moved into my own apartment. Our casino chip scheme wasn't the only thing to end in disaster.

I was thinking I made $250 and got laid—
all in three hours. Not a bad job!

NOW THAT I was *persona non grata* at the Chicken Ranch, I needed to hook up with someone who had dough so I could continue to make that 18 percent at Sheri's Ranch. I found just the guy, Joe Zullo, an ex-fighter who did a little time in Leavenworth for beating up a military officer, but he was far from a bad ass. Carefree Joe danced down the street like a guy sidestepping his opponent in the ring. All Joe wanted in life was to play Texas Hold'em. As luck would have it, he was such a lousy player, I think he never won a single pot. One time Joe held two aces and threw them away on account of raises. When two more aces showed up on the flop, Joe threw a fit calling the dealer a cheat, which nearly got him thrown out of the poker room, but the card room manager had a change of heart. You just couldn't stay mad at Joe if you tried. He had you laughing in no time, and that's why everyone liked him.

Joe's rich brother gave him a monthly allowance, since Joe had no real income. It didn't take much for me to convince Joe that all we needed was a limo to cash in on the great deal at Sheri's. Joe got on the horn with his brother and, bingo! Within a week, Joe owned a slightly used Plymouth Voyager. Our business mushroomed, but I knew we could do even better if Joe went along with my new fail-proof idea.

I was on a losing streak at the Holiday poker room and the button had passed to the next guy, when in walked Joe. I cashed in my chips and we moved to the coffee shop. I heard somewhere that, after golf courses, coffee shops were the most popular places to clinch a deal.

"Listen Joe. I know how we can get a lot more business by working with the Las Vegas cab drivers. They're already making 18 percent, just like us, but we can increase their business and ours if they use my perfect prop."

I told Joe I had menus made up exactly like those used by the Chicken Ranch. They described all the stuff the girls will do with a john like a "straight lay" and a "reversed half and half."

I whipped out a menu. "Here's the cover, Joe. I've got the menu price of five dollars right above the map to Sheri's. And there's our phone number in big black print."

"You mean we can make more money this way?" Joe was a little slow sometimes, punchy from years of being beaten around the head.

"Yeah, Joe. We're gonna come out with more business."

Then me and Joe hit the cab lines in front of the hotels with our menus. Joe had no trouble approaching the cabbies. What he lacked in brains, Joe made up in vitality—just like the Energizer Rabbit that kept ticking and ticking.

And I made my pitch. "Now you have something to show your customers," I told one cabbie. "You can sell these things or give them away for a bigger tip. It's up to you. Whatta you say?"

The cab drivers went nuts for the idea, so we gave each guy 20 menus at no charge. Our phone number appeared on the menu promoting our "free limo service," which meant a lot of customers called us directly instead of taking a cab. The cabbies didn't care because they actually did more business with their new bait to lure prospects. Our cell phones rang non-stop and everybody was happy.

Sometimes a girl would hit the jackpot with an "out date," which meant the john would arrange to take her to Las Vegas for dinner, a show and a night of sex. The girl's fee could go all the way up to $10,000, depending on her sales skills. No matter what the agreed price, the madam always approved the final deal. Boy, did I love those out dates! I could make $1,800 in a single night.

It was typical on the return trip to Las Vegas for a guy to boast that he was so good in bed, he had the girl moaning for more. Wow, I thought. This guy must really have something. Then I'd drive the same girl to town, and all she could talk about was her old man this and her old man that, not a word about the john. The more I heard, the more confused I got.

I was driving Sugar, a platinum blonde, back from an out date. She looked at me and said, "You're awfully quiet, Slick. What's bothering you?"

"I just don't get it. Maybe you can set me straight," I said.

"Try me, Slick." Sugar ruffled her blond curls. Her little girl's voice matched the innocent look in her enormous blue eyes. But Sugar was about as innocent as Linda Lovelace in the porno film, *Deep Throat*, which brings me to my question.

"How come a guy will brag how a girl was so hot for him, she begged for more, but the next time I see the girl, she doesn't so much as mention the guy?"

Sugar giggled. "That's because our job is to play a role, Slick. Like me and the baby doll look. It's all part of feeding a guy's ego. The better we are at making his dreams come true, the bigger the tip. And what guy doesn't love to think he's the best lay in the world?"

"Yeah, I get it. Some guys go for the little girl type. What I can't figure out is, if you're so innocent, how could he be the best lay you've ever had?" I never got an answer to that one.

The strangest thing happened about a month after I began working with Joe. I got a call from a customer at the ritzy Alexis Park Resort out on East Harmon, the only Las Vegas hotel without a casino. The square-looking guy had a woman with him—maybe his secretary, judging by her looks. She had her dark hair pulled into a severe knot and wore a no-nonsense plain black skirt, white blouse and low-heeled shoes, her pale mouth frozen into a tight little smile.

I led them to my limo, talking up Sheri's "foreplay specials." As for the limo, me and Joe invested our recent earnings in a used Lincoln Continental in bad need of a paint job. I hit on a color no one could miss. "Look for a shocking pink limo," I told customers. Even a blind man could feel the vibes coming from that car, which is exactly why some customers preferred I park it around the corner to avoid attention.

"Can I take her along?" The guy nodded toward "miss prim-and-proper."

Sure," I answered. "We even take single girls out to Sheri's who like other women."

He smiled and slid into the back seat, next to his silent partner.

On the drive out, I kept up my pleasant bullshit. There wasn't a peep from the back seat. Call it intuition, but I had the uneasy feeling maybe the lady was jealous. Or, maybe they were playing some kinky game? Mr. Square checked out the line-up, picked a girl and got right down to business. Me and Jackie (she finally told me her name) waited in the lounge.

We were sitting on the couch when Jackie asked, "Is there a restaurant nearby?"

"Yeah, about five miles from here."

"Will you take me there?"

"Sure."

We drove toward Pahrump, watching the sun fade into the naked desert. About a mile up the road Jackie said, "Stop here."

I pulled over and she told me to get in the back. In no time, she had her glasses off, her hair down and her skirt way up to reveal a pair of shapely long legs. A Pepsodent smile lit up a surprisingly pretty face. Wait a minute. Didn't Dorothy Malone pull this same stunt on Humphrey Bogart in *The Big Sleep?*—change from a plain Jane into a sexy siren in nothing flat? Jackie sure didn't look the type, but why complain. I was getting laid.

After maybe an hour, I told Jackie, "We better get back or your friend is in for a big surprise."

Reluctantly, she straightened herself up and we headed back. I looked over at the prim-looking woman on the seat next to me, hair once again pulled into a severe knot. Was this the same broad who gave me one of the best blowjobs I ever had?

It was a photo finish. No sooner did we sit down, than out walked Mr. Square. I had a hard time keeping a straight face. He spent $500, meaning my share was $150.

I pulled up next to the Alexis and opened the limo's pink door. Jackie said, "Give him a nice tip. He was very patient." The faintest hint of a smile played across her poker face. Well, the guy peeled off another C-note from his wad of hundreds. After they left, I was thinking I made $250 and got laid—all in three hours. Not a bad job.

Then there was the string of celebrities I drove to Pahrump—who will remain unnamed to protect their privacy—except for one. That's because I'm sure Charlie Sheen has nothing to hide. The famous actor brought his friends to the Ranch on a regular basis. And generous Charlie paid for everything by check. The way he went for the girls, I could tell he wasn't one of those funny boys. Listen, Charlie. If you happen to read this—I still have that knife you left under the limo seat by accident.

While I waited for calls from horny guys, I played poker at the Tropicana. I knew through the grapevine that Leslie was dealing Pai Gow Poker there, and I wanted badly to see her. I bumped into her "by accident" on her break.

"Hi, Leslie. It's good to see you." On Leslie, the standard dealer's uniform looked like a designer original. I kept up the small talk, hoping I still had a chance with her. "How long have you been dealing at the Trop?"

Leslie eyed my cellular phone with disapproval, her voice dripping with sarcasm. "So, you're doing that again."

"Yeah, but it's no big deal. Say, how about we get together after your shift . . . just coffee?" Seeing Leslie again made me realize how much I missed her. But I didn't want to scare Leslie off by moving too fast.

"Okay. Meet me at the casino time office at eight o'clock tonight."

I arrived early, Leslie showed up and we walked to my car. She took one look at my pink limo, sighed and shook her head.

"We'll take mine," she said.

Next thing you know, Leslie started coming over to my place. It looked like the old flame still burned, but the smallest breeze could blow it out. I made up my mind. If Leslie turned stubborn, I'd bend like the "Rubber Man" in a circus.

One day watching Leslie deal Pai Gow, an idea hit me. With that lax floorman on duty, and perfect timing, I knew a way we could take off some games. We practiced on my kitchen table until the moves were as natural to us as making love. I continued to play poker at the Trop and every once in a while I'd check out Leslie's table. If everything seemed right, I'd sit down and we went into action.

Now I had four red chips worth five dollars each capped in my right hand. When the floorman was looking the other way and the players concentrated on their hands, I threw down a $20 dollar bill, meaning I wanted change. Leslie quickly grabbed three or four black $100 chips out of the tray. When our hands met, I took the black chips and released the red chips, which looked like she was making change for $20. We did this only once and then I'd leave, not wanting to push our luck.

Over a two-month period, we pulled our Pai Gow con game only 30 or 40 times. Greed would have killed us, the same way it takes out all fools stupid enough to test their luck. Casinos feed off greedy suckers who ignore the formidable odds so stacked against them they might as well throw their money directly in the drop box and eliminate the middleman. Yeah, and I'd be a millionaire if I followed my own advice.

I got a call on my cell one day from a hooker named Tina who needed a lift into town. I knew Tina was a lesbian, but that stuff never bothered me.

"I need a favor, Slick. Me and my girlfriend don't have anywhere to go. Do you think I can take her to your place during my week off? I promise we won't be any bother."

"No problem, Tina. I'm usually at Leslie's anyway."

Well, after Leslie's shift that same night, she noticed I wasn't in the Tropicana poker room and decided to pay me a visit at home. Meanwhile, a couple of customers called from the Fremont Hotel for a ride to Sheri's. Leslie knocked on my door and Tina answered, wearing only a pair of panties.

"Come on in, Leslie. Slick's taking two guys to the Ranch, but why don't you wait for him?"

Leslie saw the other girl sitting on the couch, naked except for a bikini bottom. When I came home, Tina filled me in.

"Leslie took off so fast I couldn't explain what we were doing at your place and that you weren't involved. I'm sorry, Slick. If I knew Leslie was coming over . . ."

"That's okay, Tina. If it wasn't you and your friend, it would have been something else."

I phoned Leslie and tried to tell her what happened. She was so hot, her words left scorch marks on my ear. I thought I'd better let her cool off for a few days.

A couple of long days later, I bumped into Leslie's friend. By the look on her face, I could tell it was bad news. She said Leslie met a Chinese guy in Taiwan who now owned a bunch of restaurants in Portland, Oregon. He'd been begging Leslie to move up there and marry him. She decided to take him up on his offer. Not only did I lose Leslie, I drove her into another guy's arms. Then AIDS hit Las Vegas like the plague and Sheri's business started to fall off. Now what was I gonna do? For the first time in my life, depression threw me into a tailspin. I guess I was still going against the turn of the world.

One good thing came my way and not a minute too soon. Jerry Lewis needed a security guard the month before his annual Muscular Dystrophy telethon in September. Seemed that Jerry had fired his maid. Her husband, a convicted felon, threatened to kill Jerry so he went to Official Security to hire a bodyguard. Kitty knew I could use a few extra bucks (pay was $20 per hour), so on an overcast Thursday, she called to see if I was interested.

"Yeah," I answered, trying not to sound too excited. "I guess I could do it."

Joe hung out in the poker rooms while I shadowed Jerry around his building in North Las Vegas, the site of the TV broadcast. If one of our customers called, I'd tell Jerry I needed to run an errand or give the guy Joe's number. I didn't want Jerry to find out I was moonlighting at Sheri's. But now that I know him, I'm sure he would have laughed his ass off.

Jerry had more get-up-and-go than a ten-year-old on uppers. For example, we kept this golf cart outside Jerry's office inside this big trailer. My job was to check out visitors before they entered. The next thing you know, there was Jerry in the golf cart flying off to the sound stage. If I wasn't quick enough, he'd get away from me. But one time I managed to jump aboard. We passed through a huge area where some of the guys were throwing around a baseball. Jerry couldn't resist the action. He screeched to a halt and joined in. A fastball whizzed past Jerry nailing me in the chest. The force knocked me down and there I sat gasping for air. I looked up to see Jerry's concerned face hovering over me.

"Are you all right, Slick? Should we call an ambulance?" Right then I felt about as useful as a kid armed with a water pistol chasing a robber.

Speaking of guns . . . More than once Jerry asked, "Are you packing, Slick?"

"Yeah," I answered, patting my coat pocket where I stashed my heavy cellular phone. He'd just nod thinking he was safe. How could I tell Jerry that, with my felony record, I'd do prison time if I was caught carrying a weapon? Once Jerry tossed me a box he got from some fan, fearing it might be a bomb. I became the lucky owner of a beautiful cashmere sweater.

A famous star called Jerry at the last minute to say she couldn't appear on the live telecast in person. Jerry read her the riot act. If words were bullets, he could shoot down an inflated ego faster than a skilled marksman. But Jerry always treated little guys with respect, quick to share his Colonel Sander's fried chicken with guys like me. Only one person I knew, Vince Eli, could match Jerry's incredible memory. Jerry remembered everyone's name—simple stagehands—who had worked for him 10 years earlier. They loved him for that.

Performers Jerry had known for years, like Robert Goulet, dropped by to bullshit. But on the afternoon of the telethon, Sammy Davis's beautiful wife, Altovise, came by in tears. She delivered the sad news that doctors diagnosed Sammy with throat cancer.

It's a good thing my boss liked to drive. Otherwise, he might have answered a call on my cell phone and got a little surprise. Which brings me to an interesting story. It was the day before the telethon. The set buzzed with laborers, technicians, and the big man himself making sure there were no slip-ups. Wouldn't you know, my cellular phone died. Me and Joe needed all the business we could get. I spotted a big shot from the phone company, introduced myself and handed him this line of bullshit.

"You see, I've got a big problem," I said. "President Reagan is supposed to call Jerry on the air tomorrow night on this cellular phone. This is the only number that's been cleared by White House security, so could you please fix the phone?"

The guy must have been ex-military because he checked himself in the middle of a salute. "No problem, Mr. Hanner. I'll see to it right now, personally." He took my phone and walked away.

A little while later, the phone company guy came back with my cell phone. "It's all set to go, Mr. Hanner, and there's no charge." There was a long pause, then he continued. "A funny thing happened. The minute I had it working, the phone started ringing. I answered thinking it was the White House testing the line." Another long pause. "But it was some guy asking how much is a half-and-half?"

"Really?" I said. "That's strange."

29

"Seeing as how I'm having a nervous breakdown and Loreny's threatening to kill people,
I think this might be a good time to leave."

WITH THE AIDS scare running off our business, I didn't know how much longer my limo driver job would last. One incident threw things over the edge. I got a call from a customer at the Lady Luck. Me and Joe drove over together. Right off the bat, the guy eyeballed our shocking pink Lincoln and told us we looked like a couple of fags. I laughed off the remark but it rubbed me the wrong way. Lately, a lot of things rubbed me the wrong way. On the way out to Sheri's, the guy began to open up about his situation.

"Ya know, I've been doing time in the joint for the past two and a half years and all I could think about was getting laid. The price don't matter."

We got to Sheri's, he picked out a girl, and they went to her room. Me and Joe figured he'd be a long time, but the guy was back in less than an hour. Gee, I thought. That was quick work. In the limo, I noticed the guy didn't say a word.

"What's wrong?" I asked. "You don't seem too happy."

"What's wrong?" he repeated. "I'll tell you what's wrong. I've been waiting over two years for a woman. I found out it's just like a fucking medical exam. She won't do this or that, orders me to put on a condom, she won't kiss me. Shit. I had better sex in prison."

We rode the rest of the way in silence. When I dropped him off and he didn't tip, I knew it was time to find another job.

Soon after the ex-con incident, I paid my old boss, Ron Zuber, a visit at the Nevada Palace. Ron was an all or nothing guy, meaning he either yelled at you or clammed up. Ron couldn't stomach people who complained about their problems, and he walked away if someone asked about his family. I got right to the point.

"Hey, Ron. You need any help?"

"Your timing's perfect, Slick. If you want to take a job on the floor for a couple of weeks, I'm getting ready to fire my swing shift manager. When it opens up, you can have his slot."

I quit my job at Sheri's and went to work at the Nevada Palace. Nothing much had changed. Ron still screamed all the time. In two weeks, I took over swing shift.

My life had more ups and downs than a rollercoaster ride and this was definitely one of the down periods. Then I met a blackjack dealer named Martha who was born in Thailand. I have to admit, at first I was attracted to Martha because she reminded me of Leslie. But it was Martha's offbeat sense of humor that slowly lifted my spirits, and I felt myself breaking out of that tunnel of gloom. In a way, Martha saved my life. I guess self-pity and laughter don't mix too well. Martha landed a better job at the Dunes, but not before we got real chummy.

Within a month, Bill Wortman gave Ron Zuber the axe. We carried on for a while without an actual casino manager. Things went swell. I only wish it could have stayed that way. Then Wortman made his friend Bob, an ex-Metro cop on the "dog patrol," acting manager. Nothing official came down, but Bob sure acted like it had. He threw his weight around without knowing shit about the casino business. When you figured his last partner was a German Shepherd, maybe his behavior made sense? Bob was so bad that almost everyone missed Ron the screamer.

I ignored Bob and did things my way. That pissed Bob off so much he searched for a reason to get rid of me. He didn't have far to look. Even though my pink card allowed me to work legally, my felony gave Bob the ammo he needed to shoot me down. Bob's reasoning was how could I possibly be honest? He hid behind potted plants and slinked around like Inspector Clouseau in the Peter Sellers movie. (I think Bob took acting lessons from Phil Diaguardi, my ex-boss at the Stardust.) Bob would show up unexpectedly during my shift trying to catch me stealing. What a joke. He even third degreed one of my floormen about my so-called suspicious behavior. Turned out the floorman, who lusted after my job, told Bob everything he wanted to hear. They became great buddies. These are the thanks I got for promoting that SOB from a dealer to a floorman.

It all came to a head one day. Bob and the floorman were giving me a hard time over some procedure, just as an excuse to move me out.

"Listen Bob," I said. "You can leave the pit. As for you," I reminded the floorman. "You work for me."

The minute they left, I laid odds on what was gonna happen next. Wortman called me into his office, didn't buy my explanation and I quit. I swear this was the Landmark all over again.

Loreny from my old gang, now retired in Las Vegas, invited me to stay with him. Our boyhood bond still held strong but Loreny was such a wacko that I didn't trust him. Some people mellow over time, but not Loreny. When he was over the edge, looking into his eyes was like staring down a double-barreled shotgun. The worst part was you never knew exactly what set Loreny off. His anger could go from 0–60 mph in nothing flat. I still remember years ago how he hit that woman in the face with a brick when she tried to protect her old man. I kept telling myself, "Don't make waves."

As for finding work, things just weren't the same in this town. It was the late 1980s. Now you had to go through something called "human resources" and wade through all this paper work before they'd even consider you. Gone were the days when a mob guy juiced you into a job and nobody asked any questions how you got there. The new breed of college guys operating the casinos ran everything on the up-and-up. They brought in guys just like themselves—casino management types—who promoted from inside. With my pink card dragging me down like a lead ball, I was all washed up in Las Vegas.

Playing poker offered an escape for a while but I just couldn't concentrate anymore. The Las Vegas I knew was a thing of the past. Pretty soon, I hit rock bottom. I shouldn't have been surprised what happened next. They closed the Dunes, so now Martha was out of work, too. I invited her to move in with me at Loreny's. Naturally, I got Loreny's okay first. I wasn't nuts for Martha staying there, considering Loreny's yen for violence, but she had nowhere else to go. Besides, I figured we'd be gone soon. Later, I could have kicked myself.

Martha pulled up in front of Loreny's in the Caddy her ex-husband had given her. Things went so well at first, I thought maybe I was making a big deal out of nothing. Then it happened. Martha had been at Loreny's a little over a week when I walked in to find him banging Martha's head against the wall. If I hadn't been there to pull Loreny off of Martha, I think he would have killed her. Martha cried and threatened to call the police. I quieted her down and took her outside where we could talk. She told me Loreny tried to make a pass at her and she pushed him away.

"Okay, you lousy freeloading bitch. If you want to stick around you can clean the toilet," he yelled.

It didn't click yet that Loreny could kill her. She told him she wasn't a maid, which got him boiling hot. That's when I walked in.

Martha wouldn't set foot again inside Loreny's house, so I packed up our things. The raging psychopath had temporarily turned back into a human being.

Loreny tried to stop me. "Gee, I didn't mean her any harm. Don't let her go to the cops."

Maybe I was wrong to walk out right then and do nothing. I guess our old bond kicked in. I felt guilty as hell bringing Martha over to Loreny's. Somehow, I had to make it up to her.

A guy who owed me a favor got us a comp for a few days at the Aladdin. I made some calls and found out that riverboat casinos were making a splash in Joliet, my old stomping grounds just south of Chicago. We threw our belongings in the Cadillac and headed east. What a trip! After you're in Las Vegas for a while, you forget all about those Midwest winters. It snowed so hard, we would have made better time with a dogsled.

In Joliet, I looked up a guy I hadn't seen in 40 years. Tennessee was still the young redneck I remembered from the Arcadia Roller Rink.

"Well, it's Billy. I'll be darned." He talked in a southern drawl thicker than dark molasses. Tennessee took us in like long lost relatives. The trailer was about all he had to his name except for a rebuilt Ford pickup and an old motorcycle parked out front. Why am I laughing, I thought. Tennessee owned more than I did.

I drove the 60 miles to Chicago in Martha's car. My sole purpose—to see my old friend, Sam Gambino, back with the Chicago police force. I banked on Sam's connections getting me and Martha into one of the riverboat casinos. We took a ride out to Maywood Park, a harness-racing track that doubled as the Outfit's "conference room." Sam introduced me to a bigshot conducting business in his private box. Sam and this Frankie threw around the ritual bullshit for a while, until Sam turned the subject to me.

"You've got all this pull, Frankie. Can't you get Slick here a job on the riverboat?"

Frankie threw his head back and laughed. "Whatta you think we are, magicians?" Then Frankie turned to me. "Look. If it was ten years ago, we would have just walked on the boat and told the owner we'll let him run it for us. But now, if you don't keep a low profile, the FBI's all over you and you wind up in jail."

Frankie's words stunned me. Geez, I thought. It's not just Las Vegas that's down the tubes. So, now what was I going to do? I came up with a backup plan on the return drive to Joliet. On a hunch, I called Jimmy Zambutero, a friend in Biloxi, Mississippi. Great. Jimmy had a contact for Martha. I'd be dead there on account of my felony, but Martha was clean. The hard part was convincing her to go without me.

"I've never driven anywhere alone, Slick. Please come with me. Maybe they'll skip the background check on you?"

"Aw, you can do it, Martha. It ain't that big a deal. Once you're there you just look up Jimmy and he'll take you through the ropes."

After hours of back-and-forth, finally Martha agreed. At least I found her work and it would kind of make up for the Loreny mess. I kept up a strong front for Martha's sake. Inside I was mush. Sam thought maybe a little poker would cheer me up. He picked me up at Tennessee's and staked me to a Hold'em game on a riverboat casino in Joliet. Luck was on my side. My winnings paid for a plane ticket back to Las Vegas. Sam wanted me to live with him, but I turned him down, not wanting to overstay my welcome.

Sam had every opportunity to rise high in the police force, especially since he was connected, but Sam didn't have that kind of ambition. How could they promote him when Sam only wrote one ticket in his entire career, a ticket he was forced to write or lose his job? Sure he was Tony Spilotro's cousin. Sure he knew his share of Outfit guys. But Sam was no mobster, because he always stuck his neck out for the underdog. That didn't mean Sam took shit off anybody. If you crossed Sam, he'd grind you into mincemeat, no exceptions. The two of us were cut out of the same cloth.

With no bankroll, I didn't have too many choices. I decided to risk moving back with Loreny, gambling he wouldn't flip out on me. Loreny could only act normal until some incident triggered another pathological outburst. Geez, I thought. I gotta get away from this guy before he goes completely berserk. My perfect out materialized that same day when a boyhood chum from our old gang rolled his RV up to Loreny's curb. I recognized the easy gait and lanky body. It was Leroy Smolen, my old rap partner, who I hadn't seen since he worked with Mugsy. The three of us sat around Lorney's kitchen table reliving old times like 37 years never happened. We laughed about the time in Cook County Jail when Leroy sneaked into my bullpen through the dumb waiter. No one outside our gang could understand the bond we had that brought psychopaths like Loreny together with happy-go-lucky fuck-ups like me. Hell, I could hardly figure it out myself.

Later, when Loreny took off to buy groceries, Leroy showed me around his RV. "Hey, Billy. Why don't you come down to Florida with me? It'll be just like old times."

"Seeing as how I'm having a nervous breakdown and Loreny's threatening to kill people, I think this might be a good time to leave."

"Yeah. Stick around Loreny and you could wind up nuts or dead," Leroy added in that humorless way of his.

I followed Leroy's RV in my car. If it hadn't been for my daughter Betty loaning me $100 and Leroy helping with gas and food, I couldn't have swung it. On our way through Biloxi, I looked up Martha. The old feelings welled up, but I kept them in check. Everything seemed to be going good for her and I didn't want to butt in. Martha saw right through my act.

I was about to push on when she said, "You don't want to go to Florida. Why don't you stay here with me?"

I thanked Leroy and moved in with Martha. Two days later, we came up for air. I got on the horn with Jimmy Zambutero.

"Glad you're here, Slick. Since I started running the poker room at the President in Biloxi, I found out that if a guy's application looks good, sometimes they don't bother to do a background check. Besides, the FBI charges a ton of money. Maybe you'll get lucky."

"I have nothing to lose, Jimmy. You got any leads?"

"As a matter of fact, my friend Dave Sugar, manager of our new President Casino in Tunica, Mississippi, needs help in the worst way. Tunica's over 400 miles from Biloxi, so you'd have to relocate, Slick. Dave's training our dealers in Memphis, Tennessee, only 50 miles from Tunica until the President opens. If you want, I'll give him a call."

Nice to see there were a few places left where the juice still flowed. Dave Sugar hired me on the spot. I drove back to Biloxi and broke the good news to Martha.

"Gee, Slick. That's terrific. Maybe they'll forget about a background check. You know, it's strange. If they could pardon Hirohito after what he did to Pearl Harbor, you'd think they could pardon a 19-year-old kid who didn't kill anybody."

For the next month, I trained break-in poker dealers in Memphis. The President Casino opened a few weeks later on a Mississippi riverboat. The good news—I was hired to run swing shift. The bad news—if they gave the U.S. an enema, Tunica is where they'd insert the tube. What a dump. I commuted back and forth on "Death Highway" between Memphis and Tunica for a while, but decided my chances of surviving road rage were a lot better if I moved to Tunica. Hey, I couldn't complain. I had a decent-paying job for an entire year until the President floundered due to massive flooding on the river. For a while, you couldn't get there unless you had webbed feet. Then there were the power outages from winter ice storms. By 1990, the President Casino pulled up anchor and sailed down river.

Patting my bankroll, I headed to Biloxi and looked up Martha. She was as happy to see me as ever, but confessed that her ex-husband convinced her to come back. He lived down on the "Redneck Riviera," better known as Panama City, Florida. Good. With his retired military officer's pay, Martha wouldn't have to worry.

"That's great, Martha. Now you can buy all the grits and hog jowls you want," I teased.

The next few years were a blur—one poker room after another—until my daughter Kathy called me from New Mexico where she just finished law school. She had passed the bar in that state and was working for a law office in Albuquerque.

"Dad, you just have to come to New Mexico. The governor signed a bunch of compacts with the Indians, which gives tribes the legal right to have Class III gaming. That includes blackjack, craps, roulette, poker and all the other table games. And Dad, nobody here knows how to play poker."

"That's all I needed to hear, baby. I'll be right out."

EPILOGUE

HERE IT IS, 2005, and life is good. All my kids made something of themselves. Considering their father's a convicted felon and ex-thief, that's a major accomplishment. My daughter Billita writes a successful newspaper column in northern Illinois. Mandalay Bay Hotel and Casino in Las Vegas honored Mary as employee of the year. Her name blazed in lights on their giant marquee. Betty and her husband Danny, casino employees, plan to retire young on their savings. I hear Tom and his wife are doing fantastic due to years of hard work. My dream is that one day Tom will realize how much I love him, in spite of my failures as a father. Katherine (as she prefers to be called) practices law in Las Vegas. She's committed to helping the underdog.

After many years, Kitty met the daughter Kitty's parents forced her to give up. Without that burden of guilt hanging over her, most of Kitty's anger disappeared.

Bob Mauro and Vince Eli both passed on to that big racetrack in the sky (or strip joint, depending on your point of view). I sure miss them. We'll have one hell of a reunion.

As for me, Kathy once feared I'd eat dog food and live in a dump. The only dog food around my palm-shaded apartment overlooking the yacht harbor is the stuff I feed to Herman, my German Schnauzer. Me, I play poker and eat steak any time I want. Casinos need guys like me to teach them how to spot cheaters. No fancy surveillance equipment in the world can substitute for first-hand knowledge. Casino consulting gives me a good income, but I sure ain't rich.

Looking back, would I do it all again? More than likely. I'm not proud of being a thief but I'm not ashamed, either. A lot of guys change their tune when they write their story. Not me. I've tried to tell about my life as honestly as I can—no whitewashing, no excuses.

My exciting times may be winding down, but when I put on the old music and close my eyes, it's like it happened yesterday. . . .

ACKNOWLEDGEMENTS

SLICK AND I both want to thank all those friends who remembered important incidents in Slick's life, especially Bob Mauro, Vincent Eli, Jack Kearns, Leroy Smolen and Loren Rodgers.

For encouraging and supporting me through nine arduous years of writing, my heartfelt thanks go to J.J. Gamble and Gerald Wolf; Cynthia Adams; Kay Davis; my cousin and her husband, Patricia and John Olson; my blackjack teacher and friend Larry Smith; Dana Susa; Kathleen Brown; Kary and Osvaldo Zarate; the Raul Morales family; and my father and mother, Earl and Annabelle Bohat, for believing I could do it.

For inspiring me with their writing, I'm indebted to my friend and mentor, Roger C. Parker, author of over 36 books; Bill Roorbach, author of *Writing Life Stories;* John L. Smith, author and *Las Vegas Review-Journal* columnist; Slim Randles, *Albuquerque Journal* columnist; author Rick Porrello; and Randy Wayne White, best-selling author (plus Doc, Tomlinson and the whole gang).

Special thanks to: Hank Kaplan, world-renowned sports writer for taking the time from his busy schedule to set me straight on a few boxing facts, and probably the only guy in the world who knew what kind of toothpaste Ali used in 1964 before he TKO'd Liston in the 7th; Lyle Stuart and his fantastic team at Barricade Books (when Lyle called to tell me he was offering us a publishing contract, I nearly fainted); good friend, Tony Montana, who immediately sent our manuscript to a literary agent and continues to work doggedly to promote *Thief!* and its potential as a movie; and finally, Edward Becker, our literary agent and my friend and mentor, who helped us realize our dream. I'll never forget Ed's kindness and encouragement well beyond the publication process.

Cherie Rohn

INDEX